TEACH YOURSELF...

MICROSOFT PUBLISHER 3

FOR WINDOWS 95

TEACH YOURSELF...

MICROSOFT PUBLISHER 3

FOR WINDOWS 95

DEVRA HALL

MIS: PRESS

A Subsidiary of
Henry Holt and Co., Inc.

First Edition—1996

Printed in the United States of America.

Library of Congress Cataloging-in-Publication Data

Hall, Devra.
Teach yourself-- Microsoft Publisher 3 / by Devra Hall.
p. cm.
ISBN 1-55828-466-4
1. Microsoft Publisher. 2. Desktop publisher. I. Title.
Z253.532.M53H35 1995
686.2'2544536--dc20 95-26025
CIP

10 9 8 7 6 5 4 3 2 1

MIS:Press books are available at special discounts for bulk purchases for sales promotions, premiums, fund-raising, or educational use. Special editions or book excerpts can also be created to specification.

For details contact: Special Sales Director
MIS:Press
a subsidiary of Henry Holt and Company, Inc.
115 West 18th Street
New York, New York 10011

Editor-in-Chief: Paul Farrell

Managing Editor: Cary Sullivan

Copy Edit Manager: Shari Chappell

Copy Editor: Genil Breeze

Editor: Mike Sprague

Production Editor: Maya Riddick

ACKNOWLEDGEMENTS

Creating a book—any book—is a time-consuming and exhausting process. And, it is a process that requires the cooperation and talents of a number of people. I'd like to take the time here to thank a few of those people who rarely get acknowledged and who do most of the actual work after the writing process is complete.

Most of the work of laying out the pages of this book falls on the shoulders of a single person. Maya Riddick put forth the creative energy that translated a double-spaced manuscript into a *teach yourself...* book. Creating a series look and feel can only be done if there's a single person holding the reins. Shari Chappell is the person who oversees the editing process and keeps each *teach yourself...* book looking like every other. And, perhaps the most forgotten of all people who create books is the person who manages the entire printing process. Kurt Andrews cajoled and threatened some poor printing company into producing this book in far too short a time period—thereby getting you a book in the same year the software released. Thank you all!

MICROSOFT PUBLISHER 95

TABLE OF CONTENTS

CHAPTER 2: WORKING WITH TEXT 31

CHAPTER 3: WORKING WITH IMAGES 83

CHAPTER 6: DESIGN OBJECTS AND ELEMENTS 219

CHAPTER 7: PUTTING IT ALL TOGETHER 259

CHAPTER 1

GETTING STARTED

- Examining the startup dialog window for creating new publications
- Exploring the Publisher working environment
- Glancing at menu options
- Bar hopping: toolbars, rulers, and the status bar
- Getting acquainted with the objects

In this chapter, you'll examine the three tab pages of the startup dialog window. Then you'll take a good look around the Publisher desktop, noting the various working environment elements such as the screen, menus, toolbars, and speedbuttons available to help you create your Publisher masterpieces. You'll also get acquainted with the various elements—text, pictures, tables, borders, etc.—that are the building blocks of every publication.

THE STARTUP DIALOG WINDOW

When you launch Microsoft Publisher, the program opens and the startup dialog window appears on top, as shown in Figure 1.1. This startup dialog window has three tab pages: PageWizard (this tab page should be on top), Blank Page, and Existing Publication. Let's take a look at them one at a time.

FIGURE 1.1 OPENING SCREEN WHEN YOU FIRST LAUNCH MICROSOFT PUBLISHER.

Click on the **Existing Publication** tab to bring that page to the top. This page has three sections and, assuming that you have not yet created and saved any publications, all three sections are still blank, as shown in Figure 1.2. The top left section displays a list of the most recently used Publisher files (so far, none). When you select a publication from the list, you will see a miniature image of that publication's first page appear in the preview section. Of course, for now, you'll just have to take my word for it.

TIP

When Publisher is already open and you want to open another existing file, you'll find that the last five publications you worked on are listed at the end of the File menu. You can click on one from there to open it.

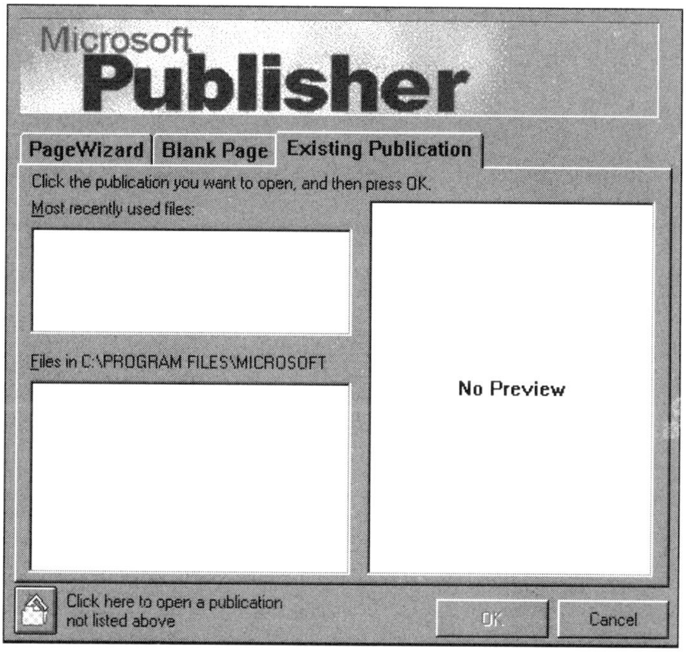

FIGURE 1.2 THE EXISTING PUBLICATIONS TAB PAGE FROM THE STARTUP DIALOG WINDOW.

Immediately below the list of most recently used files is a section that displays a list of the files found in the named folder. In Figure 1.2 the named folder is C:\PROGRAM FILES\MICROSOFT PUBLISHER (the last word is cut off due to limited space in the window). This is the folder on my system that contains the Publisher program. If you want to search for publication files in another directory, you just click on the button shown in the bottom-left corner, the one that says *Click here to open a publication not listed above*. This brings up the Open Publication dialog window (see Figure 1.3) from which you can navigate through the various drives and folders available to your system.

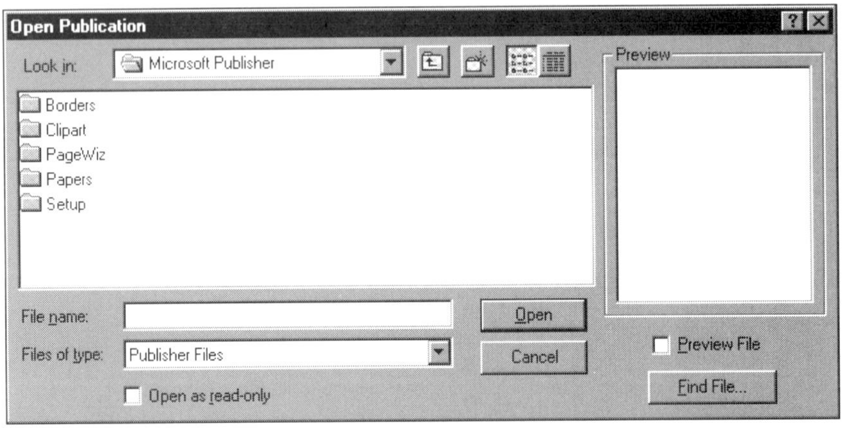

FIGURE 1.3 THE OPEN PUBLICATION DIALOG WINDOW USED TO FIND PUBLICATION FILES IN OTHER FOLDERS OR ON OTHER DRIVES.

When you click on the tab that says **Blank Page**, your dialog window should look like the one shown in Figure 1.4. From here you can select a particular page layout. Choices include **Full Page**, **Book Fold**, **Tent Card**, **Side Fold Card**, **Top Fold Card**, **Index Card**, **Business Card**, **Poster**, and **Banner**. All these layouts are blank as far as content or design elements are concerned. However, when you select one of these predetermined sizes, the layout guides (the blue and pink dotted lines) are set up for you and are available consistently on each page of your publication. (I say "available" because you can decide whether you want the guides to be visible.)

In the bottom-left corner of the Blank Page dialog window is a button labeled **advanced Page Setup options**. In Chapter 6, you'll use that button to bring up a dialog window that allows you to set your own size and page orientation guidelines.

FIGURE 1.4 THE BLANK PAGE TAB PAGE FROM THE STARTUP DIALOG WINDOW.

Now let's go back to the PageWizard tab page. PageWizards automatically create professionally designed documents based on the style and formatting choices you make and information you provide when prompted. Microsoft Publisher has 19 different PageWizards, but as you can see from the icons shown in Figure 1.5, you can only access 16 of them from this dialog window. (If you can't see all 16 icons on your screen, use the scroll bar to scroll down.) You'll see how these work when you use one to create your first Publisher document in Chapter 2, but first I want you to get familiar with Publisher environment.

FIGURE 1.5 THE PAGEWIZARDS TAB PAGE FROM THE STARTUP DIALOG WINDOW.

For now, either select **Full Page** from the Blank Page tab page and click on **OK**, or select **Cancel** to get rid of the startup dialog window and show the Publisher desktop.

YOUR WORKING ENVIRONMENT

Depending on whether you have selected an object and what type of object (text, picture, etc.) it is, your environment will change in small but helpful ways. For instance, some of the menu options will change, and I'll remind you of those changes again when I introduce each object type in the following chapters. Also the buttons available on the Format toolbar will change, and I will highlight these for you as well. But the basic features are always there, so that's where we'll start. Your basic working environment looks like the one shown in Figure 1.6.

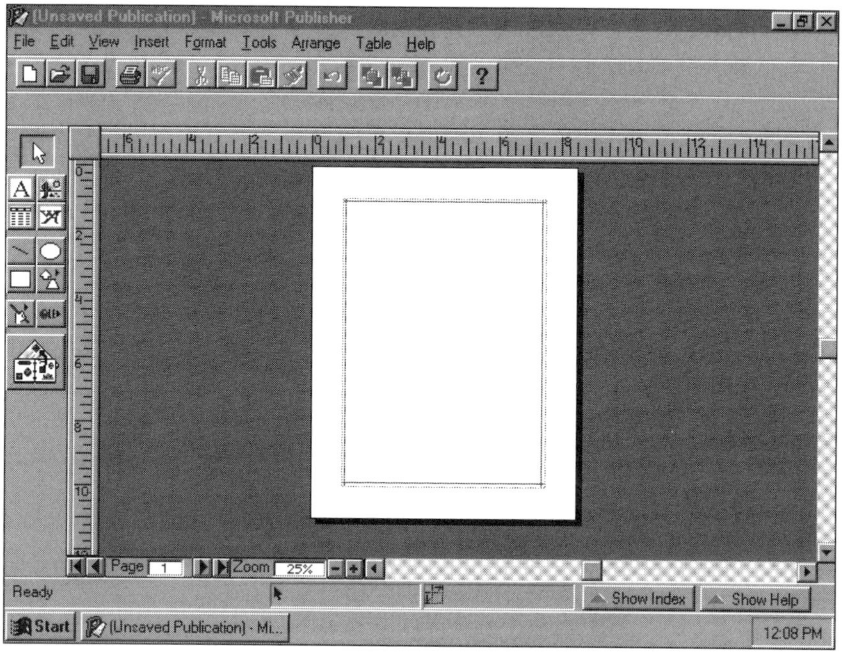

FIGURE 1.6 THE BASIC MICROSOFT PUBLISHER WORKING ENVIRONMENT WITH A BLANK PAGE.

At the very top is a title bar showing the name of your publication and the application name Microsoft Publisher. Because you haven't saved this publication, the title bar reads *[Unsaved Publication] - Microsoft Publisher.* Just below the title bar is the menu bar, and right below that is a toolbar. Actually, there are two toolbars, but at the moment no tools are shown on the second bar.

Menus

Publisher has nine menus across the top. File, Edit, View, Insert, Format, Tools, Arrange, Table, and Help. Conceptually, many of these menus are similar to those found in most Windows programs, and you will find some menu options that are identical to the ones in other programs that you use. You'll become familiar with the options of the various menus as you begin using them to work on the sample publications in this book, as well as on your own projects. For now, I'll just show you a picture of each menu, and give you the nutshell descriptions.

File

The File menu, shown in Figure 1.7, contains the options for opening, closing, and saving publications. It also contains the options for finding files, as well as handling page setup and printing. The newest feature is the **Send...** option, used to send a publication out through email—a feature that is new to the Windows 95 operating system and only available if you installed Microsoft Mail.

FIGURE 1.7 THE FILE MENU.

Edit

The Edit menu contains the customary **Undo**, **Cut**, **Copy**, **Paste**, **Delete**, **Find**, and **Replace** commands, plus a few others shown in Figure 1.8. As you work with Publisher, you will find that the Edit menu options change, depending on what you are doing in the publication. For example, the **Cut** option will say **Cut Text Frame** if you have a text frame selected at the time you open the menu. If you have a picture frame selected, the menu option will read **Cut Picture Frame**. And so on for tables and other objects. The same applies to the **Copy** and **Delete** options as well. The **Edit Object** option at the bottom of the Edit menu also changes from **Edit Object** to **Edit Story in Microsoft Word** when a text frame is selected, and to **Microsoft WordArt 2.0 Object** when a WordArt frame is selected.

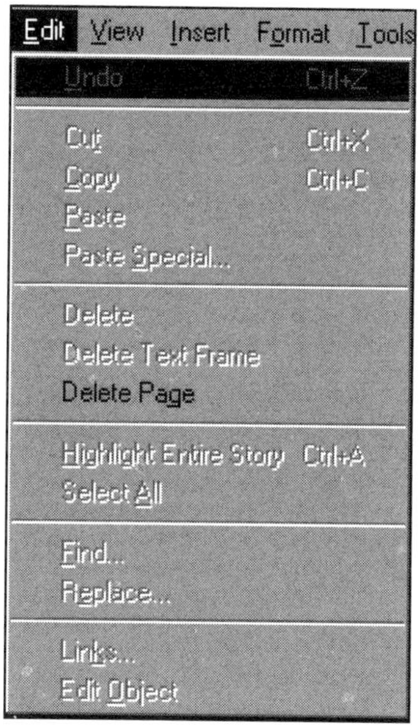

FIGURE 1.8 THE EDIT MENU.

View

The View menu options, presented in four sections as shown in Figure 1.9, deal primarily with what you see on your screen. The first three options deal with the size at which you see your publication page or pages. The workspace has enough room to show you a two-page spread where each page is seen at 25% of actual size. The **Full Page** option shows only a single page, also at 25% of actual size. If you prefer keystrokes over menu selections, you can use the **F9** key to toggle between full and actual size.

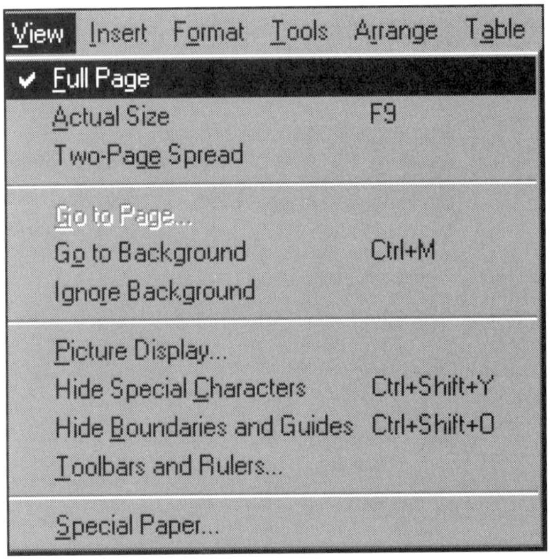

FIGURE 1.9 THE VIEW MENU.

The second section of this menu contains three options. The first brings up the **Go To Page** dialog window that tells you how many pages your publication contains. You enter the number of the page that you want to see, and Publisher jumps directly to it. This is handy when you have a publication with many pages. (Even though it is not indicated on the menu, you can also use the **F5** key to bring up to Go To Page dialog window.) The second option allows you to switch back and forth between the background and foreground of a publication. The last option in this section allows you to ignore (or hide from view) anything placed in the background. The purpose of a background, and how you work with it, is discussed in Chapter 6.

The next group of options on the View menu allows you to hide or show various elements. The **Picture Display...** option is more than a simple hide/show toggle switch. It gives you a middle choice, i.e., to show pictures on your screen with less detail than they actually contain. This is sort of like a draft version; you can see the image, but it doesn't take as much time to show up on your screen.

The two View menu options relating to special characters, and to frame boundaries and layout guides, are straightforward toggle switches that allow you to hide something visible or show something hidden. *Layout guides* are pink and blue dotted grid marks that mark sections and help you position objects in your publication. A *boundary mark*, shows the outer edge of each object—the frame itself.

The **Toolbars and Rulers** option, on the other hand, brings up the dialog window shown in Figure 1.10, where you also have some control over the size and color of the toolbar buttons and whether toolbar tips are active. (You can also bypass the menu option and access this dialog window by pressing **Ctrl-K**.)

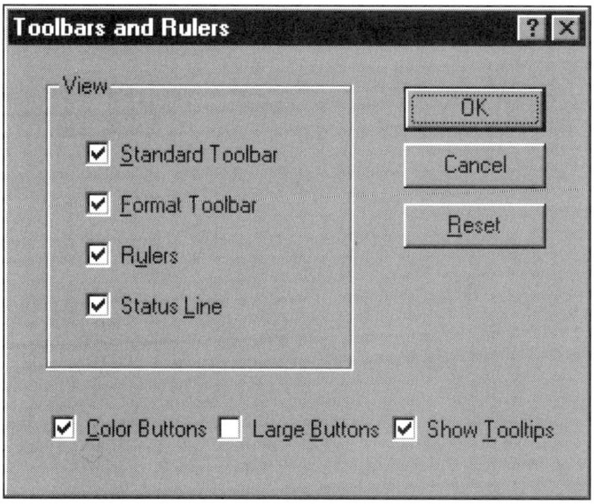

FIGURE 1.10 THE TOOLBARS AND RULERS DIALOG WINDOW.

The final section on the View menu relates to the use of Special Paper sold by Paper Direct. Figure 1.11 shows the Special Paper dialog window from which you may preview and select a special paper. The paper's design becomes visible on your layout so that you can visualize where to place your objects. Of course, the paper itself already contains the "design," so even though the design appears on your screen it doesn't print out.

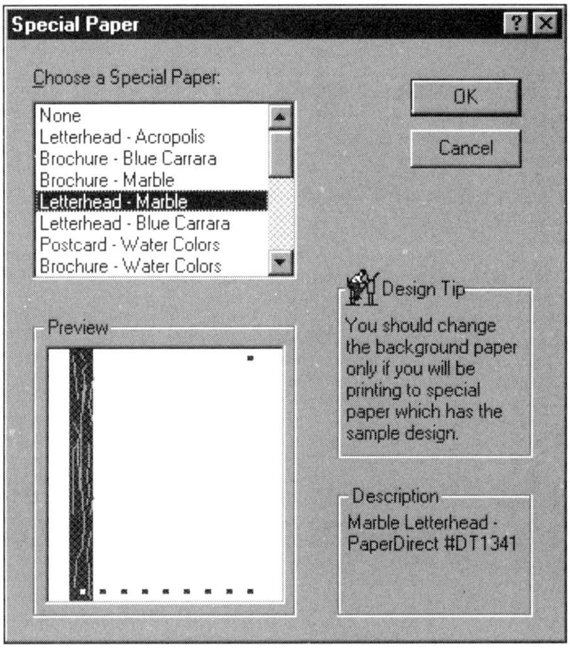

FIGURE 1.11 THE SPECIAL PAPER DIALOG WINDOW.

Insert

When you want to insert existing text, picture, clip art, or other object files, you'll find the options you need on the Insert menu, shown in Figure 1.12. In addition to bringing in existing files, the Insert menu also contains options for inserting the system date and/or time and page numbers into a text frame.

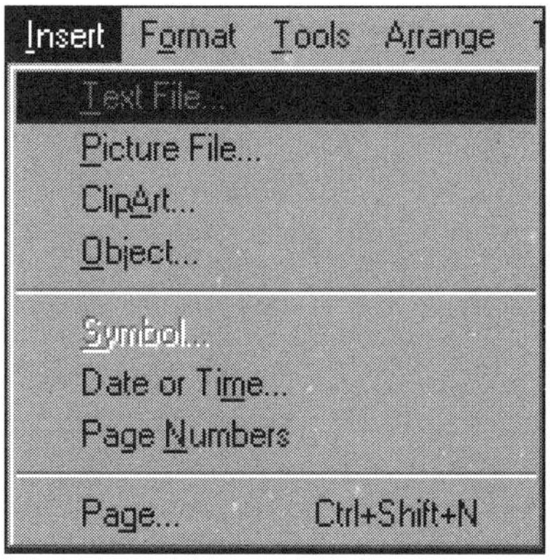

FIGURE 1.12 THE INSERT MENU.

To add a new page to your publication, you use the last option, **Page...** to bring up the dialog window shown in Figure 1.13. Not only can you specify how many pages you want to add and whether they should be inserted before or after the current page, but you can tell Publisher to create a text frame for you, or even copy all the objects from some other page.

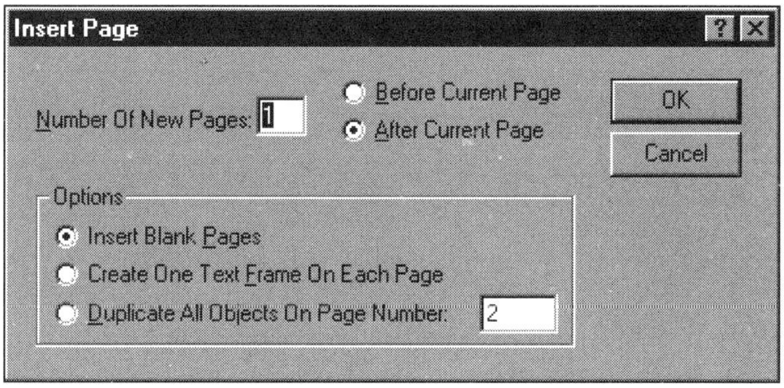

FIGURE 1.13 THE INSERT PAGE DIALOG WINDOW.

Format

As with the Edit menu, the Format menu options change depending on what type of frame/object is selected. When you are working with a text or table frame, the Format menu includes options that allow you to format the text—specify text style, characteristics, spacing between character and lines, fancy first letter, tabs, lists, etc. When you are working with WordArt and picture frames, your options change to allow you to scale, crop, and recolor objects as well as alter the shape around which text will wrap.

Regardless of the active frame/object type, the Format menu also contains the options for working with borders, fill colors, patterns and shading, and shadows. Most objects (all except lines and shapes) also have an object Properties option. Object Properties include such things margins and text wrapping specifications. I'll talk more about each property when I discuss the object types in Chapters 2-5. If you open the Format menu without first selecting an object (for example, a text frame), the menu options will appear as shown in Figure 1.14.

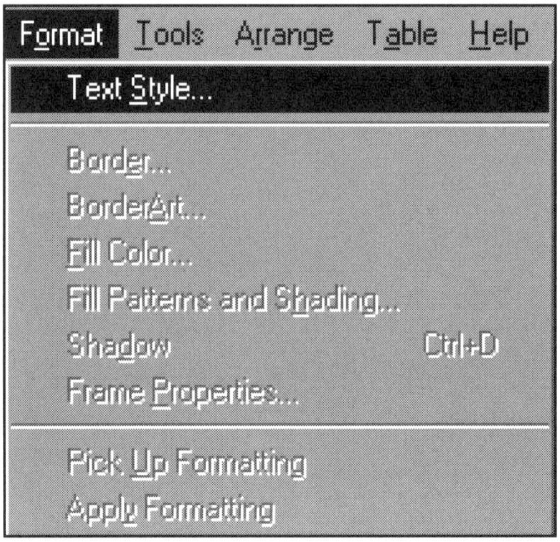

FIGURE 1.14 THE FORMAT MENU (NO ACTIVE OBJECT).

Tools

Surprise! Tools for spell checking, hyphenation, and layout are found on the Tools menu, as shown in Figure 1.15. There you also have the options to make your objects snap to guides, ruler marks, or one another. You can also gain access and add new elements to the Design Gallery using the first two options on the Tools menu. (I'll talk about the Design Gallery in Chapter 6.)

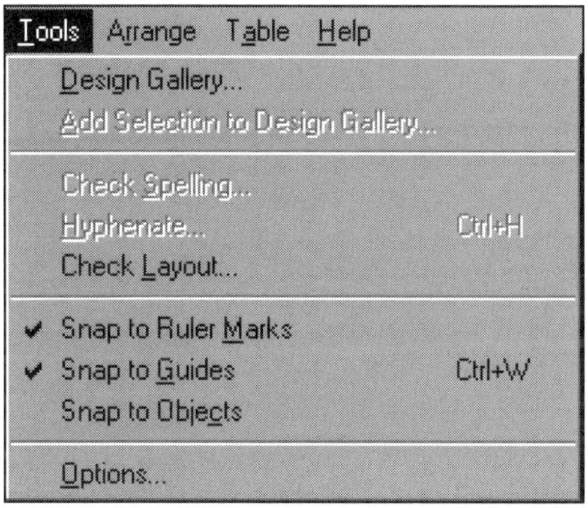

FIGURE 1.15 THE TOOLS MENU.

Additional options, such as which page number to being with; whether you want your layouts measured in inches, centimeters, picas, or points; and whether you want Publisher to open with the startup dialog window examined earlier, can be set in the Options dialog window by selecting **Options...** from the Tools menu. Figures 1.16 and 1.17 show the Options and More Options dialog windows with the default settings. I'll explain various options as they become relevant to your tasks in this book.

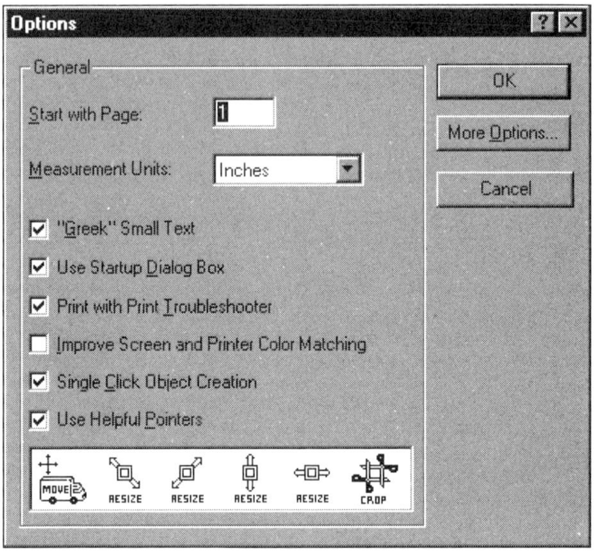

FIGURE 1.16 THE OPTIONS DIALOG WINDOW THAT APPEARS WHEN YOU SELECT **OPTIONS...** FROM THE TOOLS MENU.

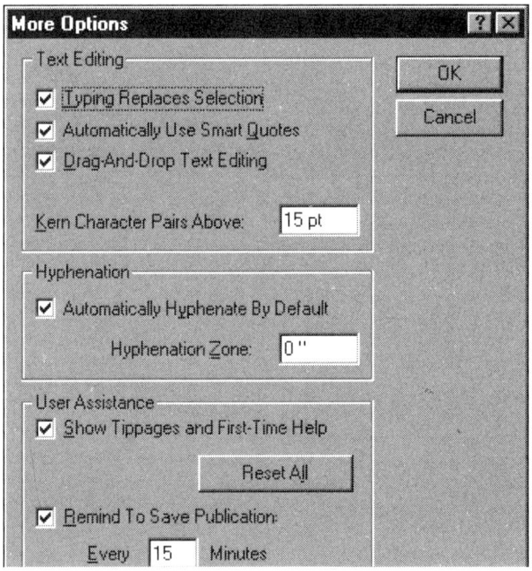

FIGURE 1.17 THE MORE OPTIONS DIALOG WINDOW.

Arrange

When you decide to do some of your own layout and design work (instead of letting the Wizards to it all), you'll use the Arrange menu (see Figure 1.18) to set up layout and ruler guides; group, lineup, and nudge objects into position; and layer, rotate, flip, and clip objects. You'll have plenty of use for this menu in Chapter 6 when you create a publication from scratch.

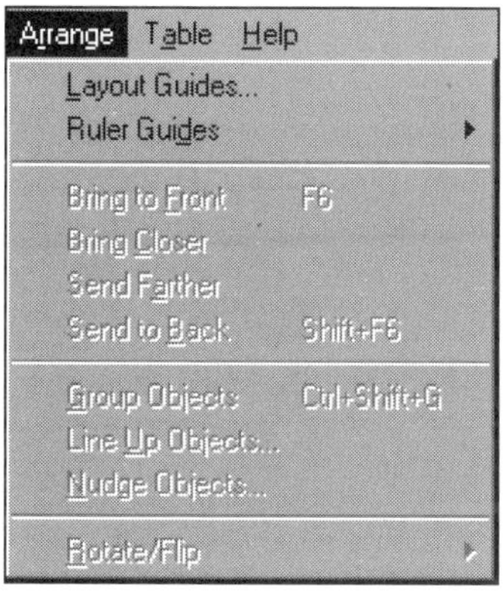

FIGURE 1.18 THE ARRANGE MENU.

Table

Figure 1.19 shows the Table menu where you'll find the commands for all table operations such as inserting or deleting rows and columns, merging cells, and filling in values. Chapter 4 is devoted to working with tables.

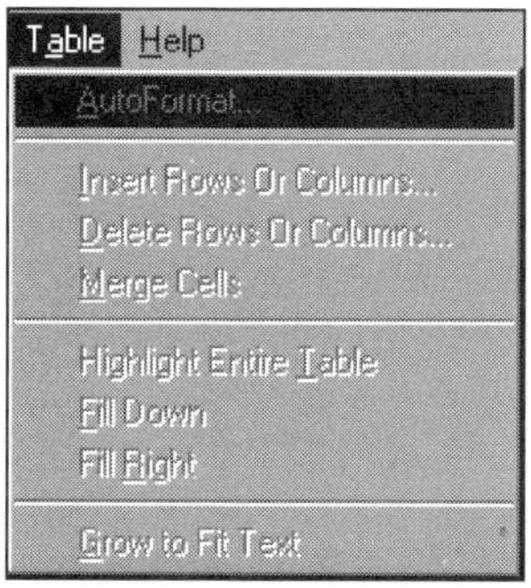

FIGURE 1.19 THE TABLE MENU.

Help

The last menu is the Help menu, and as shown in Figure 1.20, it contains more than just the usual **Contents** and **Index** options. Open the Help menu and take a look.

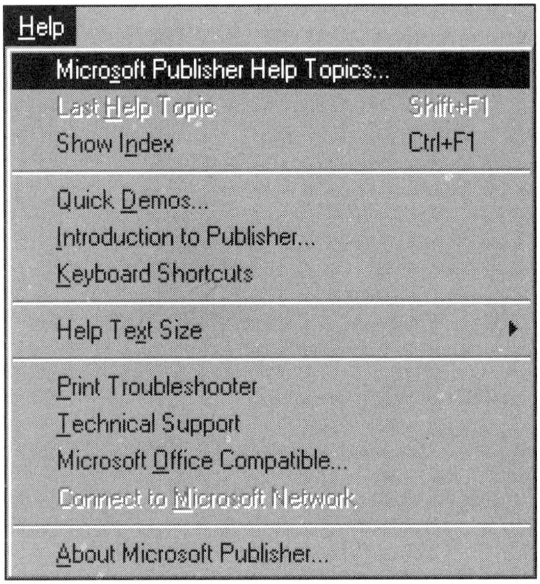

FIGURE 1.20 THE HELP MENU.

As shown in Figure 1.21, the Microsoft Publisher **Help Topics...** option opens a window that stays open on the right of your screen until you click on the **Hide Help** button at the bottom. Try it now and take a look at the topics.

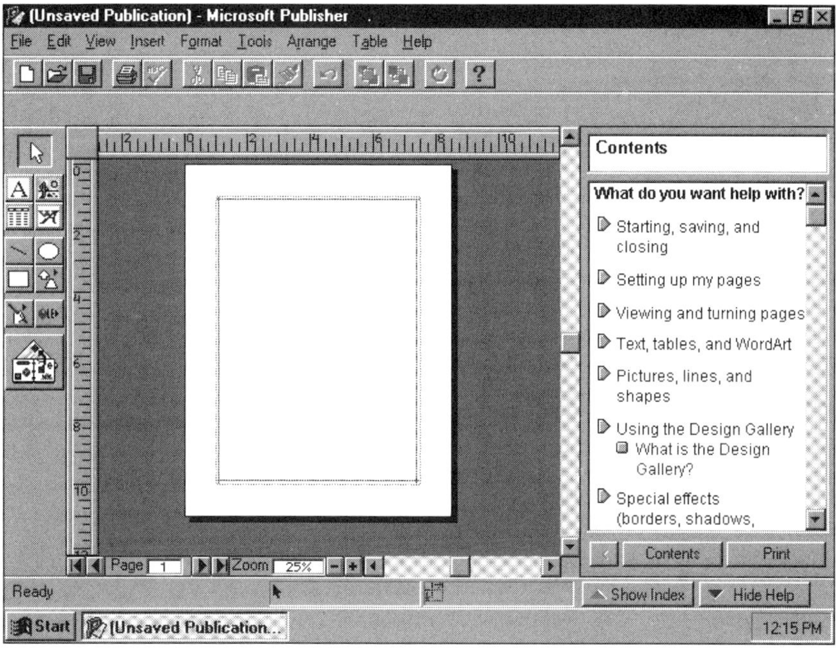

FIGURE 1.21 PUBLISHER SCREEN WITH HELP TOPICS DISPLAYED.

When the help panel is not displayed, you can also bring it up by clicking on the **Show Help** button. When help is displayed, the button changes to **Hide Help**. (It's what is known as a *toggle button*, automatically switching to the opposite value.) The same is true of the Index. Click on the **Show Index** button at the bottom of your screen, or select it from the Help menu, and take a look at the second help panel that appears. Your screen should look similar to the one shown in Figure 1.22.

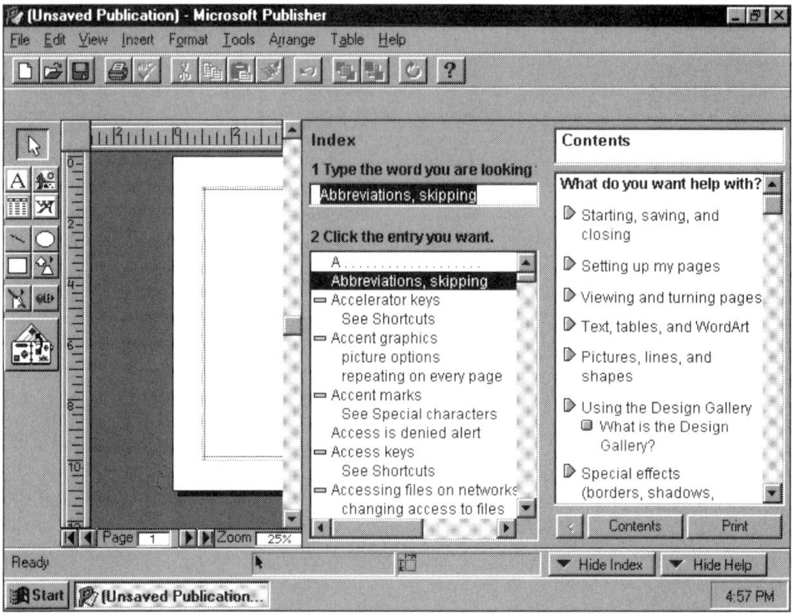

FIGURE 1.22 THE PUBLISHER SCREEN WITH BOTH HELP TOPICS AND INDEX DISPLAYED.

Unlike the help panel that can appear alone, the index panel always displays together with the help panel. This doesn't leave much room on the screen to work, so chances are you'll want to hide the index when you're not using it. Depending on your eyesight and the size of your monitor, you may want to alter the size of the help text by choosing the **Help Text Size** option from the Help menu and selecting **Smaller**, **Normal**, or **Bigger** from the submenu.

Publisher comes with a dozen *Quick Demos*, mini tutorials that explain various concepts and procedures such as background, preparing your publication for print by an outside printer, and wrapping text. Select **Quick Demos...** from the Help menu to see a complete list of the demo topics.

Introduction to Publisher... is a 13-screen presentation that explains the main program features. When you select **Keyboard Shortcuts** from the Help menu, the help panel opens to provide four categories of shortcut information. Publisher supports so many keyboard alternatives that you'll be grateful that the help panels are broken into various groups and subgroups of activities. Throughout the book, I'll mention some of the keyboard alternatives.

The **Print Troubleshooter** option is a subject that I'll get to in Chapter 9. If you want information about **Technical Support**, select this option from the Help menu to bring up the help panel with information on obtaining technical support and how to use the Microsoft Network Publisher Forum to get even more help.

If you select the **Microsoft Office Compatible...** option from the Help menu, the Microsoft Office Compatible window appears (provided that you have MS Office installed on your system).

And finally, the last Help option, **About Microsoft Publisher**, displays an informational window with the copyright notice and serial number.

Standard and Format Toolbars

Immediately beneath the menu bar is a toolbar, or *speedbar*, containing a number of buttons as shown in Figure 1.23.

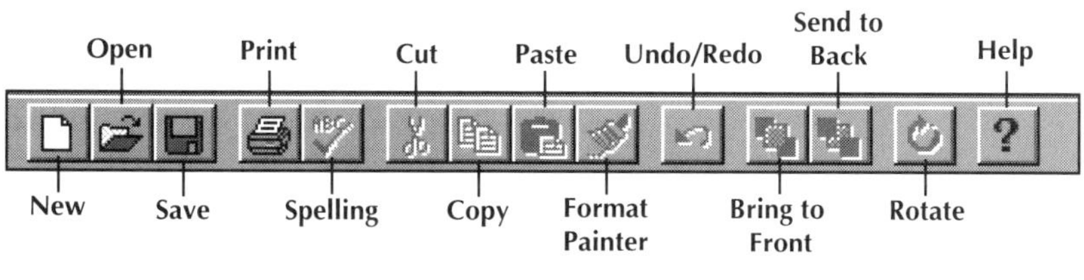

FIGURE 1.23 THE STANDARD HORIZONTAL TOOLBAR.

The **New**, **Open**, and **Save** buttons have the same effect as selecting those same options from the File menu. Similarly, the **Cut**, **Copy**, **Paste**, and **Undo/Redo** buttons are the same as their counterparts on the Edit menu. The **Format Painter** button is a composite of the **Pickup Format** and **Apply Format** options on the Format menu. The **Spelling** button is the same as the **Check Spelling** option on the Tools menu. The **Bring to Front**, **Send to Back**, and **Rotate** tool buttons serve the same function as the identical options on the Arrange menu. Finally, the **Help** button brings up the help panel containing the most recent help topic you looked at.

Depending on what type of object you select, various tool buttons appear on the second horizontal toolbar, known as the Format toolbar. I'll describe them when discussing the specific objects in Chapters 2-5. You can choose to hide or show the various toolbars. Right-click on any toolbar (horizontal or vertical) to display the pop-up menu, as shown in Figure 1.24, and make your selections from there. As you can see from the pop-up menu you can choose to hide or show the menu bar, horizontal toolbar, vertical toolbar, and status bar; or you can bring up the Rulers and Toolbars dialog window. The dialog window (shown earlier in Figure 1.10) offers the same four options and allows you to change your buttons from color to black-and-white (or vice versa), change between large and small buttons, and specify whether you want to see the button tool tips.

NOTE

Tool tips are the little descriptors or identifiers that appear when you hold your mouse over a button.

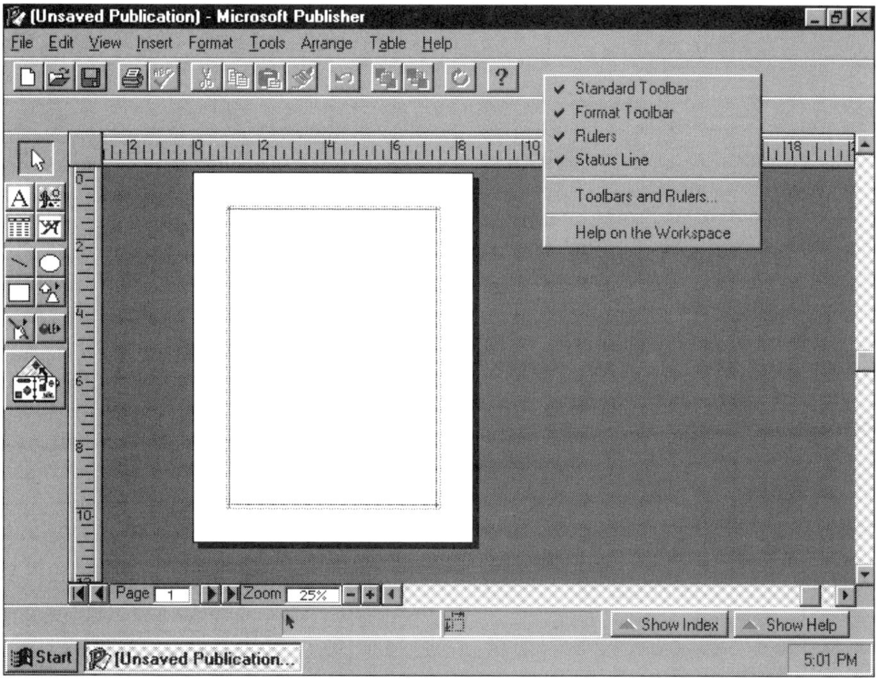

FIGURE 1.24 TOOLBAR POP-UP MENU DISPLAYED BY RIGHT-CLICKING ON A TOOLBAR AREA.

Rulers and Scroll Bars

The central work area is surrounded by a horizontal and vertical ruler on the top and left respectively, and by scroll bars on the right and bottom. You can drag the rulers over into the layout area, as shown in Figure 1.25, or you can use the **Ruler Guides** option on the Arrange menu to add an additional ruler guide that displays on your screen as a green dotted line. You may wonder why you'd want to do this, but you'll find it useful when you want to precisely position your objects on the page.

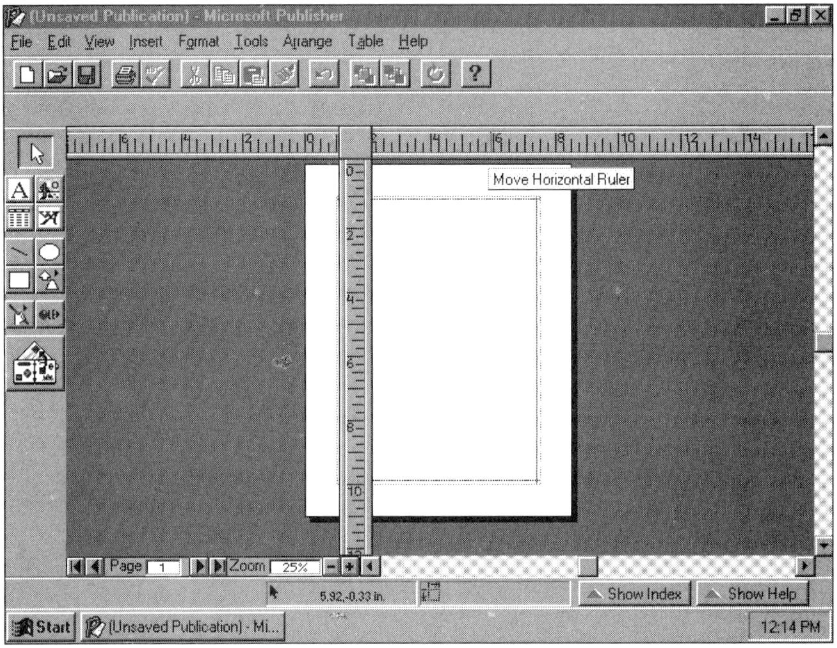

FIGURE 1.25 BLANK PAGE LAYOUT WITH RULER BAR MOVED INTO LAYOUT.

The default measurement unit for the rulers is inches; however, you can change that. In the discussion of the Tools menu earlier in this chapter, you saw the Options dialog window where you could choose to change the unit of measurement. The rulers will reflect any change you make.

The horizontal scroll bar along the bottom contains some additional indicators that can also be seen in Figure 1.25. On either side of the page number indicator are buttons to move forward and backward. Just to the right of that is the Zoom indicator showing the percentage of reduction or enlargement at which you are currently seeing the publication. **100%**

is full size. You can enlarge or reduce the display by clicking on the + and - buttons.

Status Bar

Immediately below the horizontal scroll bar is the five-section status bar shown in Figure 1.26. Publisher uses the far left section to display various status or helpful messages. If you highlight a menu option, a brief description appears. If you hold your mouse over a tool button, you'll see a description in the status area, and that's in addition to the tool tip descriptor that appears next to the button in question.

The second section on the status bar indicates the position of your cursor in a text frame, or the location of the top-left corner of the selected object frame. And the third section tells you the size of the selected frame. If this section is blank, that means that you have not selected an object (or perhaps, you have not created one yet).

The last two sections are actually buttons, **Show Index** and **Show Help**, discussed earlier in this chapter.

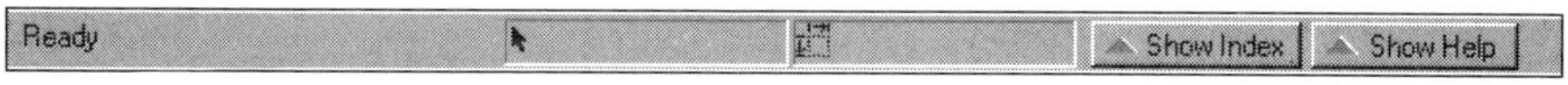

FIGURE 1.26 THE STATUS BAR.

Vertical Toolbar

The vertical toolbar shown in Figure 1.27 holds the tools needed to create your text frames, picture frames, and other objects as described in the next section. In addition to a button for each of the basic objects, you'll also find a button to reestablish your pointer (useful for canceling a prior tool selection), a button to call up a PageWizard to create a special object, and a button to gain access to the Design Gallery containing special design objects.

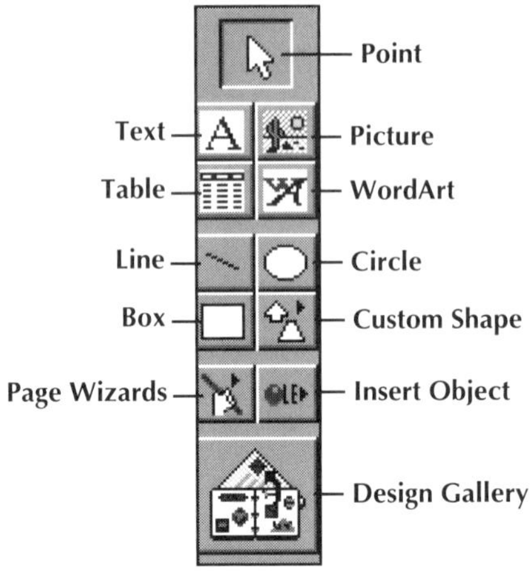

FIGURE 1.27 THE VERTICAL TOOLBAR CONTAINING THE FRAME.

THE OBJECTS

All objects are created equal. Well, what I really mean is that you create all objects the same way: Click on the desired object tool, drag out the object frame area, and add in the content. Actually, that's not entirely true. That's one way to do it. But there is another way that does not involve dragging out the frame area.

Earlier in this chapter, you saw the Options dialog window (Figure 1.16). One of the options is **Single Click Object Creation**, and it is selected by default. What this means is that once you click on an object tool, you can just click anywhere in your workspace and the Publisher creates the object in a default size, placing the top-left corner of the object wherever you clicked. You can then resize and position the object as you choose.

NOTE

This would be a good time to point out that your workspace is not limited to the actual page, but consists of the entire central area on your screen. Your workspace is the area bordered by the rulers and scroll bars. And you can place objects anywhere on your workspace.

After you have content in the frame, you can stylize both the frame and content, as well as position the object properly within the document. That's the nutshell description. In Chapters 2-7, you'll examine many sample publications and experiment with the creation, placement, and styling of object frames and their content. Most of your publications will contain a combination of text and images with a sprinkling of design objects such as lines, shapes, and border art.

Basic Elements

Text: As you'll see in Chapter 2, you can import existing text from other programs, or type your verbiage directly into a text frame. And you have all the typical formatting options to stylize your text.

Picture: Chapter 3 is devoted to the use of pictures, both photographic and clip art. You'll find everything you need to know about importing, scanning, cropping, and scaling images.

Table: A table contains columns and rows of text, so many of the formatting and display options are the same as those used for text objects. Topics such as inserting/deleting columns and rows and filling and merging cells are the subject of Chapter 4.

WordArt: This is sort of a hybrid type of object. The content is text, but it is rendered as a bitmap image. This allows you to shape and size your words in unusual ways and add special effects as discussed in Chapter 5.

Lines and Shapes

Line: Line objects come in different thicknesses and colors, with or without arrowheads of varied designs.

Circle and Box: You can apply borders, fill colors, patterns, and shading to any circle object, whether perfect or ovoid in shape. The same applies to box objects, both square and rectangular.

Custom Shapes: Publisher comes with 36 additional shapes ranging from a thunder bolt to bubble quotes and triangles. As with other shapes, you may apply borders, fill colors, patterns, and shading to any custom shape object.

At first you may think that you'll seldom have use for lines and shapes, but you'll soon find that individual lines and shapes can be grouped together to form a composite object that you can use for design or ornamentation. You'll get a closer look at lines in shapes in Chapter 5.

PageWizard Objects

The PageWizard objects available to you when you click on the **PageWizard** button are not the same as those available from the startup dialog window that appears when you launch Publisher. These are elements that you want to include *inside* a publication, as opposed to being a publication in and of themselves. The four PageWizard objects are: Calendar, Ad, Coupon, and Logo.

NOTE

Okay, you caught me. Calendar is also one of the PageWizards on the startup dialog window, but you use that one to create a calendar as the whole publication, and this one to include a small calendar as one element within another publication.

Other Objects

When you click on the **Insert Object** button, a dialog window appears listing all the applications available on your system that support OLE (Object Linking and Embedding). You'll examine the Insert Object dialog window and the concept of OLE in Chapter 8.

Design Gallery

A few moments ago I suggested that you could create composite objects for design or ornamentation use. Publisher's Design Gallery contains **Headline**, **Ornament**, **Pull Quote**, **Sidebar**, **Table of Contents**, and **Title objects**; and they come in **Classic**, **Jazzy**, **Modern**, **Plain**, and

Other styles. The best feature of the Design Gallery, however, is the capability you have to create and save your own design objects for future use as described in Chapter 6.

SUMMARY

- The Publisher startup dialog window has three pages: PageWizard (containing icons to launch Design Assistants for 16 different types of publications), Existing Publications (allowing you to select recently used Publisher files or files stored within a particular folder), and Blank Page (containing various size and page folding choices).
- Publisher has nine drop-down menus: File, Edit, View, Insert, Format, Tools, Arrange, Table, and Help.
- The Edit and Format menus change depending on what type of object you select.
- The newest feature on the File menu is the **Send...** option, used to send a publication via email—a feature that is new to the Windows 95 operating system and only available if you installed Microsoft Mail.
- Publisher allows you to reduce or enlarge the display of a publication using options on the View menu, or the **+** and **-** Zoom buttons to the left of the horizontal scroll bar.
- You can control the color and size of the toolbar buttons, and turn the tool tips on or off.
- Your layout can be measured in inches, centimeters, picas or points. The default is inches, but you can change this setting in the Options dialog window.
- The Publisher Help window appears as a panel fitted to the right side of your screen, making it convenient to keep Help visible while working on a publication. You can **Hide** or **Show** the Help panel at the touch of a button. The Help Index appears as a separate panel immediately to the left of the Help panel.

- **Introduction to Publisher...** is a 13-screen presentation that explains Publisher's main program features. Publisher also includes a dozen **Quick Demos**, mini tutorials that explain various Publisher concepts and procedures. You can select both options from the Help menu.
- Publisher has two toolbars below the menu bar. The first is the standard toolbar, containing speedbuttons for frequently used functions such as opening and saving files, editing options such as undo and copy, as well as formatting, spelling, and arranging functions. The second is the Format toolbar, where the available speedbuttons depend on the type of object you select.
- The toolbar pop-up menu allows you to hide or show the menu bar, horizontal toolbar, vertical toolbar, and status bar. You can also access the Rulers and Toolbars dialog window from there.
- You can drag rulers onto the design page.
- The page number indicator and buttons that allow you to move back and forth among the pages are located to the far left of the horizontal scroll bar.
- Immediately below the horizontal scroll bar is a five-section status bar: 1) displays brief descriptions of menu options and speedbuttons; 2) shows cursor position or location of top-left frame corner; 3) shows size of a selected frame; 4 and 5) the **Show/Hide Index** and **Help** buttons, respectively.
- The vertical toolbar holds the object tools: Point, Text, Picture, Table, WordArt, Line, Circle, Box, Custom Shapes, PageWizard, Insert Object, and Design Gallery.
- To create an object, click on the object tool, and then click on the layout page or in your workspace. If the **Single Click Object Creation** option is not selected, you have to drag out the frame area on the page.
- Four PageWizards are available from the vertical toolbar: Calendar, Ad, Coupon, and Logo. These are objects that you want to include inside the publication and should not be confused with the PageWizards available in the startup dialog window.

CHAPTER 2

WORKING WITH TEXT

* Creating and saving a publication
* Identifying, moving, and resizing text frames
* Editing and formatting text: specifying fonts, attributes, and character spacing
* Inserting symbol characters and wingdings
* Grouping objects and connecting frames
* Creating lists and bullets
* Greeking small text
* Coloring text and objects
* Using the Format Painter
* Defining text styles
* Setting line spacing
* Spell checking
* Examining the text object pop-up menu

All data elements in a Publisher document must be contained within a frame, and text is no exception. Once you have a text frame, the basics of working with text in Microsoft Publisher are much the same as working with text in any word processing program. Characters may have different fonts, sizes, colors, and other attributes such as bold, italic, and underline. Setting these characteristics is generally referred to as *character formatting*. You can also format a paragraph, justifying the text to the left margin, right margin, or both margins (this is called *flush*); or you can center the text within the frame. You can also set tabs and indent paragraphs. These are the simple basics. The Business Card PageWizard is a good place to begin examining these simple basics, and you can get familiar with where all the tools are located. Then I'll use some of the other designs to illustrate other text-based features.

SAMPLE BUSINESS CARD

Launch Microsoft Publisher, if you have not done so already, select **Business Card** from the PageWizard tab page, and click **OK**. (The Business Card icon is on the second row, second from the right.) If your Publisher program is already open, select **Create New Publication...** from the File menu to bring up the startup dialog window.

While a few of the Wizard's designs do not require any input from you, most of the designs prompt you for some information. In the case of the business card, the first decision you must make is one of style. The Wizard has nine styles of business cards from which you may choose. As shown in Figure 2.1, the default is the first style, **Classic**. If you click on another style, the preview picture on the left changes to reflect your selection. This way you can get some idea of how each style will look.

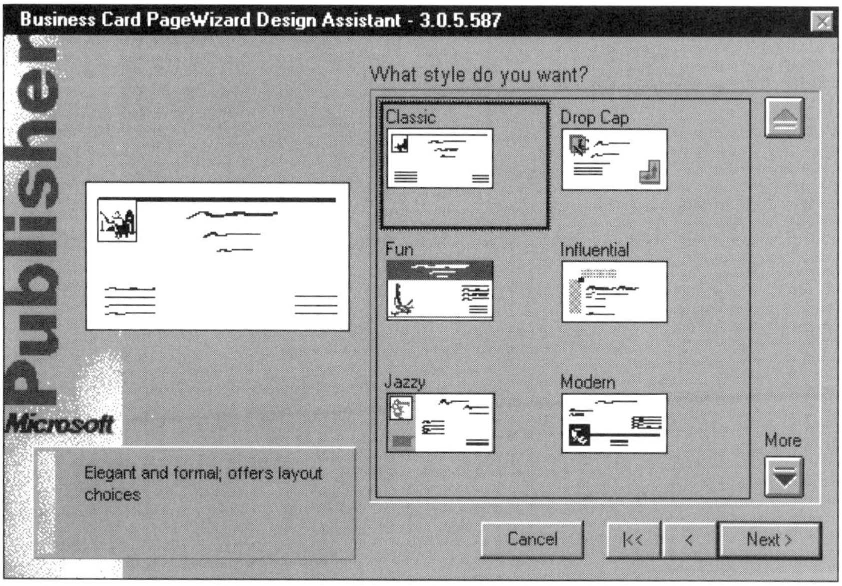

FIGURE 2.1 BUSINESS CARD PAGEWIZARD DESIGN ASSISTANT PROMPTS YOU TO SELECT A STYLE.

For our first example, let's stick with classic. Make sure that **Classic** is selected, and then click on **Next>**. The Wizard now wants to know whether you want to use a picture on your card. Your other option is to use initials instead of a picture (see Figure 2.2). If you want to use a picture on a business card, you'll want to use an image that relates to your business, or even better, the company logo. For now, however, you don't have to worry about this. Publisher will use a default image as a placeholder, and you will be able to change it later. Again, you can see your choice reflected in the preview picture on the left. For now, leave **Include a picture** selected and click on **Next>**.

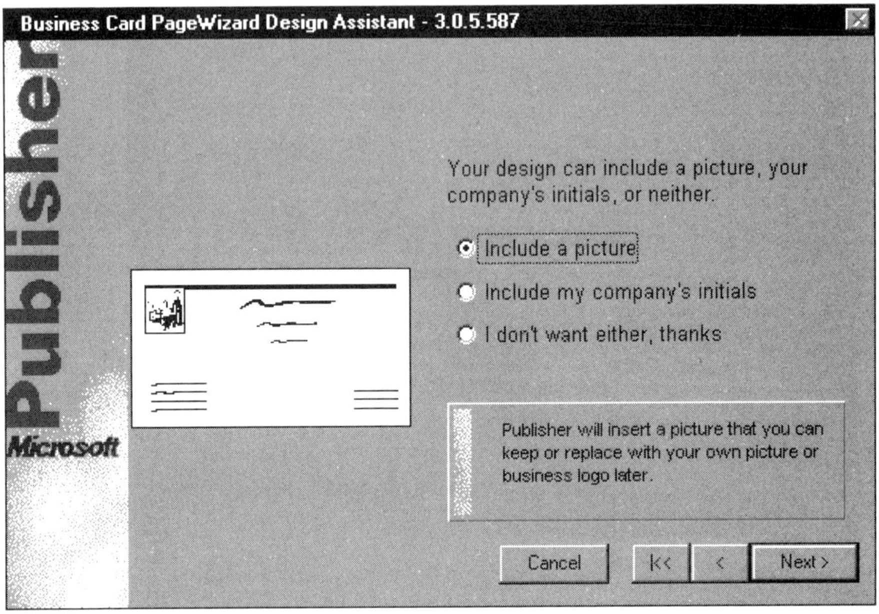

FIGURE 2.2 BUSINESS CARD PAGEWIZARD DESIGN ASSISTANT ASKS WHETHER TO INCLUDE A PICTURE OR INITIALS.

Now you need to provide the Wizard with your specifics. First, your address. Publisher will keep track of three different addresses for you: business, personal, and other. Make your selection, and enter your address, including company name if appropriate. Figure 2.3 shows my entry. I chose to provide a business address, but because I don't have a company name, I used my name on the first line. You'll see why in a moment.

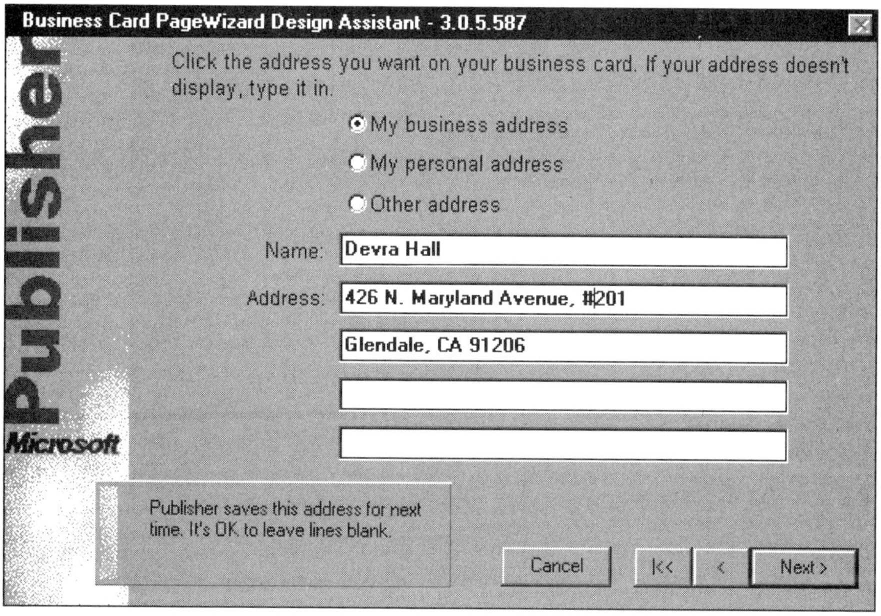

FIGURE 2.3 BUSINESS CARD PAGEWIZARD DESIGN ASSISTANT PROMPTS YOU FOR YOUR BUSINESS, PERSONAL, OR OTHER ADDRESS.

The next prompt screen allows you to specify your name, title, phone number, fax number, and email address. Each item is optional. If you want to include title, for example, click on the radio button next to the word **Title**, and type your title into the text box that appears. My selections are shown in Figure 2.4. You'll notice that because I used my name in the previous screen, I left it blank here.

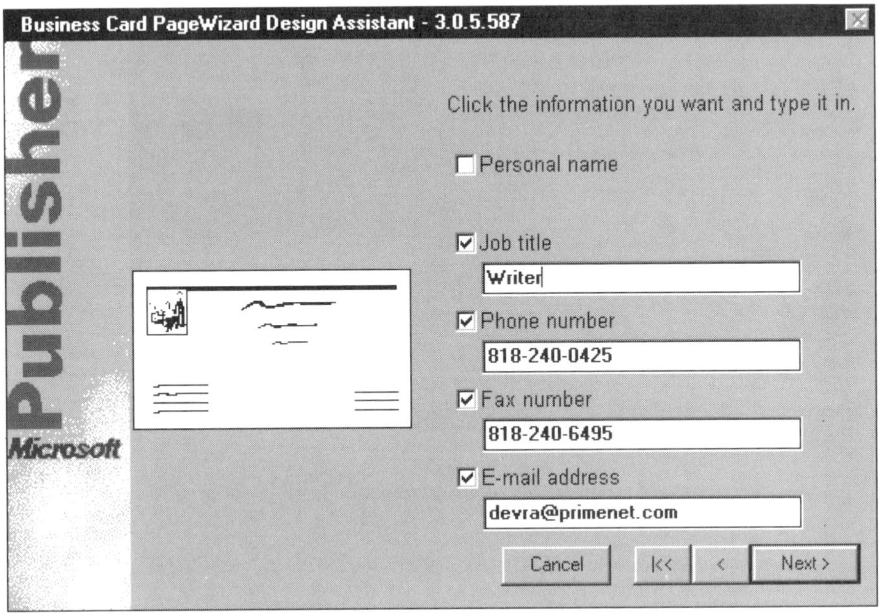

FIGURE 2.4 BUSINESS CARD PAGEWIZARD DESIGN ASSISTANT PROMPTS YOU FOR NAME, TITLE, AND CONTACT INFORMATION.

Finally, the Wizard wants to know if you want to lay out multiple card copies on a single page (ideal if you are going to print out your own cards), or if you want to see just one centered on a page. If you are producing camera-ready art for a printer, you will probably want just one image. For our purposes at the moment, select **One in the center** as shown in Figure 2.5, and click on **Next>**. When the next Wizard screen appears, click on **Create It!** and, as the Wizard says, sit back and relax. Don't fall asleep though, because the Wizard is a pretty fast worker.

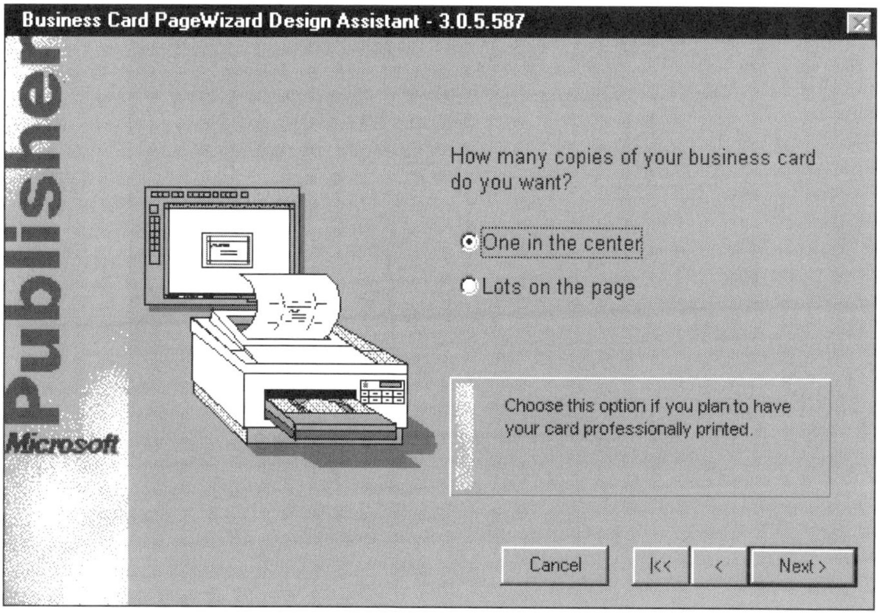

FIGURE 2.5 BUSINESS CARD PAGEWIZARD DESIGN ASSISTANT ASKS WHETHER YOU WANT TO CREATE A SINGLE CARD OR MULTIPLES ON A SINGLE PAGE.

When the PageWizard is done, you have a choice of requesting step-by-step help to assist you in completing your business card. For now, select **No** and click on **OK**. Your screen should now look something like the one shown in Figure 2.6.

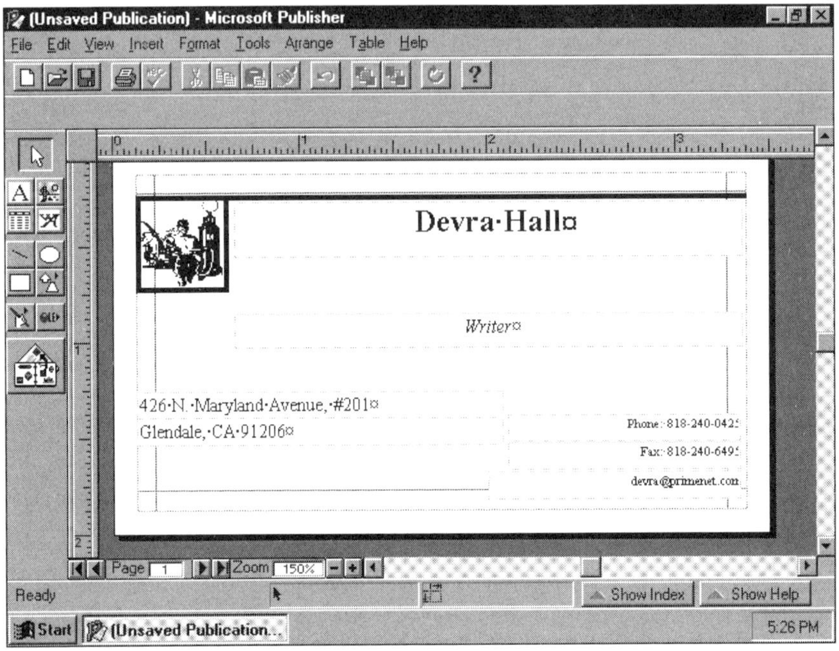

FIGURE 2.6 DEVRA'S SAMPLE BUSINESS CARD AS CREATED BY THE PAGEWIZARD.

Identifying Text Frames

Notice all the individual text frames. If you think back to each individual line of data you provided, you'll see that there is a frame for each one. I provided three address lines (one was the company name, or in my case, my name, plus two address lines), a title, phone number, fax number, and email address. You should be able to make out seven text frames in Figure 2.6.

The only other elements in this business card design are a line and a picture frame. The line I am referring to is the wide one at the top. If you look at Figure 2.6 again, you'll also notice some thin dotted lines. These are not design elements. The dotted lines represent the boundaries of each frame, and the others are layout guidelines.

So how do you know these are text frames? Well, it's obvious because they contain text. But if they were empty frames, would you be able to identify them as text frames? The answer is yes; there are many telltale signs.

Without actually selecting a frame, you can tell at a glance by checking to see if there is an end-of-file character in the frame. Depending on the size of your screen and the zoom factor, this character is sometimes hard to see. Take another look at Figure 2.6 and check out the last character after my name, my title, and each address line. You should be able to find this character at the end of the text in each of the text frames of your sample business card publication. Now try deleting the text on one of the frames. The end character remains even when no text is in the frame.

If you actually select a text frame by clicking on it, you'll see eight handles appear around the frame (one in each corner and in the middle of each side), and a little button appears at the bottom of the frame as shown in Figure 2.7. You will only see this particular button on text frames, and the single diamond indicates that all the text associated with that frame is currently visible within the frame.

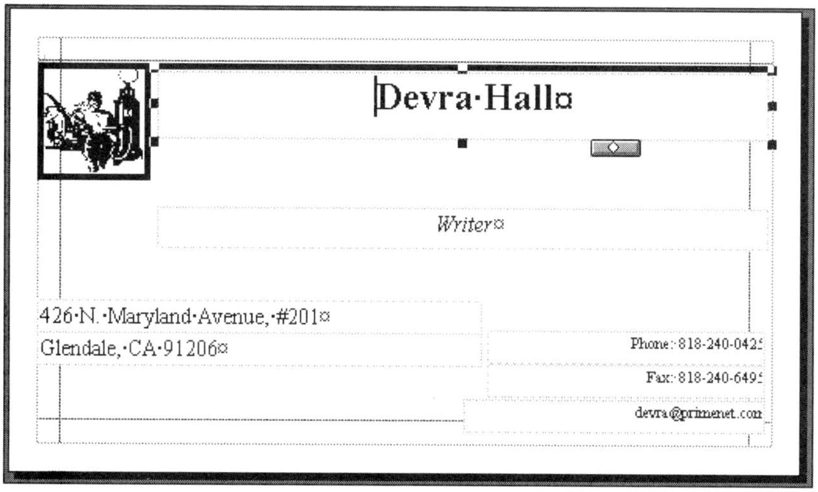

FIGURE 2.7 DEVRA'S SAMPLE BUSINESS CARD WITH THE TOP TEXT FRAME SELECTED.

Yet another way to tell what type of frame you have selected is to take a look at your desktop environment. When you select a text frame, changes occur in the Edit and Format menus, as well as on the second horizontal toolbar, known as the Format toolbar. Figure 2.8 shows the three drop-down list boxes and twelve speedbuttons that appear when you work with a text frame. You'll get a chance to use the buttons on this toolbar as this chapter continues. But for the moment, I want to continue talking about text frames and other changes to your working environment.

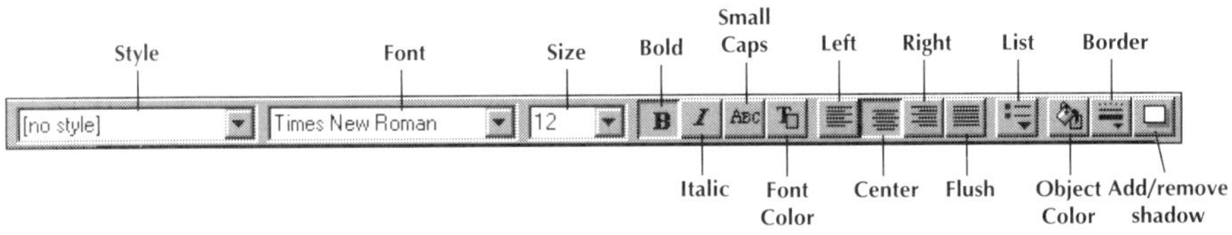

FIGURE 2.8 WHEN YOU WORK WITH TEXT, THE FORMAT TOOLBAR CHANGES TO DISPLAY THESE THREE DROP-DOWN LIST BOXES AND TWELVE SPEEDBUTTONS.

In Chapter 1 I mentioned that the Edit and Format menu options change depending on what type of object you select. When you select a text frame, the Edit menu's **Cut**, **Copy**, **Delete**, and **Edit Object** options change to read **Cut Text Frame**, **Copy Text Frame**, **Delete Text Frame**, and **Edit Story** in Microsoft Word. The changes to the Format menu are more extensive. In addition to changing the **Frame Properties...** option to **Text Frame Properties...**, Publisher adds six additional options for working with text. The Format menu with the additional options is shown in Figure 2.9. You'll examine these options as you continue to work with the samples in this chapter.

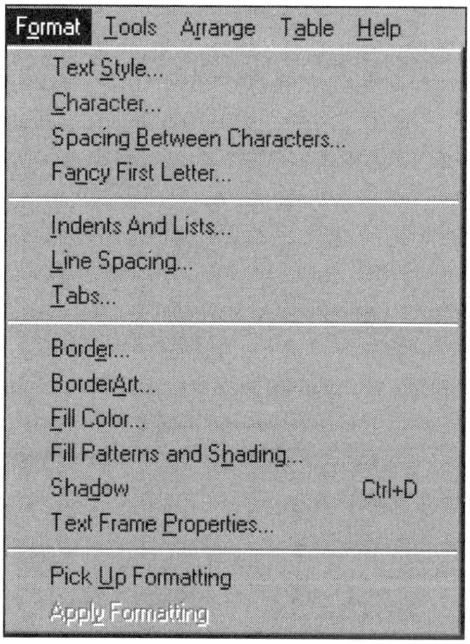

FIGURE 2.9 WHEN YOU WORK WITH TEXT, THE FORMAT MENU CHANGES AND INCLUDES ADDITIONAL OPTIONS.

Moving and Resizing Text Frames

Before we move on to character formatting, there is something bothering me that I need to fix. The business card design created by the PageWizard using the data I provided looks lopsided to me. Of course, depending on whether you provided the same lines of data that I did, your own layout may look a bit different, or you may like the design as is—but for the sake of the exercise, humor me.

I imagine that a professional designer would explain that the placement of the phone, fax, and email lines at the bottom-most right corner is supposed to balance the top left picture, and I would probably agree. It's the two address lines that bother me. I want to move them down farther, but I don't know yet whether I want the bottom line to match the bottom line of the email frame or whether the two address lines should be centered within the three contact lines. The final decision is a matter of your own taste or preference. What is important, however, is that even when you use a PageWizard, you can easily make whatever changes you want.

Moving frames around is easy. First select the frame and then move your mouse around over the frame; when the cursor/pointer changes into the Move cursor, as shown in Figure 2.10, click and hold down your mouse button while you drag the frame to the new location. When your frame is in position, release the mouse button.

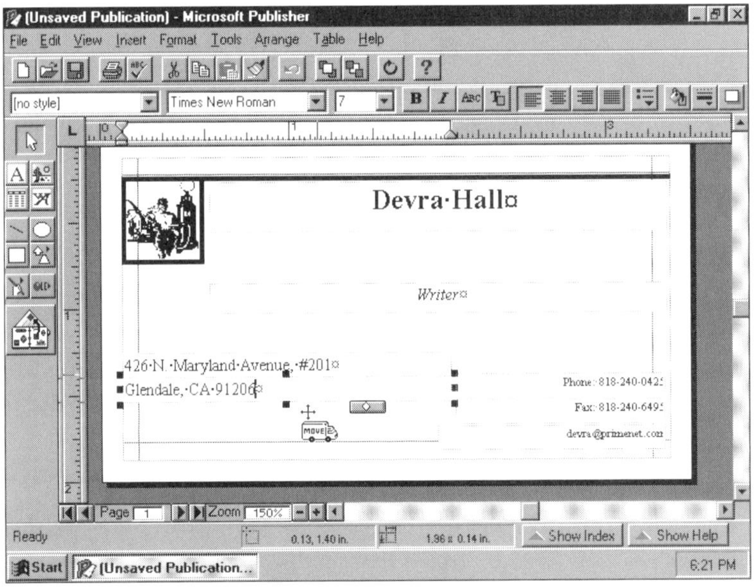

FIGURE 2.10 THE MOVE CURSOR.

Resizing a frame is just as easy. Select the frame and move your mouse over one of the frame handles until the pointer changes into a resize cursor; then click and hold down your mouse button while you push or pull your frame to the desired size. If you choose either the top or bottom handle, the resize cursor allows you to resize vertically, changing the height of the frame. If you choose either the left or right handle, the resize cursor allows you to resize horizontally, changing the width of the frame. If you choose either of the corners, the resize cursor allows you to resize diagonally, changing both the height and width simultaneously. Figure 2.11 shows the various resizing cursors.

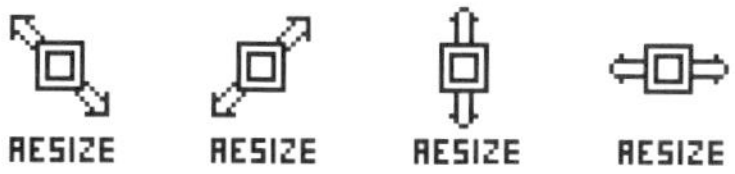

FIGURE 2.11 WHEN RESIZING A FRAME, YOUR CURSOR WILL LOOK LIKE ONE OF THESE.

Select one of your address text frames and resize it horizontally so that the frame becomes too small to display all the text. Figure 2.12 shows one of my address text frames when I resized it horizontally. Notice the button attached to the bottom of the text frame. It's different from the one I showed you in Figure 2.7. Now instead of showing a single diamond indicating that all the text is visible, the button shows three small black squares to indicate that there is more text than what you can see in the frame. If you enlarge the frame again to display all the text, the button will revert to the single white diamond.

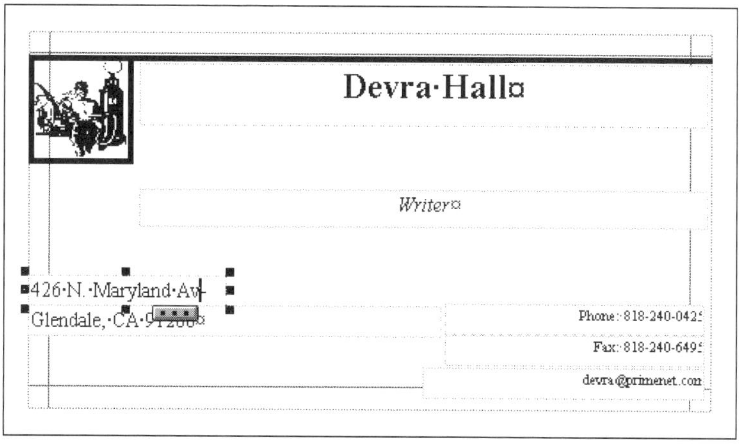

FIGURE 2.12 THE RESIZED ADDRESS FRAME, NOW TOO SMALL TO SHOW ALL THE TEXT.

Editing Text

The simplest way to put text inside a text frame is to click on the frame and begin typing. When you use a PageWizard you'll find some text already inside the various text frames. Usually, the text says something useful, such as a reminder or clue as to what the PageWizard had in mind when designing the layout. However, in the business card layout, you already provided the correct text, so the Wizard inserted it for you; but that doesn't mean you can't make changes.

If you want to change the text that is already there, you may do so. Try inserting or deleting a middle initial in your name. Make sure that the text frame containing your name is selected; then place your cursor in position. You can also select text and copy, cut, paste, or delete it.

NOTE

You can use the keyboard to highlight text. Place your cursor just before the letter where you want to start the selection; then hold down the **Shift** key and use your right and/or down arrow keys to move across and down. You can use your left and up arrow keys as well.

Assuming that you haven't done any customizing of your Publisher environment on your own, when you highlight some text and then start typing, the highlighted block is automatically deleted and replaced with whatever you type. Try highlighting your name and then type in a different one. See how that works?

Your ability to do this depends on the option settings. In the last chapter, you examined the Tools menu and discovered the More Options dialog window (refer to Figure 1.17). When the option labeled **Typing Replaces Selection** is checked, you can type right over an existing block of selected text. However, when this option is not checked, your selected text will not be disturbed, and any new text will simply be inserted. Once your text is in place, you can format it.

Setting Basic Text Characteristics

Before moving on to another sample publication, let's look at a few of the features and tools for basic character formatting. Basic text characteristics include the font type and size, as well as attributes and effects such as bold, italic, underlines, capitals, color, shadow, and character spacing. When it comes to font types, you have at least 48 fonts (41 of which are TrueType) ranging from Algerian and Arial, to Wide Latin. In addition, you have symbols and three sets of wingding characters (see the "Symbols and Wingdings" sidebar). If you have Publisher's Deluxe version, you have more than 60 available font types.

SYMBOLS AND WINGDINGS

Symbols are special characters that include foreign letters, fractions, and other symbols such as the copyright mark. Symbol characters look slightly different when rendered in different fonts.

Unless you are intimately familiar with the symbol font and know exactly which letter converts to which symbol when the symbol font is applied, it is far easier to use the **Symbol...** option from the Insert menu. This option brings up the Insert Symbol dialog window shown in Figure 2.13.

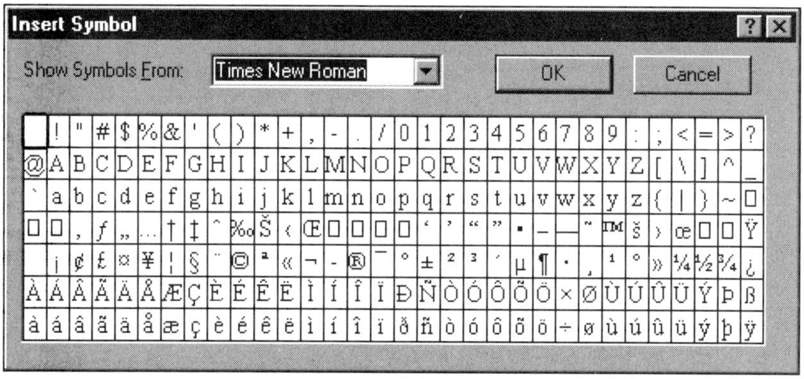

FIGURE 2.13 THE INSERT SYMBOL DIALOG WINDOW.

The name of the font you are currently using will be visible in the drop-down list box, and you can change to another font if you so desire. Select the symbol you want and click on **OK**.

T I P

If you want to see the symbol enlarged slightly before inserting it, click on the symbol but hold down your mouse button.

You can also use the Insert Symbol dialog window to view and insert wingdings. *Wingdings* include such things as bullet characters, arrows, smiley faces, check marks, and more. You have three groups of wingding characters, available by choosing **Wingdings**, **Wingdings 2**, or **Wingdings 3** from the drop-down list of fonts. Figures 2.14, 2.15, and 2.16 show the three groups of wingding characters.

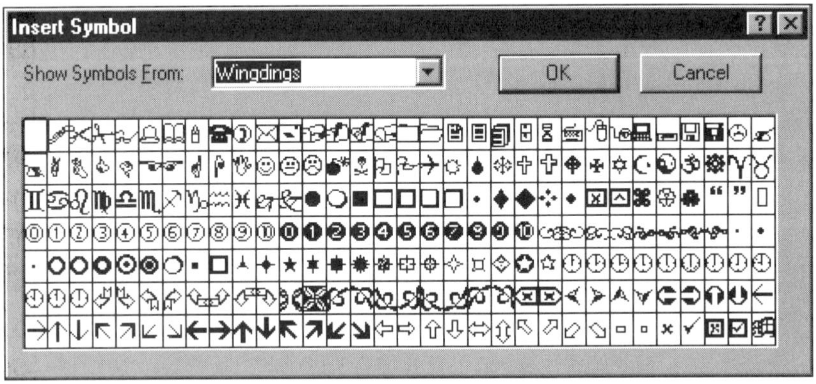

FIGURE 2.14 THE WINGDINGS CHARACTERS DISPLAYED IN THE INSERT SYMBOL DIALOG WINDOW.

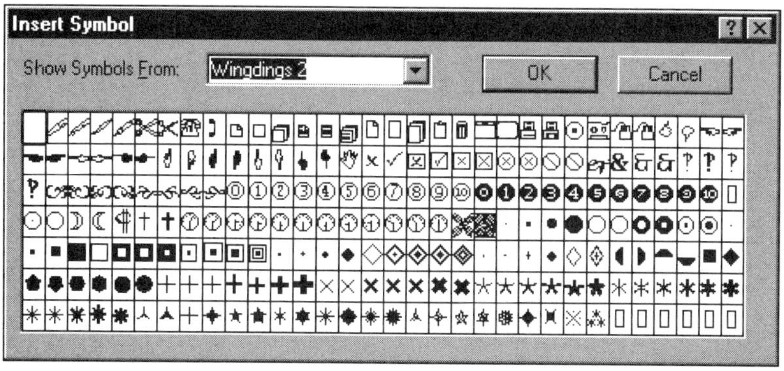

FIGURE 2.15 THE WINGDINGS 2 CHARACTERS DISPLAYED IN THE INSERT SYMBOL DIALOG WINDOW.

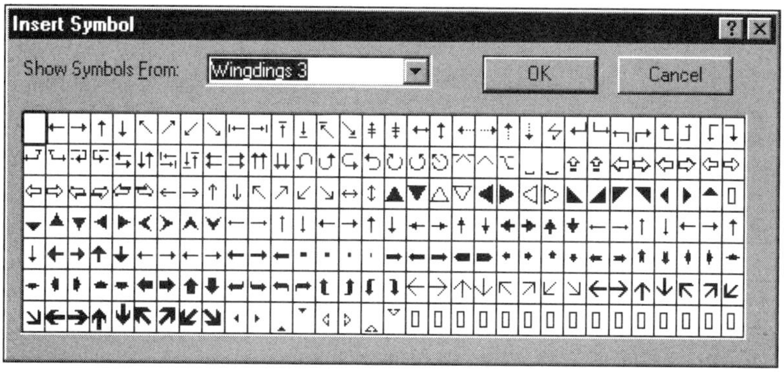

FIGURE 2.16 THE WINGDINGS 3 CHARACTERS DISPLAYED IN THE INSERT SYMBOL DIALOG WINDOW.

Selecting Fonts

You can choose a font for your text by selecting it from the middle drop-down list on your Format toolbar (the second horizontal toolbar; see Figure 2.8). If you select some text before choosing a font, then Publisher only applies the new font to the selected text. If you pick a font without first selecting text, Publisher looks at the position of your cursor and only applies the new font to any new text inserted at that point.

If you are not familiar with text formatting, try experimenting a bit with the text in the sample business card. For example, change the font of your name or company name from **Times New Roman** to **Ultra Shadow**. Don't forget to select the text first.

Assigning Attributes

From this same Format toolbar you can also specify the size of the font and assign the Bold, Italic, Small Capitals, and Color attributes. The same rules apply; if you select **Bold** or change a color without first selecting text, the change will only apply to new text inserted at that position.

Experiment some more. Change the size of your name from **12 point** to **16 point**. If you included a title on your sample business card, you'll see that it is formatted as italic. Try removing the italic attribute. Try making it small capitals. Change the text color.

Alternatively, you can select the **Character...** option from the Format menu to bring up the Character dialog window as shown in Figure 2.17. The Character dialog window provides some options not available on the Format toolbar. Only from the dialog window can you specify **All Capitals**, **Underlining**, and **Super-** and **Subscript**. Of course, some keyboard shortcuts will allow you to bypass both the Format toolbar and the Character dialog window. For example, pressing **Ctrl-B**, **Ctrl-I**, or **Ctrl-U** will assign bold, italic, or underline attributes, respectively, to selected text.

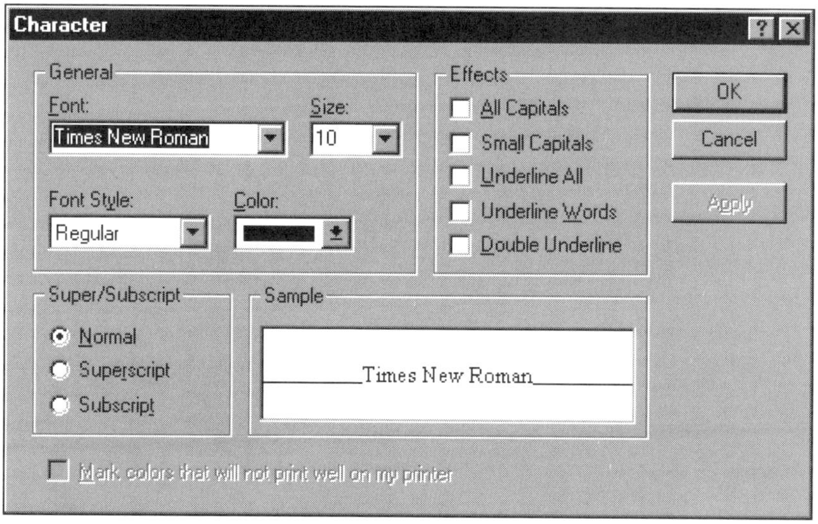

FIGURE 2.17 WHEN YOU SELECT **CHARACTER** FROM THE FORMAT MENU, THIS DIALOG WINDOW APPEARS.

Spacing Characters

The technical terms for character spacing are kerning and tracking, but you don't have to be an experienced typesetter to take advantage of Publisher's character spacing features. *Kerning* refers to the spacing between specific pairs of characters, and Publisher automatically takes care of kerning letter pairs on the fly when the font of a specified size or greater is used. This applies to letter pairs, such as *Wz*, *Wo*, and *Ya*, that normally print too far apart. The default setting for automatic kerning is *14pt* or greater, but you can change the default size to suit your needs by entering the new size in the More Options dialog window (see Figure 1.17).

Tracking refers to the spacing between all letters, not just specific letter pairs. If you're new to publishing, you may not be used to thinking about point sizes. However, you might simply want the letters to be spaced farther apart or closer together than normal. Try an experiment. Select the text frame containing your name or company name on the sample business card. Make sure that the cursor is inside the text frame. Then choose the **Spacing Between Characters…** option from the Format menu to bring up the dialog window shown in Figure 2.18.

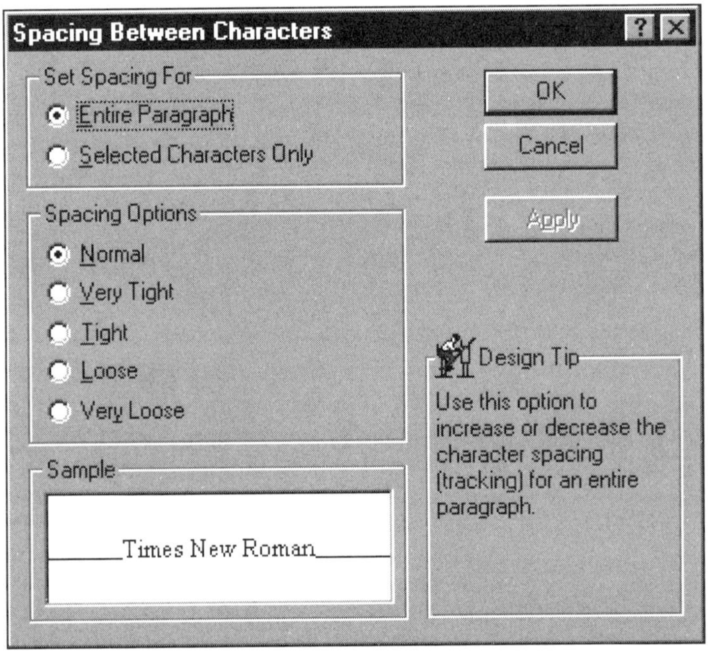

FIGURE 2.18 WHEN YOU SELECT SPACING BETWEEN CHARACTERS FROM THE FORMAT MENU, THIS DIALOG WINDOW APPEARS.

The top section of the dialog window lets you choose whether you want your spacing selection to apply to the whole paragraph (i.e., whichever paragraph the cursor is in) or just to the selected text. If you followed my instructions, you did not select any text, so the **Entire Paragraph** option is appropriate.

Next, your spacing options are: **Normal**, **Very Tight**, **Tight**, **Loose**, and **Very Loose**. Select the **Very Tight** option and click on **OK**. After you check out the results, select **Undo Format** from the Edit menu to return the text to its previous state. Then try it all again, this time selecting **Very Loose**. You might want to keep experimenting until you get a feel for how text looks when spacing is altered.

TIP

Ctrl-Z also works to undo the formatting.

When you want to set the character spacing for selected text, you have the opportunity to specify the exact amount of points by which you want to squeeze together or move letters apart. Figure 2.19 shows what the Spacing Between Characters dialog window looks like when you choose **Selected Characters Only**.

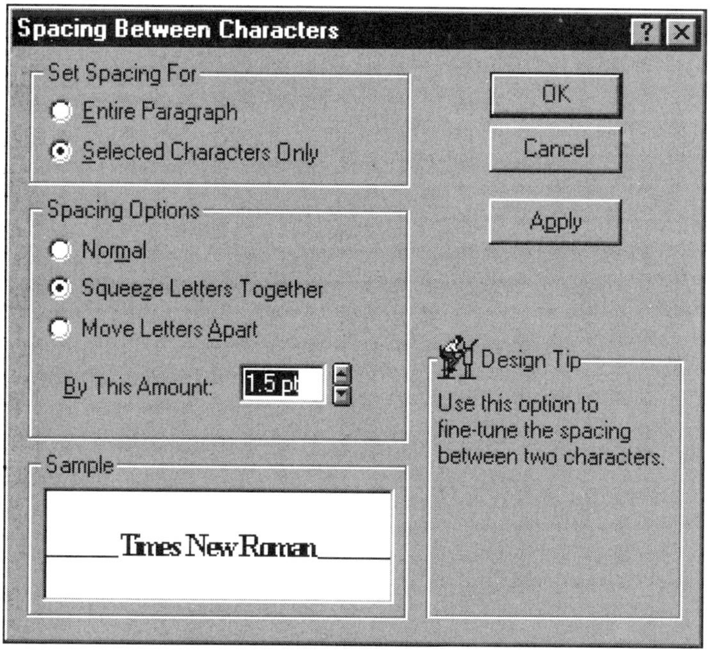

FIGURE 2.19 SPACING BETWEEN CHARACTERS DIALOG WINDOW WHEN USED FOR **SELECTED CHARACTERS ONLY**.

Saving a Publication

If you want to save the business card you've been working with, you can do so by clicking on the **Save** option in the File menu. Because this is a new publication that you have not yet saved, the Save As dialog window appears, as shown in Figure 2.20. Select the folder in which you want to store your publication, and give your publication a name (don't forget, this is Windows 95, so you can use a long filename if you want to). When you're ready, click on **OK**. It's also a good idea to check the **Save Preview** option so that you can see the preview on the Open Existing Publication page of the startup dialog window as discussed in Chapter 1. If you try to exit from Publisher or open a new publication before saving your current work, Publisher will ask you if you want to save it.

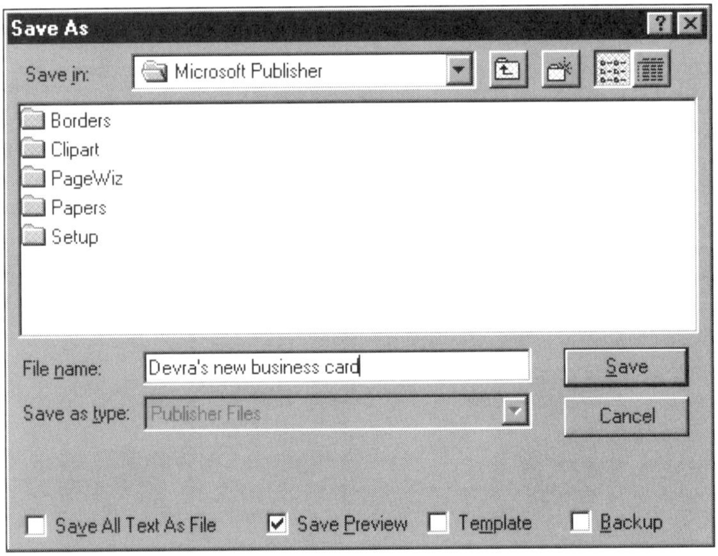

FIGURE 2.20 THE SAVE AS DIALOG WINDOW.

I could continue to use the Business Card design, but because I want to show you as many of the different PageWizards as possible, I want to use different designs for each example or group of topics throughout the book. If you want to save your business card, you can do so now. Don't forget, however, that there are other business card styles than the Classic style I used for this example.

On your own, you might want to experiment with some of the other styles. You will find that the Business Card PageWizard acts differently, depending on the style you select. For example, the **Drop Cap** style does not allow you to make any choices in the beginning, but the Wizard prompts you for information on the fly. Similarly, the **Influential** and **Water Color** styles do not allow you to make any choices because they are designed for use with special paper.

Enough with the business cards. It's time to look at another PageWizard.

SAMPLE RECIPE CARD

Click on **Create New Publication...** in the File menu. If you saved your previous work already, Publisher will bring up the PageWizard screen directly. If you did not save your work, Publisher will ask if you'd like to do so. The choice is yours. If you took a break after the last section and exited from the Publisher program, launch it again now.

Select **Specialty** from the PageWizard tab page (it's on the third row, second from left). When the Specialty PageWizard screen appears to ask what you want to make, select **Recipe Card** as shown in Figure 2.21; It's the last choice, so you may have to scroll down to find it.

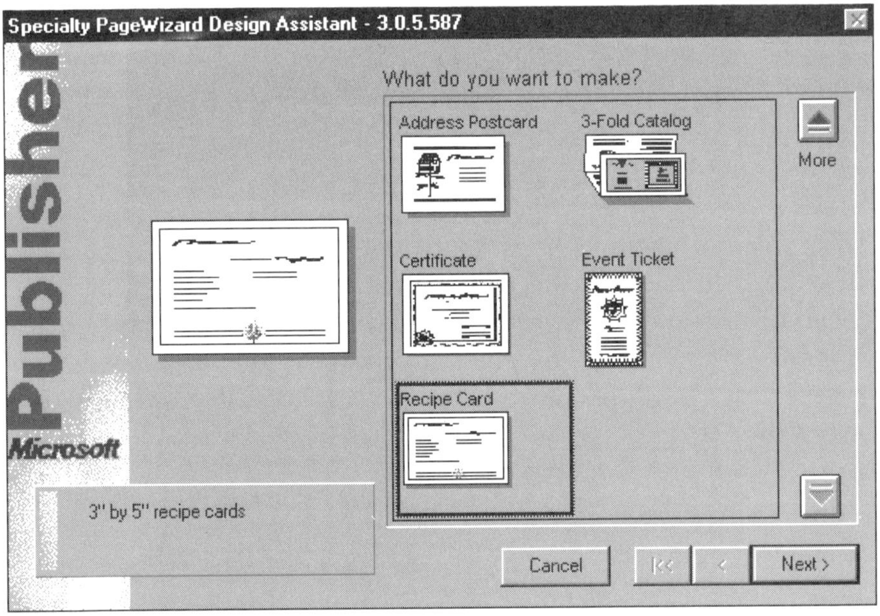

FIGURE 2.21 A SPECIALTY PAGEWIZARD SCREEN WITH THE RECIPE CARD ICON SELECTED.

When you click on **Next>** you'll find that no more preparation is required. Click on **Create It!** and let the Wizard do its stuff. After the PageWizard begins to prepare the layout, it will pause briefly to ask you to input your name, and then it completes the layout. When it's done, your screen with the new Recipe Card layout should look something like the one shown in Figure 2.22.

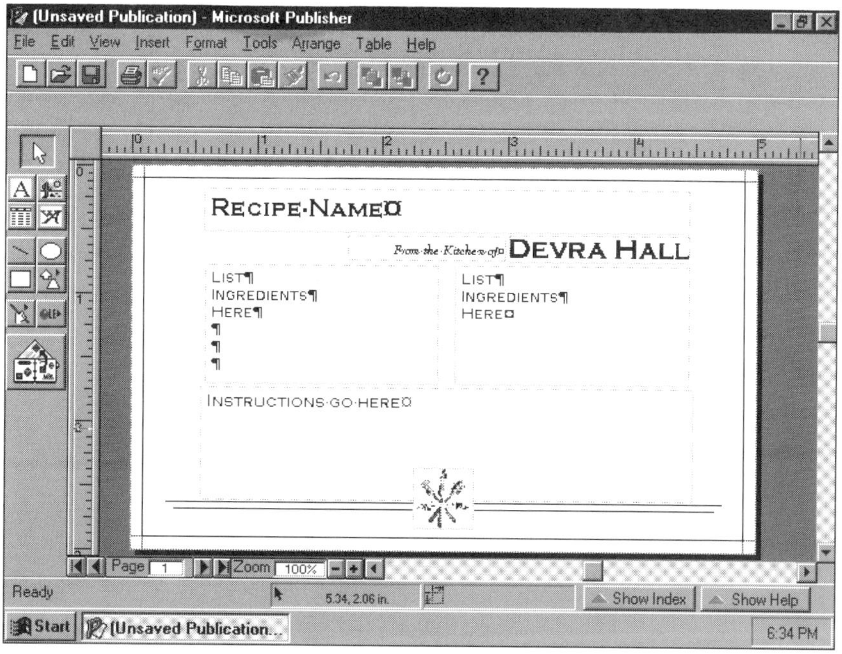

FIGURE 2.22 THE RECIPE CARD AS DESIGNED BY THE SPECIALTY PAGEWIZARD DESIGN ASSISTANT.

Take a quick look. How many frames are in this layout? You should be able to find seven frames. Although at first glance you cannot tell, one of the interesting things about the Recipe Card layout is that two of these frames have been grouped together to form a single group object. I'll show you the group object in a moment.

How many of these seven frames are text frames? The correct answer is five. Did you count six? If so, you probably counted the frame with your name in it as a text frame, but it's not a text frame; it's WordArt, which is something I'll talk about in Chapter 5. If you select that frame, no text button appears at the bottom of the frame, and there is no end-of-file character in that frame.

Oops. Did you count all the end-of-file characters visible in Figure 2.22? If you did, you only found four, and I just said that there are five text frames. Well, there are five text frames, but there are only four text files. Two of the text frames are connected so that the text that would not fit in the first frame flows over into the connected frame.

Just to confuse matters a little bit, it happens that the two frames that are connected are the same two frames that are grouped. But grouping frames or objects and connecting frames are two totally separate activities that have nothing to do with each other.

Grouping Objects

Try to select one of the two text frames that contain the words *LIST INGREDIENTS HERE*. It doesn't matter which you click on, you will end up selecting the two together, as shown in Figure 2.23. Notice that the frame handles surround both text frames together. Now try moving the group frame and see how the two text frames move as if they were one. The main purpose of grouping objects is so that you can move or rotate multiple objects simultaneously while maintaining their relative position to one another.

TIP

If you want help moving the frame back into its original position, select **Undo Move** from the Edit menu.

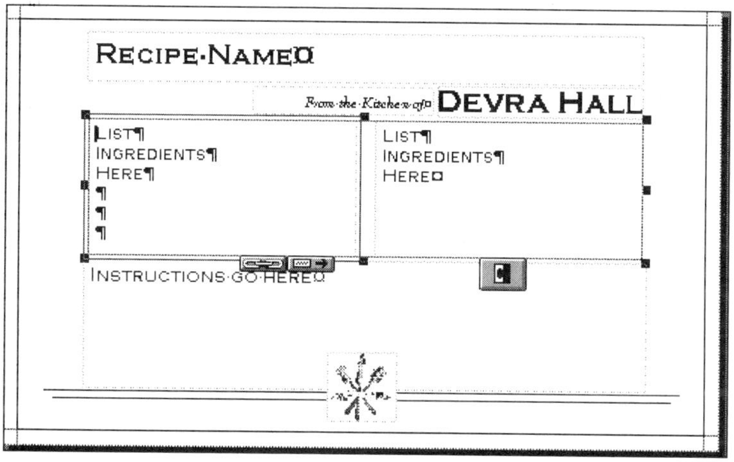

FIGURE 2.23 TWO TEXT FRAMES GROUPED TOGETHER. THE BUTTON WITH THE JIGSAW PUZZLE PIECES INDICATES THAT THE GROUP IS TOGETHER.

Now take a look at the frame button on the right, the one that looks like two pieces of a jigsaw puzzle fit together. Go ahead and click on that button to ungroup the two text frames. When you do so, the button changes. Now the jigsaw puzzle pieces are no longer fit together, reflecting the fact that the group is undone, as shown in Figure 2.24.

FIGURE 2.24 A GROUP OF TWO TEXT FRAMES JUST SEPARATED. THE BUTTON WITH THE JIGSAW PUZZLE PIECES INDICATES THAT THE GROUP IS NOT TOGETHER.

If you want to create the group again, all you have to do is click on the left text frame to select it and then hold down the **Ctrl** key and select the right text frame. When you do this, the group button appears, and when you click on it the objects become a group. Try it if you want to. Re-create the group, and then ungroup the objects again. When you are done experimenting, make sure that the two text frames are no longer a group.

TIP

If you ungroup an object by mistake, you can select **Undo Ungroup Object** from the Edit menu.

Connecting Frames

Twice earlier in this chapter I talked about the button that appears on the bottom of a text frame. The first time I mentioned it, I showed you the single diamond on the button indicating that all the text was visible in the frame. The second time I mentioned the text frame button, I showed you the three little squares indicating that the file contained more text than was visible in the selected text frame.

When there is more text than can fit in one frame, you need to connect it to a second frame (assuming you want to see the remaining text). And if there is still more text than can fit in the two frames combined, you connect the second frame with a third one. And so on. Connecting and disconnecting frames is quite simple.

Select the left text frame that is meant to contain the recipe's ingredients. At the bottom of that frame you should see two buttons, as shown in Figure 2.25. The button on the right has three squares, indicating more text, and a right arrow. The button on the left looks like three connected links of a chain and indicates that this frame is connected to another frame.

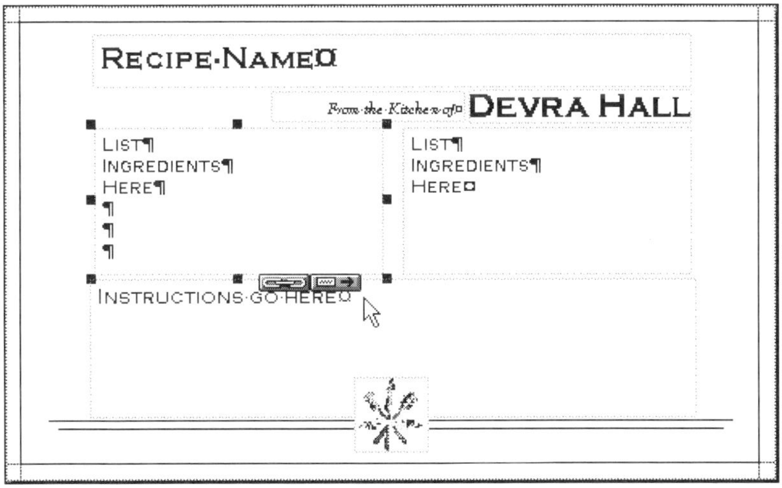

FIGURE 2.25 A TEXT FRAME WHERE THE FRAME BUTTONS INDICATE THAT THE TEXT OVERFLOW HAS BEEN PLACED INTO A CONNECTING FRAME.

Now select the text frame on the right. At the bottom of this frame you should see one button. This button has a single diamond, indicating no more text, and a left arrow, as shown in Figure 2.26. Because there is no more text, there is no need to connect this frame with a third frame. The chain link button is only used to indicate forward links, so it does not appear on this frame.

FIGURE 2.26 A TEXT FRAME WHERE THE FRAME BUTTONS INDICATE THAT THIS FRAME CONTAINS A CONTINUATION OF TEXT, AND THAT THERE IS NO FURTHER OVERFLOW.

The arrows on these two frame buttons are called *frame jump buttons.* They allow you to navigate easily between frames containing a single file. This is quite useful when a frame on one page is connected with a frame on a separate page. When you click on a frame jump button, Publisher takes you to the connected frame, wherever it is within your publication.

Connecting and disconnecting frames is just as easy as grouping and ungrouping objects. To disconnect the two text frames in your recipe card sample, simply click on the chain link button at the bottom of the first frame. Your frames will instantly disconnect; the text will disappear from the second frame; and the frame jump arrow will disappear from the first frame button. Try it.

Now that the frames are no longer connected, you have more text than can be displayed in frame one. Whenever you have more text, you will want to connect to another frame. Again, the procedure is easy. If your text frame overfloweth, you simply pour the remainder into another frame.

Here's what you should do. Click on the frame button with the three squares that indicates more text. Now move your mouse over the empty text frame and notice how the cursor changes into an overflowing cup. One click and Publisher pours your text from the cup into the empty frame. And voila, your two frames are connected again.

NOTE

If you are connecting a frame on one page to a frame on a different page, the procedure is the same. The only difference is that once you click on the frame button, you have to move to the other page before pouring your text. You can click on the **Page Forward** or **Page Back** buttons without pouring your text. Just don't accidentally click inside some other frame.

Creating Lists and Bullets

Before you move on to the next design sample, I want to show you another formatting option. If you want your list of ingredients to appear as a bulleted list, all you have to do is select the text and then use the **Indents and Lists...** option on the Format menu to bring up the dialog window. When you click on **Bulleted List**, you can select one of the six bullet types, as shown in Figure 2.27.

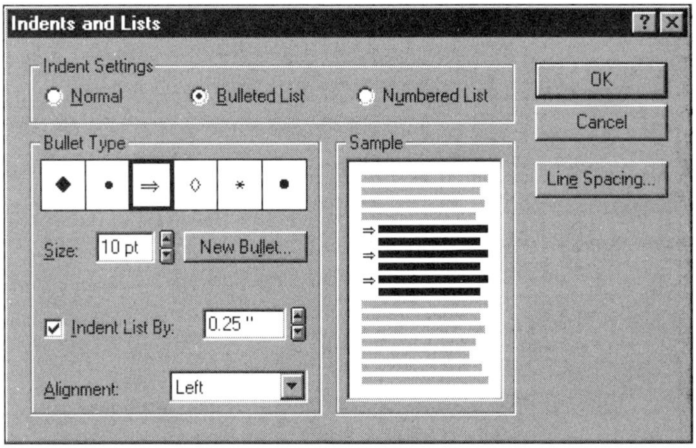

FIGURE 2.27 THE INDENTS AND LISTS DIALOG WINDOW WITH **BULLETED LIST** SELECTED.

Other settings include the character size of the bullet, amount of indentation, and alignment. If you select the settings shown in Figure 2.27 and click on **OK**, your recipe card should look like the one shown in Figure 2.28.

FIGURE 2.28 SAMPLE RECIPE CARD WITH BULLETED LIST FOR INGREDIENTS.

The idea of recipe cards is making me hungry. If you want to take a break, now would be a good time. If you prefer, you can move along to the next sample design. If you want to save this recipe card publication, do so now.

SAMPLE RESUME

Click on **Create New Publication...** from the File menu. If you saved your previous work already, Publisher will bring up the PageWizard screen directly. If you did not save your work, Publisher will ask if you'd like to do so. The choice is yours. If you took a break after the last section and exited from the Publisher program, launch it again now.

Select **Resume** from the PageWizard tab page (it's on the fourth row, second from left). This PageWizard asks which type of resume you'd like to create: chronological, entry-level, or curriculum vitae as used in the world of academia.

For this example, select **Chronological** and click on **Next>**. The only other option the Wizard gives you is one of style. The choices for style of a chronological resume are bold, gray flannel, and linear. Select **Bold**. Once you click on **Create It!**, the Wizard goes to work, pausing briefly to prompt you for your name, personal address, and telephone number. When the Wizard is done, your screen should look like the one shown in Figure 2.29.

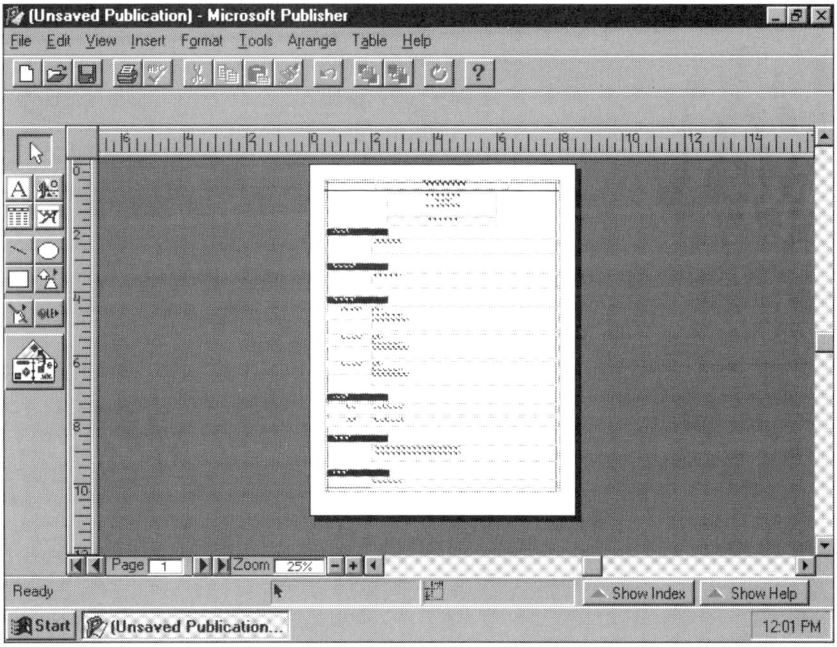

FIGURE 2.29 SAMPLE RESUME AS DESIGNED BY THE RESUME PAGEWIZARD DESIGN ASSISTANT.

Greeking Small Text

When you look at a publication at a reduced size, such as the one shown in Figure 2.29, you can't make out any of the words. However, you can see the overall shape that your text takes. You can see that there are lines of text, and that the lengths of these lines vary. However, the line lengths you see may or may not be accurate. It depends on an option setting.

When you reduce the size of a display, it becomes more and more difficult for Publisher to accurately space the characters. So Publisher provides you with an option called **Greek Small Text**. When this option is selected and you reduce the display size of a publication such that the characters become illegible, Publisher stops using characters and instead displays lines to show where text occurs. These line lengths are accurate.

The **Greek Small Text** option is selected by default. If you want to turn it off, you can access the Options dialog window from the Tools menu and clear the check mark. This may not make much of a noticeable difference to you, but you should be aware that when you work with a reduced size display and no greeking, the line lengths you see may not be accurate.

Coloring Text and Objects

One of the things that interests me visually about bold style resume design is the use of *reverse text* (white on black instead of black on white) for the headings. Sometimes reverse color text can be difficult to read. In this example, however, the readability is enhanced because the text is in small capitals.

Although Publisher does not have an automatic reverse attribute for text, you can create this effect by coloring the text frame black and changing the color of the text itself to white. The tools for this operation are the **Font Color** and **Object Color** speedbuttons on the Format toolbar. Figure 2.30 shows the Format toolbar again, this time identifying only these two buttons. Don't forget, these buttons can't be found on the toolbar unless you have selected a text frame.

FIGURE 2.30 THE **FONT COLOR** AND **OBJECT COLOR** SPEEDBUTTONS AS THEY APPEAR ON THE FORMAT TOOLBAR.

Go ahead and select the first heading text frame, the one that says *Objective*. Then click on the **Object Color** speedbutton and change the color from **black** (the square in the bottom-left corner) to **white** (the square in the lower-right corner), as shown in Figure 2.31.

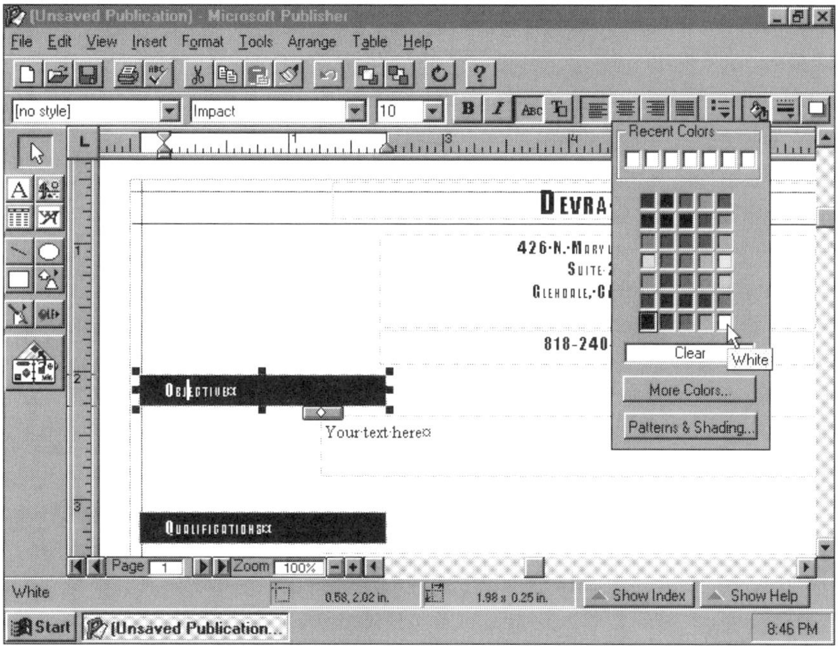

FIGURE 2.31 USING THE **OBJECT COLOR SPEED**BUTTON TO CHANGE THE COLOR FROM BLACK TO WHITE.

Oops. Your text seems to have disappeared. The operative phrase here is "seems to," because your text is really still there. It's just that you can't see a polar bear in a snow storm. All you have to do to prove it is there is change the text color from white to black and watch your text reappear. However, there is a small catch. In order to change the color of the text you have to select it first, and how can you select it when you can't see it?

There's a menu option to help you. The menu option to solve your current dilemma is the **Highlight Entire Story** option found on the Edit menu. First make sure that your text frame is selected. When you click on **Highlight Entire Story**, Publisher will select all the text in that text frame. If you want to bypass the menu, you can select the frame and press **Ctrl-A** to achieve the same results. Once the text is selected, you can click on the **Font Color** speedbutton and change the text color from **white** to **black**, as shown in Figure 2.32. Then watch your text magically reappear. Of course, with all this experimenting, the text in that frame is now different from the other heading frames. You could repeat all these steps to change the text and object colors back to the way they were, but there is a much easier way!

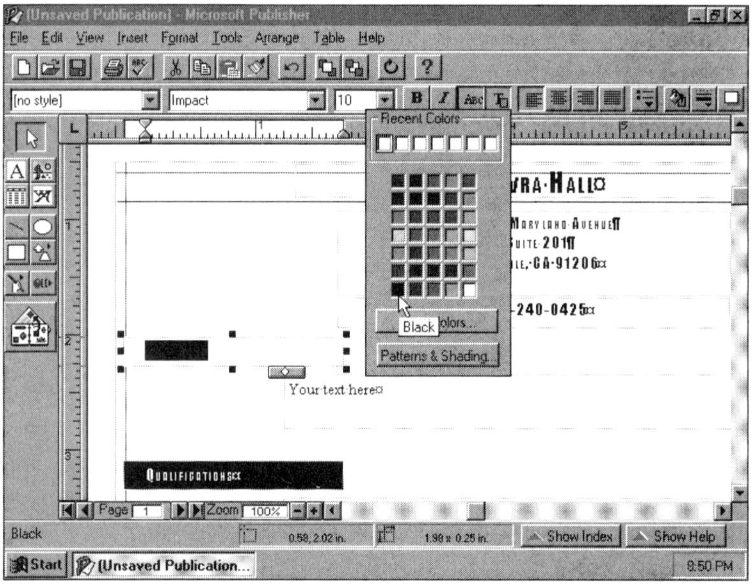

FIGURE 2.32 USING THE **FONT COLOR** SPEEDBUTTON TO CHANGE THE TEXT COLOR FROM WHITE TO BLACK.

Using the Format Painter

There is a speedbutton on the standard toolbar (that's the one directly below the menus) called **Format Painter**. It looks like a paintbrush, and it's located below the Arrange menu. The Format Painter allows you to copy the formatting of one selected object and apply it to another.

Here's what you need to do. Select the second heading text frame, the one that says *Qualifications*. Then click on the **Format Painter** speedbutton. When you do, your cursor will change into a little paintbrush with a question mark next to it. The question mark is Publisher's way of asking where you want to apply the formatting. Move your mouse down to the first heading text frame, the one you want to change back to the way it was. When your mouse enters the text frame, the question mark changes into an I-beam. Click again to release the formatting into the frame.

Working with Defined Text Styles

Using the Format Painter is a quick and easy way to copy the formatting of one object and apply it to another. However, once you complete the operation, Publisher forgets the format settings. If you want Publisher to remember the format settings so that you can use them again later, you have two alternatives.

The first alternative is what I would call semipermanent. If you use the **Pick Up Formatting** option from the Format menu, Publisher will take note of the formatting of the current selection and save it for future use. If a little while later you decide to use that formatting on some other object, you can use the **Apply Formatting** option.

Here's the catch. Publisher's memory of this formatting works like the Windows clipboard. If you **Pick Up Formatting** of another object, Publisher forgets the format from the first one. In other words, Publisher can only remember one format at a time. Also, Publisher will not remember the format once you exit the program.

If you want to save formatting for long-term future use, your best bet is to define a style. A *style* is a collection of text formatting choices that includes settings for character type and size, indents and lists (including alignment, bullets, and lists), line spacing, spacing between characters, and tabs.

NOTE

Unfortunately, styles include only text settings, not things such as object color. Text color, yes. Object color, no. So a style would only provide a partial solution if used for the example in the last section.

Creating a Defined Text Style

The process of creating a new style involves setting options on a series of dialog windows. First, bring up the Text Styles dialog window shown in Figure 2.33 by selecting **Text Style...** from the Format menu. In the style box, you'll notice that in addition to **[no style]**, our current sample resume publication already has one defined style called **impact small caps**.

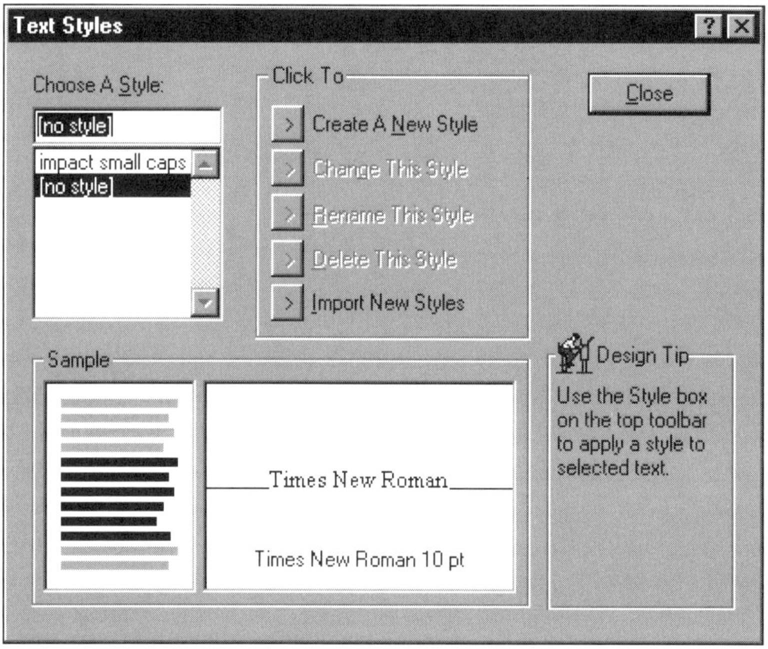

FIGURE 2.33 THE TEXT STYLES DIALOG WINDOW.

Now click on the **Create a New Style** button to bring up the Create New Style dialog window shown in Figure 2.34. The first step here is to decide on a style name and enter it in the text box where it says *Enter New Style Name*. Go ahead and enter a name.

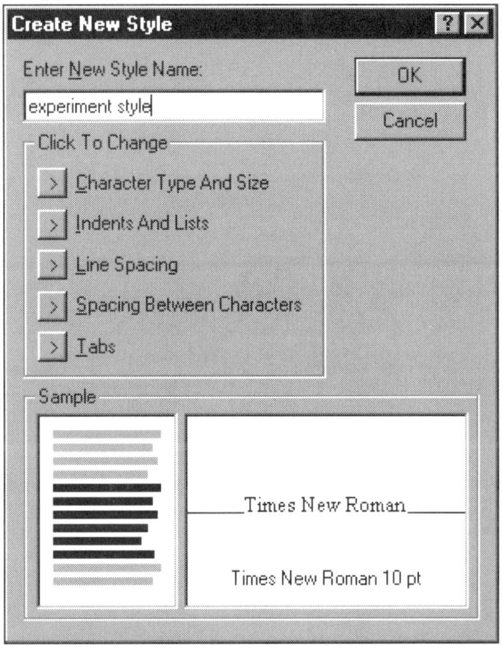

FIGURE 2.34 THE CREATE NEW STYLE DIALOG WINDOW.

The next steps depend on what setting you want to define. From here you can access the other five text formatting dialog windows listed. Let's take a look at each, even though you've seen a couple of them before. You can follow along on your screen or refer to the figures in this book.

NOTE

You may have noticed that you can access many of these dialog windows directly from the Format menu. You may do so when you are randomly formatting text in a publication. However, if you are creating a defined style, you need to access the Create New Style dialog window and continue from there.

When you click on **Character Type And Size**, Publisher displays the Character dialog window that you looked at earlier in this chapter (Figure 2.17). Character settings include font, size, style (bold, italic, etc.), color, capitals, underlining, and sub- and superscripts. Pick some fun settings, perhaps your favorite color and double underline.

The second dialog window, Indents and Lists, is also one you've seen before (Figure 2.27). This is where you specify bulleted and numbered lists, indents, and alignment. Try the **Numbered List** setting and take a look at your options. From here you can go directly to the Line Spacing dialog window shown in Figure 2.35, or you can return to the Create New Style dialog window and access it from there.

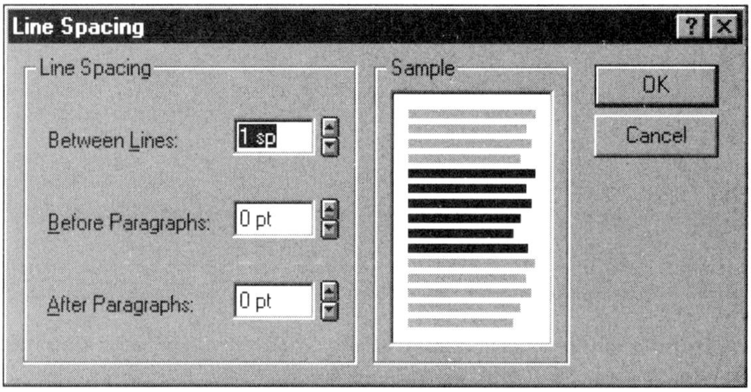

FIGURE 2.35 LINE SPACING DIALOG WINDOW.

Line spacing is automatically measured in quarter spaces, but you can enter your own decimal setting if you want to. The setting for what people generally refer to as *single spacing* is **1 sp**. Double spacing is **2 sp**. If you wanted one and two-thirds of a space between lines you would enter **1.66 sp**. You can also add additional spacing before or after paragraphs. This spacing is measured in points.

TIP

If you want, you can override the measurement type simply by typing in a different one. For example, you could enter **2 sp** in the Before Paragraph box to double space before a paragraph. You could also enter **in** for inches, **cm** for centimeters, or **pi** for picas.

Spacing Between Characters is another of the dialog windows that you have seen already (Figure 2.18). This is the one where you can make the character spacing tighter or looser for an entire paragraph or select specific spacing for selected text.

Finally, the Tabs dialog window is shown in Figure 2.36. When you use the **Tab** key, your cursor pushes forward to the next defined tab stop. Often, the default for tabs is every half inch, but when you are creating a new style, you use this dialog window to enter the precise position of each tab stop. Tabs do not have to be evenly spaced. That means that your first tab stop might be at .5, your second tab stop at 2.0, and a third tab stop at 6.5.

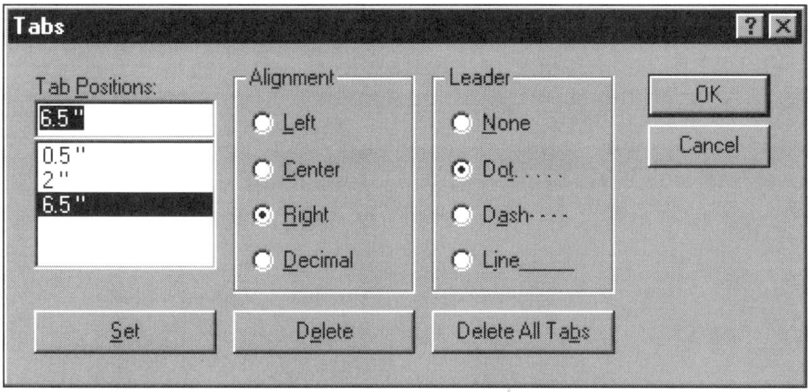

FIGURE 2.36 THE TABS DIALOG BOX WITH THREE TAB STOP SETTINGS.

In addition to entering the position of the tab stop, you can specify the alignment and leading character, if any. For example, decimal alignment is particularly useful when working with dollar figures. Or you might want to use right alignment preceded by leading dots for a table of contents. Once you enter your selections for the first tab stop, click on **Set**. Then enter your selections for the second tab stop, and click on **Set** again. If you change you mind about a setting, simply highlight it and click on **Delete**. Continue this process until you have entered all the tab stop settings you need; then click on **OK** to save the settings and return to the Create New Style dialog window.

Once you are back at the Create New Style dialog window, you can click on **OK** to save your new style and return to the Text Styles dialog window where you began this process. If you've been following along at your computer and actually created a new style, you should see the new style's name on the style list.

If you want to edit a style's settings, you just have to highlight the style on the list and click on **Change This Style**. A dialog window will appear that, with the exception of its title, is identical to the Create New Style dialog window. From that dialog window, you access the same dialog windows that you just finished examining. But this time, those dialog windows contain the settings currently defined for the style in question.

Should you want to rename a style, highlight the style on the list and click on **Rename This Style**. Enter the new name in the small dialog box that appears and click on **OK**. Similarly, you may delete a defined style by selecting the style from the list and clicking on **Delete This Style**. Publisher prompts you for confirmation before honoring your request.

The last option in the Text Styles dialog window is for importing new styles. When you click on **Import New Styles,** the Import Styles dialog window appears. Select the publication that contains the style(s) you want, and when you click on **OK** all of the styles from that publication will become available on your style list.

Using a Defined Style

When a publication includes defined text styles, applying them is a snap. Even if you did not create a new style in the last section, you can experiment using your sample resume publication because it already has one defined style.

Here's what I'd like you to do. Highlight the word *here* in one of the text frames that says *Your text here*. Then select **impact small caps** from the drop-down list on the Format toolbar, as shown in Figure 2.37. Even though you only highlighted one word, all the text changes to the impact small caps style. Does that mean that selecting a style changes all the text in a text frame? Let's find out.

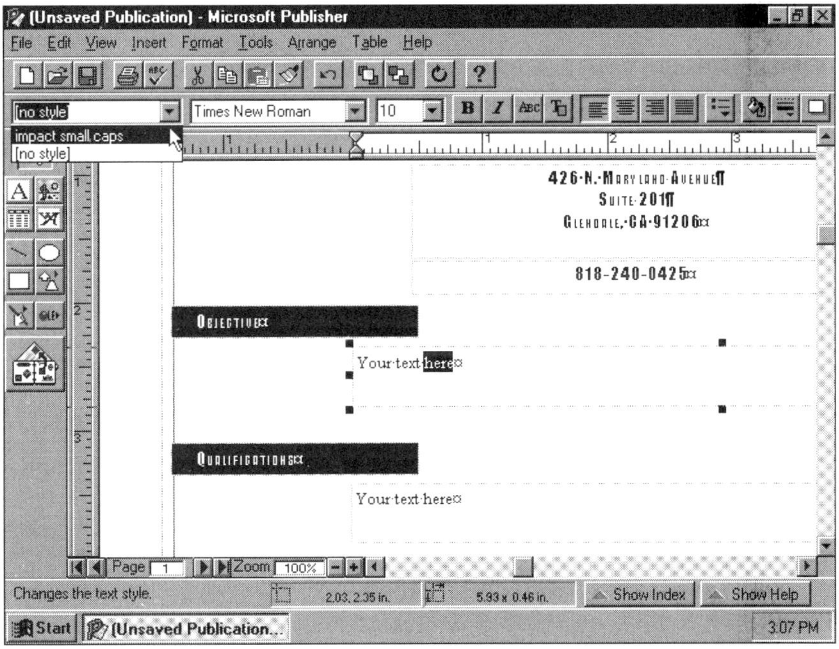

FIGURE 2.37 USING THE DROP-DOWN LIST OF STYLES ON THE FORMAT TOOLBAR TO APPLY A DEFINED STYLE TO THE SELECTED TEXT.

Select **Undo Format** from the Edit menu to return the text to its previous settings. Then move your cursor to the end of the line, press **Enter** to begin a new paragraph, and add another line of text. Finally, highlight one word from the first paragraph and select **impact small caps** from the drop-down list. This time the style changes in the first paragraph, but not the second. Now you know for sure that defined styles apply to paragraphs. If you wanted to change both paragraphs, you would have to highlight them both before selecting the defined style.

NOTE

Don't confuse paragraphs with lines. If you have a multiline paragraph and you select a word or words from one line, the entire paragraph will still change.

Spelling

Before you close your sample resume publication, you might want to take a good look at the content that this one suggests. It's a two-pager, and while not all the headings were applicable to my history, there were a couple of sections that I had not thought to include on my current resume. So, I decided to complete the data and save this particular publication. If you do the same, you'll want to know how to use the spell checker, because a resume with typos is a disaster.

The **Check Spelling...** option is on the Tools menu. If the option is grayed out (i.e., not available), that means you did not select a text object first. When I first realized that you had to select the text object before you could spell check, I thought it would be a pain, because then I assumed that you would have to select each text object one at a time. Luckily, that's only partially true. Publisher does check one text frame at a time, but *you* don't have to do all the selecting. The Check Spelling dialog window, shown in Figure 2.38, has an option to **Check All Stories**.

As long as this option is selected, Publisher will move from text frame to text frame automatically.

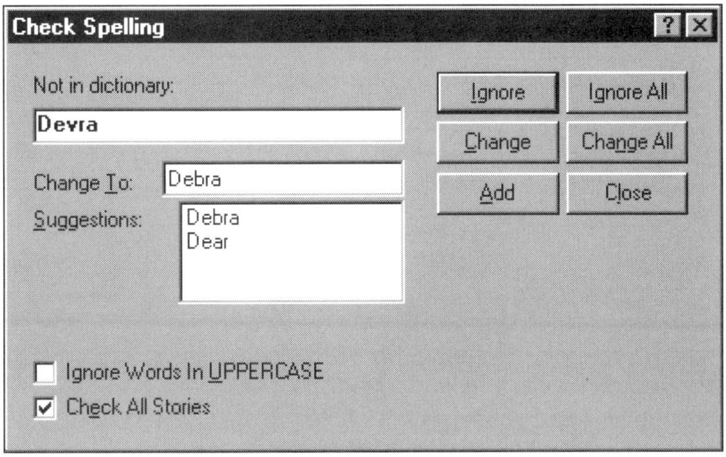

FIGURE 2.38 THE SPELL CHECKER DIALOG WINDOW.

RIGHT MOUSE MENU

I can't end this text chapter without showing you the text object menu. So far, the only menu options I have talked about are the ones on the drop-down menus across the top of your screen. Publisher also has a special pop-up object menu for each Publisher object type. To see the text object menu as shown in Figure 2.39, use your right mouse button to click on the text frame.

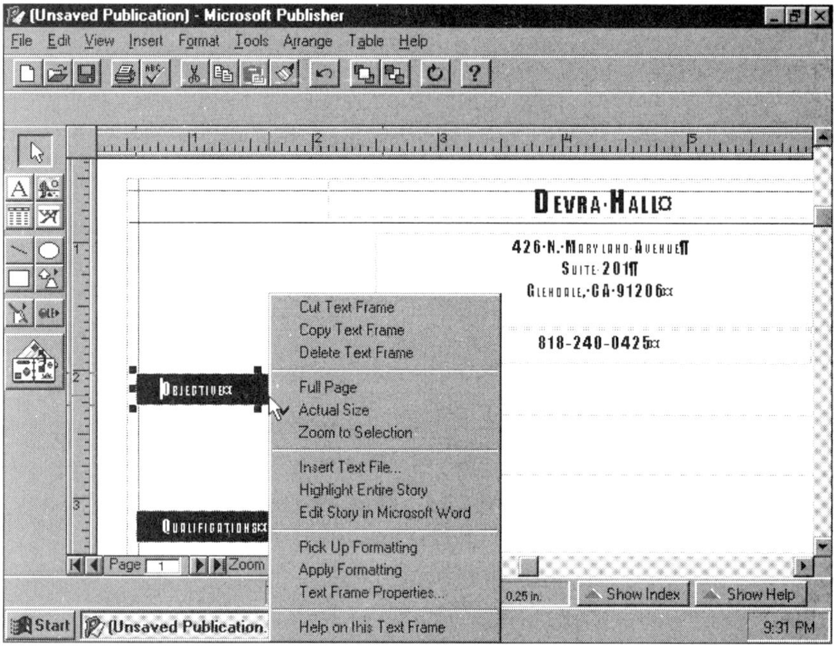

FIGURE 2.39 DISPLAY THE TEXT OBJECT MENU BY RIGHT-CLICKING ON A TEXT OBJECT.

The first group of options—**Cut Text Frame**, **Copy Text Frame**, and **Delete Text Frame**—are identical to the options on the Edit menu. The second group of options has to do with the size of the display. The **Full Page** and **Actual Size** options are identical to the options on the View menu. **Zoom to Selection** enlarges the selected frame.

The third group of options deals with the text file within the text frame. The **Highlight Entire Story** option is identical to the one on the Edit menu that you used earlier in this chapter. The **Insert Text File...** option allows you to insert an external text file. You can use the **Edit Story** option to edit the text file using the Microsoft Word program (provided you have that program on your system).

The fourth group of options relates to formatting and frame properties. The **Pick Up Formatting** and **Apply Formatting** options are identical to those on the Format menu and work the same as discussed earlier in this chapter. The **Text Frame Properties...** option brings up a dialog window as shown in Figure 2.40. As you can see, the text frame properties consist of margins, column settings, a wrap option, and two options that I'll discuss in Chapter 7.

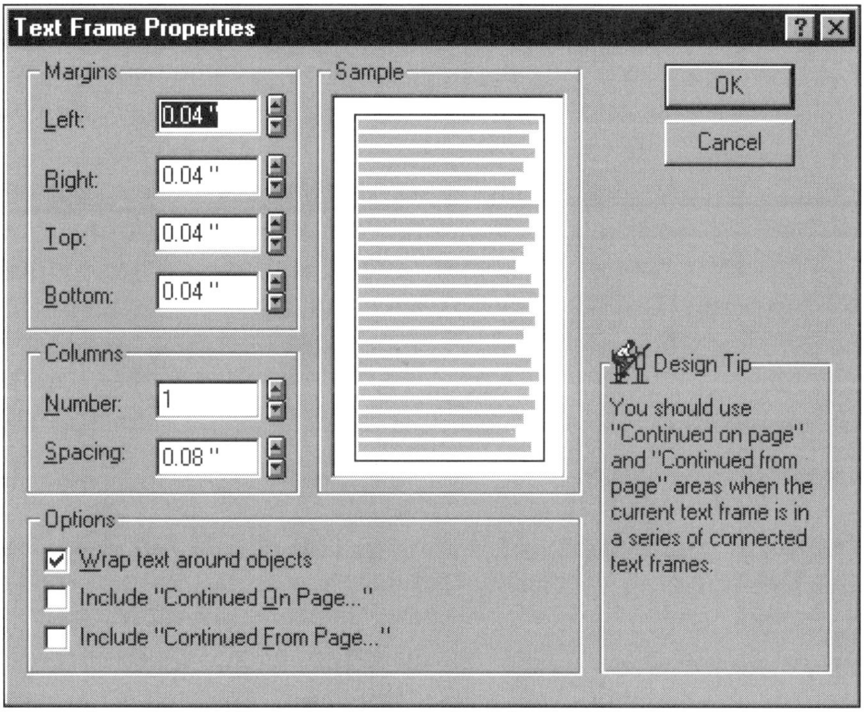

FIGURE 2.40 THE TEXT PROPERTIES DIALOG WINDOW.

The last option on the text object menu, **Help on this Text Frame**, opens the Help panel to the Text Frame subject. Here you can get help on adding and replacing text, changing the size and look of the text, making a text frame transparent or opaque (a neat feature that you'll use in Chapter 5), and other text-related topics.

SUMMARY

- To create a publication using a PageWizard, select the icon from the startup dialog window, make choices and input data as prompted by the PageWizard Design Assistant, and then sit back and relax while the Wizard designs the layout.
- The PageWizard for the classic business card prompts you for name, address, title, telephone number, fax number, and email address and asks whether you want to print out a single card on a page or multiple cards per page.
- End-of-file characters only appear in text frames. When selected, a text frame displays a button with either a white diamond indicating that all text associated with that frame is currently visible or three black squares indicating that the file contains more text than can be displayed in the frame.
- When you select a text frame, the Format toolbar displays three drop-down list boxes (style, font, and size) and twelve speedbuttons (bold, italic, small capitals, font color, left, center, right, flush, list, object color, border, and add/remove shadow).
- When you select a text frame, the Edit menu's **Cut**, **Copy**, and **Delete** options change to include the words **Text Frame**. The **Edit Object** option becomes **Edit Story in Microsoft Word**.
- When you select a text frame, the Format menu expands to include additional options: **Character**, **Spacing Between Characters**, **Fancy First Letter**, **Indents and Lists**, **Line Spacing**, and **Tabs**.
- When moving and resizing frames, your cursor changes shape to provide a visual indication of what will happen as you drag your mouse.
- You may edit the text in any selected text frame, even if it was placed there by a PageWizard. **Typing Replaces Selection** is one of Publisher's default option settings. This means that when you select a block of text and begin typing, the new text will replace the selected text block.

✱ Character formatting tools are available on the Format toolbar and in the Character dialog window, which is accessible from the Format menu. Settings include font, size, style (i.e., attributes such as bold and italic), text color, and effects such as small capitals and all capitals, underlining, and super- and subscripts.

✱ *Kerning* refers to the spacing between specific pairs of characters. Publisher handles this automatically. *Tracking* refers to the spacing between all characters. The **Spacing Between Characters...** option on the Format menu brings up a dialog window where you can choose tighter or looser spacing for selected text or entire paragraphs.

✱ *Symbols* are special characters that include foreign letters, fractions, and other symbols such as copyright marks. *Wingdings* include such things as bullet characters, arrows, smiley faces, check marks, and more. Use the **Symbol...** option on the Insert menu to select and insert both symbols and wingdings.

✱ When you save a publication you have the option of saving a preview with it. This is the preview that Publisher will display in the startup dialog window when you select an existing publication.

✱ The recipe card design is created by the Specialty PageWizard. The only input required is your name. (Actually, this should be the name of the person who made up the recipe.)

✱ The main purpose of grouping objects together is so that you can move or rotate multiple objects simultaneously while maintaining their relative position to one another. Grouping text objects should not be confused with connecting text frames.

✱ When there is more text than can fit in one frame, you need to connect the first frame to a second frame. If there is still more text than can fit in the two frames combined, you need to connect the second frame to a third one.

✱ Connect and frame jump buttons appear on connected text frames. The connect button looks like three connected links of a chain. When you click on a frame jump button with a right-pointing arrow, you jump to the next connect frame. A left-pointing arrow takes you to the previous connected frame.

- When there is too much text for the frame, click on the frame button with the three black squares to change your cursor into the overflowing cup. Move your mouse over an empty text frame (the cup tilts) and click to pour your text into the empty frame.
- To create a bulleted or numbered list, highlight the text and select the **Indents and Lists...** option from the Format menu.
- When you select the resume PageWizard, you can choose between three types (chronological, entry-level, and curriculum vitae), and three styles (bold, gray flannel, and linear). PageWizard prompts you for your name, personal address, and telephone number, and then prepares the layout.
- When the **Greek Small Text** option is selected and you reduce the display size of a publication so that the characters become illegible, Publisher stops using characters and instead displays lines to show where the text occurs. The line lengths are accurate, whereas the line lengths of minuscule text characters may not be.
- You can create reverse text by coloring the text frame black and changing the color of the text itself to white. The tools for this operation are the **Font Color** and **Object Color** speedbuttons on the Format toolbar.
- To select all the text in a frame (or a series of connected frames), use the **Highlight Entire Story** option on either the Edit menu or the text object pop-up menu. Alternatively, you can select the frame and press **Ctrl-A**.
- The Format Painter is a speedbutton on the standard toolbar that allows you to copy the formatting of one selected object and apply the format to another object. When you use this tool you must apply the format immediately.
- The **Pick Up Format** and **Apply Format** options on the Format menu allow you to copy the formatting of a selected object and apply it to another object at a later time. However, when you pick up a second format, Publisher forgets the first one.

✷ A *style* is a collection of text formatting choices; it includes settings for character type and size, indents and lists (including alignment, bullets, and numbered lists), line spacing, spacing between characters, and tabs. Style settings do not include such things as object color. To create, edit, rename, or delete a text style, select **Text Styles...** from the Format menu.

✷ The first drop-down text box on the Format toolbar contains a list of defined styles for the current publication. When you select a style from this list, Publisher applies the style to the selected paragraph(s).

✷ Use the Line Spacing dialog window to specify the measurement of space between lines and between paragraphs. Line spacing is generally measured in line spaces (sp), and paragraph spacing is generally measured in points (pt). You can override the measurement type by specifying *in* for inches, *cm* for centimeters, or *pi* for picas.

✷ Use the Tabs dialog window to enter precise tab stop positions. For every tab stop you set, you can specify alignment and select a preceding character.

✷ The **Check Spelling...** option is on the Tools menu. If you want to check spelling in all the text frames in your publication, make sure that you select the **Check All Stories** option. Otherwise, the spell checker examines only the current frame.

✷ Every Publisher object has a pop-up object menu and frame properties. Text frame properties include margins and column settings.

CHAPTER 3

WORKING WITH IMAGES

- Using wingdings as pictures
- Listing picture types
- Inserting a picture file
- Resizing and scaling a picture
- Cropping a picture
- Wrapping text around a picture
- Rotating a picture
- Recoloring pictures and picture frames
- Adding borders to picture frames
- Adding and removing picture frame shadows
- Viewing the picture object menu
- Hiding pictures
- Examining the ClipArt Gallery application
  - Finding images
  - Adding pictures to the Gallery
  - Updating preview images
  - Changing picture properties
  - Editing the category list
- Scanning photos

You should carefully consider whether you want to place images in your publications. Some images can really eat up your disk space. If you're planning to photocopy your project and your images copy well (black-and-white photos for example), you can simply create empty frames to indicate the size and placement of your images. Color photocopying is also an option, but an expensive one. If your job requires the best-possible professional quality, or if full-color is involved, you may prefer to provide artwork to an outside printer. Some printers prefer to scan prints and slides themselves, using professional laser scanners. This is done at the stage where films are being prepared. This, too, can be an expensive way to go.

Once you decide to add a picture (or several) to your publication, there are a variety of things you can do with it. You can change its look by altering the picture and/or the picture frame and change its size. When you're working with text and pictures together, you'll decide whether you want the text to wrap around the picture frame(s), or wrap around the picture itself. And then you might want to deal with the positioning of captions.

You can add pictures to your publication in a couple of different ways. Usually, when you're using Wizards to create your publications, you'll be replacing existing pictures provided by the Wizard with your own clipart selections using the ClipArt Gallery. But you also have the option of copying a picture from another publication, or even another program. You can import all types of picture files and even add images to the Gallery. Yet another option is to use OLE to embed or link a picture (see Chapter 8). You can even scan an image directly into your publication. And there's more. Other possibilities include drawing a picture with Microsoft Draw and using a picture font. But before we get into all of this, let's first clarify what is and what is not a picture.

Sample Gift Tag

The character created by a picture font is not a real picture. It is a character, and therefore it is really text. The Specialty PageWizard creates a Gift

Tag that uses just such a character. If you are not running Publisher program, launch it now. If Publisher is already running, select **Create New Publication...** from the File menu.

The Specialty PageWizard is on the third row, second from the left. When prompted to select the type of specialty item, select **Gift Tag**, click on **Next>**, and finally click on **Create It!** The PageWizard prompts you for your name, and then completes its task of creating two gift tags. Figure 3.1 shows the first tag as it appears on page one of this publication.

FIGURE 3.1 PAGE ONE OF THE GIFT TAG PUBLICATION AS CREATED BY THE SPECIALTY PAGEWIZARD.

Using Wingdings

At first glance you can't really tell that the stars are not pictures. But when you click on one of them, as I did in Figure 3.2, you see the text frame with its telltale frame button on the bottom and the text-related speedbuttons that appear on the Format toolbar. Take a good look at the Format toolbar and especially at the font shown in the drop-down text box. The font used in this text frame is Wingdings 2, and the star is one of the characters in that set.

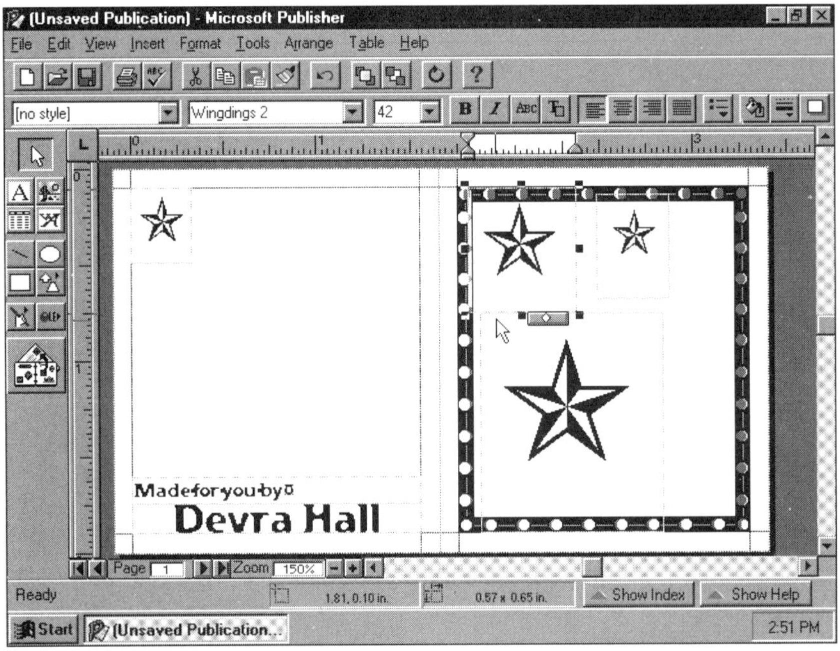

FIGURE 3.2 PUBLISHER SCREEN SHOWING PAGE ONE OF THE GIFT TAG PUBLICATION WITH ONE STAR (TEXT FRAME) SELECTED.

The stars in this publication vary in size, and this is due to the size setting for the font in each frame. For example, in Figure 3.2 you can see that the font size is 42. If you select the frame with the bigger star, you will find that the font size for that character is 72.

As I mentioned briefly in Chapter 2, you can place wingdings in your text frames by selecting the **Symbol...** option from the Insert menu. When the Insert Symbol dialog window appears, select one of the three Wingding fonts, click on your chosen symbol or character, and click on the **Insert** button. Figure 3.3 shows the Insert Symbol dialog window displaying the Wingdings 2 symbol set with the star character enlarged. You can enlarge a symbol slightly for better viewing by holding down the mouse button when you click on it.

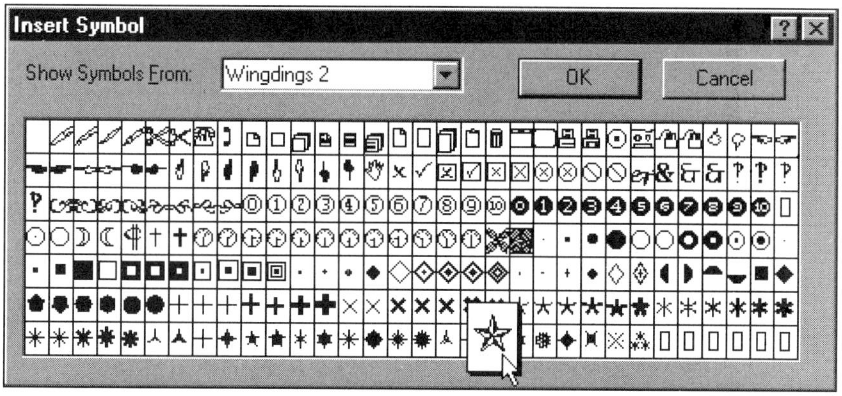

FIGURE 3.3 THE INSERT SYMBOL DIALOG WINDOW SHOWING THE WINGDINGS 2 SYMBOL SET. THE STAR CHARACTER IS ENLARGED FOR EASIER VIEWING.

PICTURE TYPES

Microsoft Publisher supports the two basic picture types: *bitmaps* and *draw-type images*. Bitmaps are composed of many tiny little dots arranged to form images. Did you ever learn about a style of painting called *Pointillism*? It's a style where the artist paints many small dots that appear to blend together when seen from a distance. In a bitmap, each dot represents a *bit*, and the word *map* refers to encoded information indicating the color of each pixel.

A good example of this style as used by computers is the art of the icon. A Windows icon is a square, 32 pixels wide by 32 pixels high. Look at Figure 3.4. This is a Zoom view of a grayscale copy of the Microsoft Publisher icon, where each box in the grid represents one pixel.

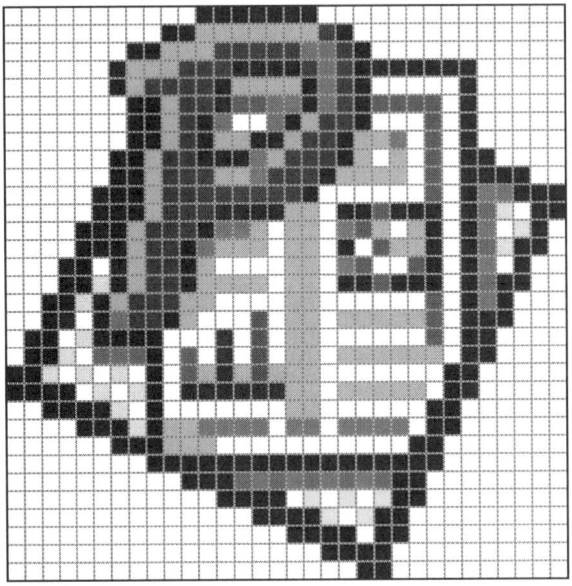

FIGURE 3.4 A ZOOM VIEW OF A GRAYSCALE COPY OF THE MICROSOFT PUBLISHER ICON.

Draw-type images are created by programs that instruct the computer to draw lines, curves, boxes, and a few other shapes at specific locations. For example, to draw a line from one point to another, the program specifies the location of each point by its X and Y coordinates, and then draws the line. To draw a square, the program specifies the top left coordinates, followed by the width and length of the box.

Table 3.1 shows the file types and filename extensions for bitmap and vector image files.

TABLE 3.1 FILE TYPES AND EXTENSIONS FOR BITMAP AND VECTOR FILES

	File Type	File Extension
Bitmap	Bitmap	BMP
	JPEG Image	JPG
	Kodak Photo CD	PCD
	PC Paintbrush	PCX
	Tagged Image Format	TIF
Draw-Type	CorelDraw!	CDR
	Computer Graphics Metafile	CGM
	DrawPerfect	WPG
	Encapsulated Postscript	EPS
	Micrografx Designer/Draw	DRW
	Windows Metafile	WMF

SAMPLE HANDICAPPED ACCESS SIGN

I'd like you to use the Handicapped Access sign to examine a picture object. Once again you can use the PageWizard. Select **Create New Publication...** from the File menu. The Sign icon is the second from the left on the second row. Select it and click **OK**. Publisher will ask whether you want to save the Gift Tag publication. The choice is yours.

When the PageWizard asks *What type of sign would you like?* select **Public Information** and click on **Next>**. Publisher has eight predefined public information signs: No Parking, Wet Paint, Restrooms, Information, Out of Order, No Loitering, No Smoking, and Handicapped Access. Select the last one (you may have to scroll down to it), click on **Next>**, and then click on **Create It!**

The Handicapped Access sign shown in Figure 3.5 contains three objects. The words are inside a text frame, just like the text frames you examined in the last chapter. You can tell at a glance that it's a text frame because you can see the paragraph mark after the word Access, and the end-of-file character following the word Available.

FIGURE 3.5 THE HANDICAPPED ACCESS SIGN AS CREATED BY THE PAGEWIZARD.

You can also see a box around the sign. This is the second object, and it could have been created by using a frame with a border. It turns out, however, that the PageWizard actually used a box shape. You'll get to work with shapes in Chapter 5.

TIP

Using a box shape is the best way to create a border around multiple objects or a whole page.

The third object is the picture. And in this example the picture is from the ClipArt Gallery. When you select the picture frame (just a single click will do it), your screen should look like the one shown in Figure 3.6.

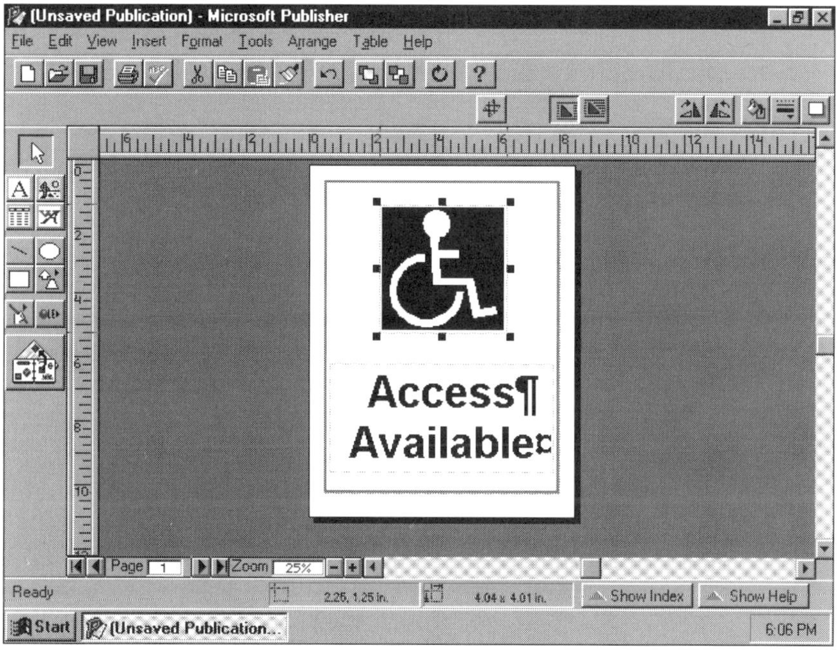

FIGURE 3.6 WHEN THE PAGEWIZARD HAS FINISHED CREATING THE HANDICAPPED ACCESS SIGN AND YOU CLICK ON THE PICTURE OBJECT, YOUR SCREEN SHOULD LOOK SOMETHING LIKE THIS.

Before you do anything with this picture, take a look at your Publisher environment and see what has changed. First notice that the position of the picture is indicated on the status bar near the bottom of your screen. The top-left corner of the picture frame is located 2.25 inches from the left and 1.25 inches from the top of the page. It also shows that the size of the picture frame is 4.04 x 4.01 inches.

In the last chapter, you saw that when you click on a text frame, text-related speedbuttons appear on the Format toolbar. So it should be no surprise that when you click on a picture frame, picture-related speedbuttons appear on the Format toolbar. Take another look at the eight speedbuttons on the toolbar. You can see them in Figure 3.6.

You will also remember from the last chapter, that when you worked with text, the options on the Format menu changed. When you select a picture frame, the Format menu options change again. Figure 3.7 shows the Format menu options available when you select the image in your Handicapped Access sign.

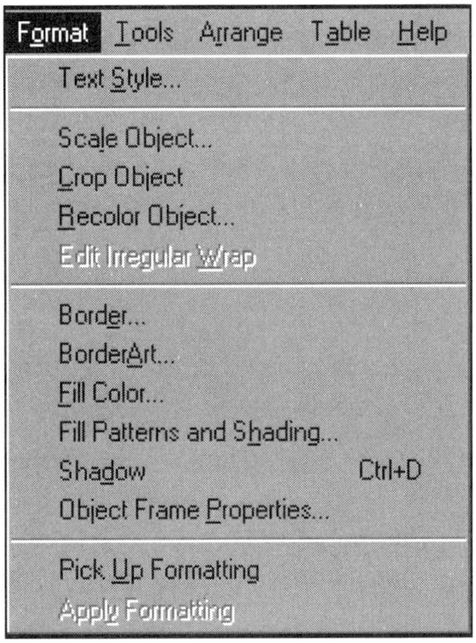

FIGURE 3.7 THE FORMAT MENU OPTIONS AVAILABLE WHEN WORKING WITH THE IMAGE USED IN THE HANDICAPPED ACCESS SIGN CREATED BY THE PAGEWIZARD.

Hmm...I thought we were working with a picture frame. Why do the options on the Format menu refer to *Object* instead of *Picture*? This can cause some confusion until you understand that Publisher is a very smart program, and it knows that the handicapped image is a draw-type image, not a bitmap picture. Publisher makes a distinction between bitmaps, which it calls *pictures*, and draw-type images referred to as *objects*.

NOTE

All the images that come with the ClipArt Gallery application are draw-type images. If you use the Windows Explorer to look at the files in the ClipArt folder, you'll see that they are all CGM files.

This distinction explains why, when you select the handicapped image, the Format menu changes its options to **Scale Object** instead of **Scale Picture**, **Recolor Object** instead of **Recolor Picture**, and so on. Functionally, from your perspective, it makes little difference because the scale, recolor, and other options can be used with both objects and pictures.

Just to keep things consistent, however, let's change the image to a "real" picture. Besides, it's as good a time as any to show you how to insert a picture into a frame.

Inserting a Picture File

The Insert menu provides one way to place a picture in a frame. Regardless of whether a frame already contains an image, you can use the options on the Insert menu to insert a **Picture File...**, **ClipArt...**, or an **Object...**. Another way to place an image is to double-click on the frame. This method, however, has limitations. If you double-click on a frame containing an image from the ClipArt Gallery (as is the case with your Handicapped Access sign) the ClipArt Gallery dialog window appears. Go ahead and try it if you'd like. Then click on the **Cancel** button to make the window go away.

Clearly then, you'll have to use the **Picture File...** option on the Insert menu to replace the ClipArt image with a bitmap picture. Let's do it. First make sure that your image is still selected, and then select the menu option to bring up the Insert Picture File dialog window, as shown in Figure 3.8. This dialog window probably looks familiar to you, as it has the same basic structure as all the Windows 95 Open and Save File dialog windows.

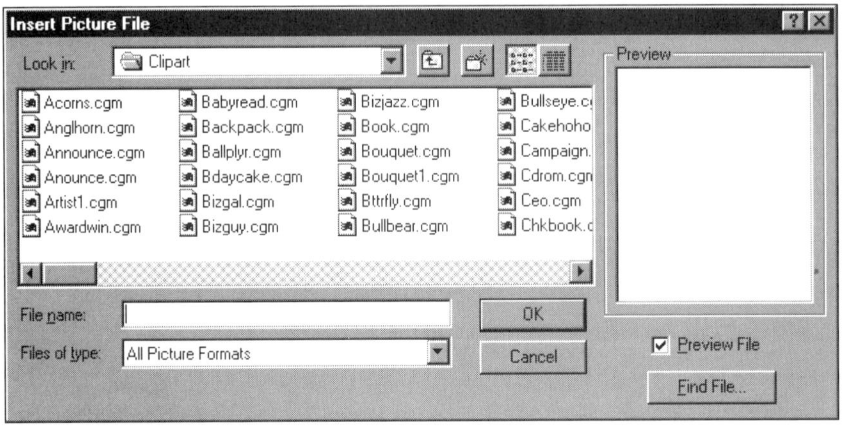

FIGURE 3.8 THE INSERT PICTURE FILE DIALOG WINDOW.

When the dialog window appears, you'll find yourself looking at the files in your Clipart folder (see Figure 3.8). No bitmap files are there. Depending on what programs you have installed, you may have a variety of bitmap files on your system. So that everyone can follow the same example, I'd like you to find the Cars file that should be located in your Windows folder.

On my system, my Windows folder is called Win. I had to move from my Clipart folder, up a level to my Publisher folder, up another level to my Program Files folder, and up once again to the top level of my hard drive. From there I moved down one level to my Win folder. When the files in your Windows folder appear, scroll right until you find **Cars**, and single click on it. Make sure to select the **Preview File** checkbox so that the image will appear in the Preview section as shown in Figure 3.9.

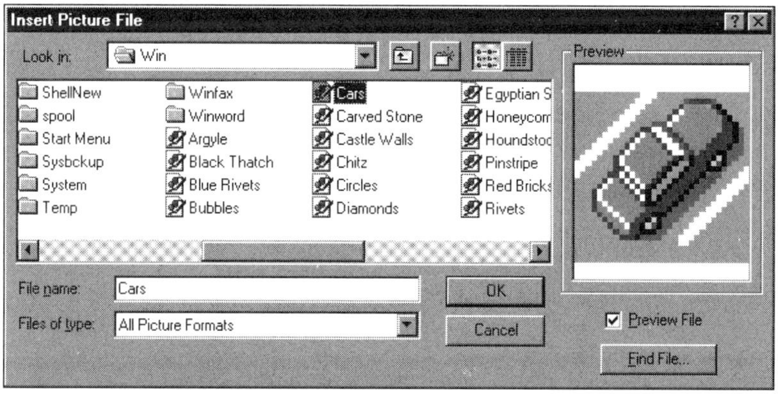

FIGURE 3.9 THE INSERT PICTURE FILE DIALOG WINDOW SHOWING THE CARS FILE IN THE WIN FOLDER.

When you click on **OK**, an Import Picture dialog window appears giving you the choice of altering the existing frame to fit the picture, or altering the picture to fit the existing frame. Accept the default choice of altering the frame and click on **OK**. Now you have an Auto Access Available sign (see Figure 3.10) and all you did was replace an image. The new frame is now located 2.24 inches from the left, 1.36 inches from the top, and it is 4.01 x 4.01 inches in size.

FIGURE 3.10 THE MODIFIED ACCESS SIGN WITH ITS NEW BITMAP PICTURE.

Now that you have a bitmap picture in the frame, take a new look at the Format menu. Providing that your picture frame is still selected, the Format menu should look like the one shown in Figure 3.11.

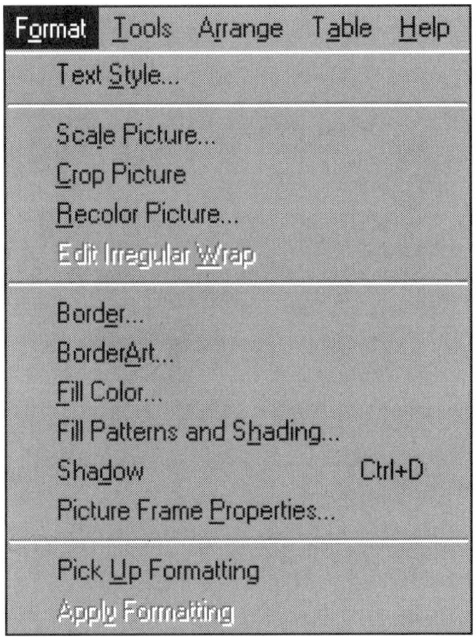

FIGURE 3.11 THE FORMAT MENU OPTIONS AVAILABLE WHEN WORKING WITH A PICTURE FRAME CONTAINING A BITMAP IMAGE.

Resizing and Scaling

In Chapter 2 you resized a text frame by clicking on the frame, moving your cursor over one of the handles, and then clicking-and-dragging the frame to the desired size. Resizing picture frames can work the same way. (See "Moving and Resizing Text Frames" in Chapter 2.) Try it. Click on the car picture and then drag the middle handle on the right side out so that the frame becomes wider. Oops! If you followed my instructions, your sign should look similar to the one shown in Figure 3.12.

FIGURE 3.12 THE ACCESS SIGN WITH A WIDENED PICTURE FRAME. THE IMAGE IS DISTORTED.

I dragged the right edge until it touched the box object serving as a border. The size of this picture is now 5.66 x 4.01 inches, and it looks slightly distorted. This is the problem with resizing bitmap images. They get distorted with simple resizing. But that doesn't mean that you can't change their size. What you need is a feature that will allow you to resize them proportionally. Let's try again. First, select **Undo Resize** from the Edit menu (or press **Ctrl-Z**) to return the picture to its original size and position.

Proportional resizing turns out to be quite easy. To keep an image in its correct proportions you need to use a corner frame handle and hold down the **Shift** key while you resize. This time you can't use the middle frame handle.

If you use the top-right corner handle, as I did, you'll find that you can't move the right edge all the way to the box because there is not enough proportional space at the top without crossing over the edge of the box. When I did it, my sign looked like the one shown in Figure 3.13. The top-left corner is still 2.24 inches in from the left, but now only .6 inches down from the top. The size of the image is now 4.77 x 4.77 inches.

FIGURE 3.13 THE ACCESS SIGN WITH A PROPORTIONALLY RESIZED PICTURE.

Not bad, but it's still not quite right. Why? Because it really should be centered horizontally. As it is now, it weighs down toward the right. So let's try it one more time. Use the **Undo** option from the Edit menu again (or press **Ctrl-Z**), and I'll show you how to resize an image proportionally while retaining the center. The key is control—pun intended. This time hold down both the **Shift** and **Ctrl** keys while dragging out a corner frame handle. Your sign should look something like the one shown in Figure 3.14.

FIGURE 3.14 THE ACCESS SIGN WITH A PROPORTIONALLY ENLARGED IMAGE HOLDING THE SAME CENTER.

NOTE

Center, as it applies to resizing, refers to the center point of the image or picture frame. When you hold down the **Ctrl** key, Publisher maintains the center point of the image as it is currently positioned. The fact that the car image in the Access sign is horizontally centered on the page is due to the fact that the original handicapped image frame was centered on the page.

Now use **Undo Resize** one more time so you can see how the **Scale Picture** option on the Format menu relates to resizing. The image as created by the PageWizard for the Handicapped Access sign was 4.04 x 4.01 inches. When you replaced the handicapped clipart with the bitmap of the car, Publisher altered the frame slightly to fit the image. The new size is 4.01 x 4.01 inches, a perfect square.

Select the image frame and choose **Scale Picture** from the Format menu to bring up the dialog window shown in Figure 3.15. According to this dialog window, the car image in our sample sign is approximately 12 times its original size—1242.4% as high, and 1242.2% as wide, to be exact. The original image at its full size (100%) is only .32 inches square (about a third of an inch in height and width).

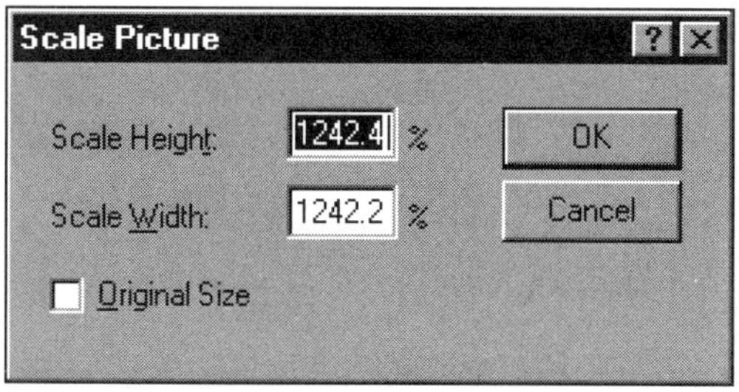

FIGURE 3.15 THE SCALE OBJECT DIALOG WINDOW SHOWING THE SCALE OF THE CAR IMAGE.

So what do you think you should enter in this dialog window to reduce the image to half its current size? Be careful, it's a trick question. If you enter **50%** for both the height and width, you would get a picture that is half its *original* size, not half its current size. That picture would be .16 inches x .16 inches.

To reduce the current image size by half, you enter **621.2%** height and **621.1%** width. The result of this action is shown in Figure 3.16. Notice that while the image is smaller, it is no longer centered. When you scale a picture, Publisher calculates the new height and width and places the resized frame by maintaining the original top-left corner position coordinates. If you look at the status bar you will see that the position is back to 2.24 inches from the left, and 1.36 inches from the top.

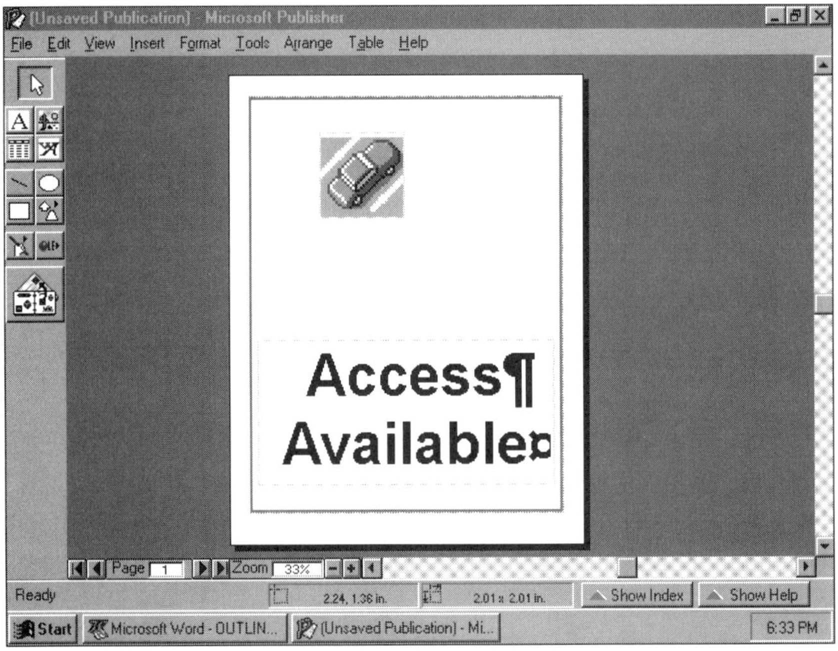

FIGURE 3.16 THE ACCESS SIGN WITH THE CAR IMAGE SCALED TO 621.2% HEIGHT AND 621.1% WIDTH. THE POSITION COORDINATES REMAIN UNCHANGED.

NOTE

To make an image larger than its original size, enter values higher than 100%. To make an image smaller than its original size, enter values under 100%. If you want to scale an image proportionally, enter the same percentage for both the height and width. When you select the original size checkbox, the image will resize to 100% height and width, i.e. its original size.

Cropping and Wrapping

The first button on the Format toolbar when working with pictures is the **Crop Picture** button. It is located almost directly below the **?** button, and you use it to cut your image. This button functions the same as the **Crop Picture** or **Crop Object** option on the Format menu. I'll come back to the subject of cropping when you examine the Change of Address card later in this chapter.

The next two buttons are **Wrap Text to Frame** and **Wrap Text to Picture**. **Wrap Text to Frame** is the default selection, and if this graphic image was sitting inside a text frame, the text would wrap around the four sides of the frame. When **Wrap Text to Picture** is selected, the text wraps around the contours of the image itself.

NOTE

If you select **Wrap Text to Picture**, you'll see an additional speedbutton appear. This button, **Edit Irregular Wrap**, applies to both picture and WordArt objects, but only appears when **Wrap to Picture** is selected. You'll examine this tool in Chapter 5.

Rotating

The next two speed buttons allow you to rotate your image, 90 degrees at a time, to either the left or the right. Try it. The car picture is currently speeding off in a northeasterly direction toward to top-right corner of your page. Click on the **Rotate Right** button and watch your car image head for the southeast instead. Click it again and the car will be upside down. Click twice more and the image will return to its right-side up position, or click on the **Rotate Left** button to move back the other way.

If you prefer, you can rotate your picture manually. Select the frame and place your mouse over one of the frame handles. Hold down the **Alt** key and then click-and-drag your frame around to the desired position. When you hold down the **Alt** key, your cursor changes to its Rotate shape.

You can have a little more control over a manual rotation by holding down both the **Alt** and **Shift** keys while rotating. This causes the rotation to proceed in 15 degree increments.

Recoloring

If you look up *recoloring pictures* in the Publisher help index, you'll find that it has several meanings. When you change the color of the space between a picture and its frame, that is called *recoloring*. To change the color of this space (you can think of it as the canvas), make sure that the picture frame is selected, and then click on the **Object Color** button to bring up the drop-down dialog window shown in Figure 3.17. The top row of colors are those that you have used most recently (none yet). Below is a small palette from which you may select a color. If you don't see what you're looking for, you can choose **More Colors...** or **Patterns & Shading...**

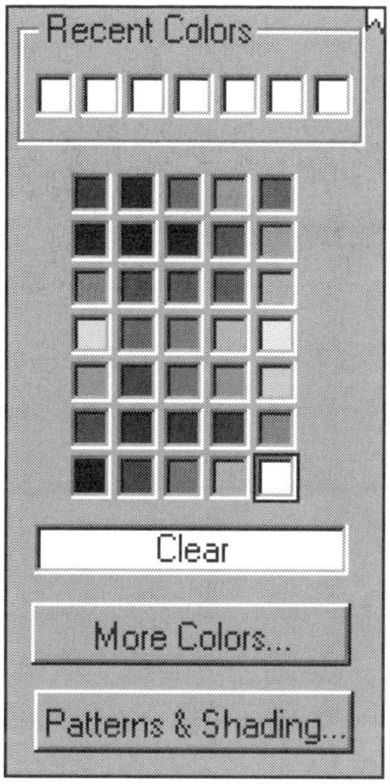

FIGURE 3.17 THE OBJECT COLOR DROP-DOWN PALETTE.

To work with a more extensive color palette, click on the **More Colors...** button to bring up the Colors dialog window shown in Figure 3.18. In the Color dialog window you can work with only basic colors, or with all colors. And for those of us with limited color taste, the Design Tip quite usefully suggests that you select colors from a single column. The colors in each column were designed to prevent color clash.

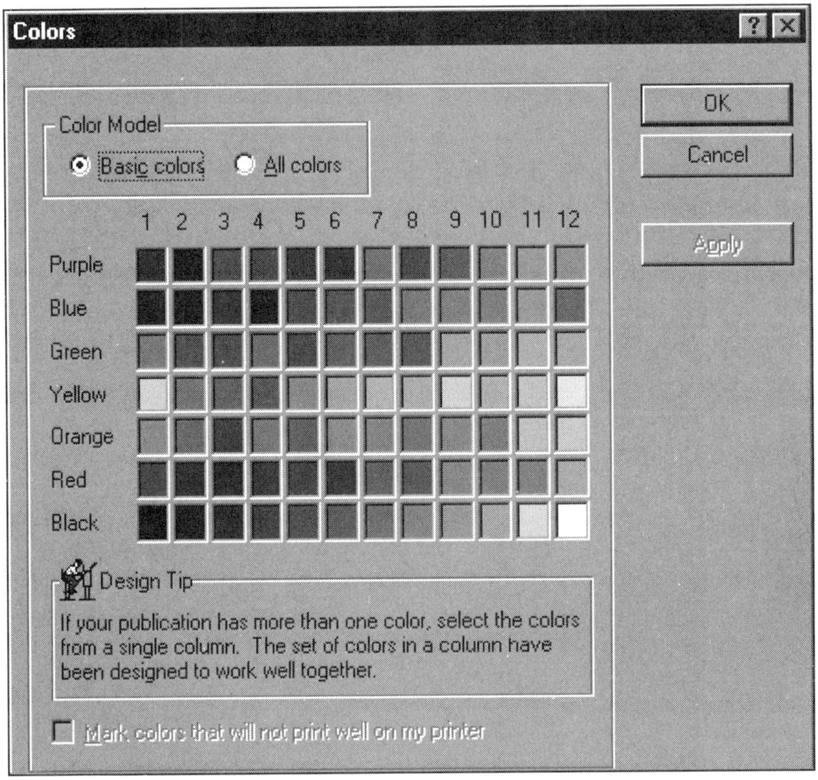

FIGURE 3.18 THE COLORS DIALOG WINDOW, WHEN **BASIC COLORS** IS SELECTED.

If you really know your colors, you can switch from Basic Colors to All Colors by making your selection on the Color Model section toward the top-left side of the dialog window. This transforms your dialog window into the one shown in Figure 3.19. Here you can enter the exact amounts of **Red**, **Green**, and **Blue** to mix your own colors.

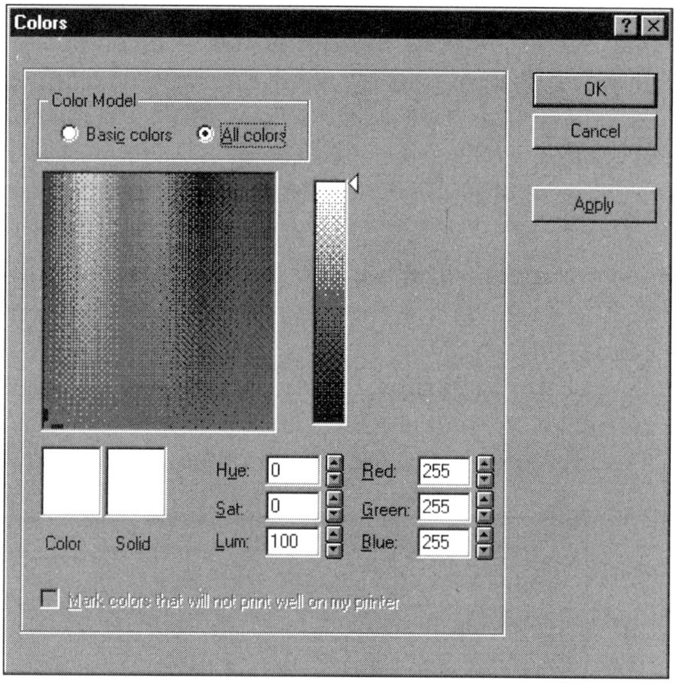

FIGURE 3.19 THE COLORS DIALOG WINDOW WHEN **ALL COLORS** IS SELECTED.

You can also set the **Hue**, **Saturation**, and **Luminescence**. *Hue* refers to the actual color. *Saturation* relates to the vividness of the hue. *Luminescence* has to do with the color's brightness. If you don't feel comfortable with the words, just use your eyes. The setting adjusts automatically when you click on a color.

If you want to work with patterns, shading, gradients, and tints, click on **Patterns & Shading** to bring up the Fill Patterns and Shading dialog window shown in Figure 3.20

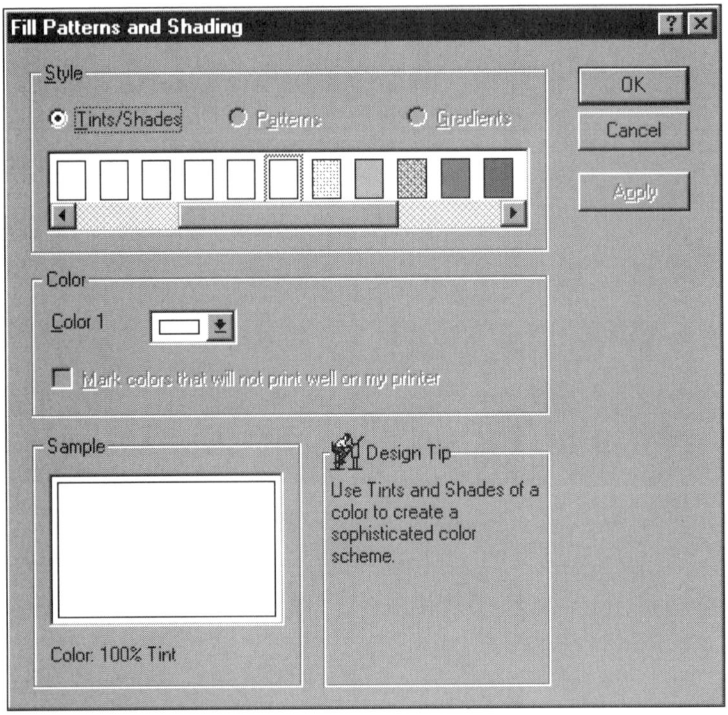

FIGURE 3.20 THE FILL PATTERNS AND SHADING DIALOG WINDOW.

The term recoloring is also used when you're working with a full-color image, and you want to change all the colors to varying shades of one single color. This is a great money-saver if you plan to use an outside print shop. Instead of printing in full-color, which is quite expensive, you can enhance your publications and get the visual impact of color using only a single color. Printers calls this *spot color.*

To use this feature, select the **Recolor Picture** option from the Format menu to bring up the dialog window shown in Figure 3.21. You can see that the left section of this window is identical to that little drop-down palette you get when using the Object Color speedbutton (see Figure 3.17), and it works the same way. The difference here is that Publisher recolors the entire image with whatever color you select.

FIGURE 3.21 THE RECOLOR PICTURE DIALOG WINDOW WITH THE BITMAP CAR PICTURE FROM THE WINDOWS FOLDER.

If your image is a single solid color (such as the handicapped picture you saw earlier), then that color is replaced by the new color you select. If your image is a multicolored image, such as the blue-yellow-gray-black car picture, Publisher recolors each color with an appropriate shade of the color you select. Try a few colors to see the effect. Then you can click on **Restore Original Colors** when you're done.

NOTE

Recolor also refers to changing the color of draw and vector images using the MS Draw program, and the colors in a bitmap image using the MS Paint program.

Adding a Border

The picture frame in our sample Access sign does not have a border. What you see is a faint gray dotted line around the picture indicating the edges of the frame. If you want to add a border, click on the **Border** speed button and select **More...** to bring up the dialog window shown in Figure 3.22. Here you can see that **None** is the current selection. Go ahead and select **4 pt**, and Publisher will place a line around the frame that is four points thick.

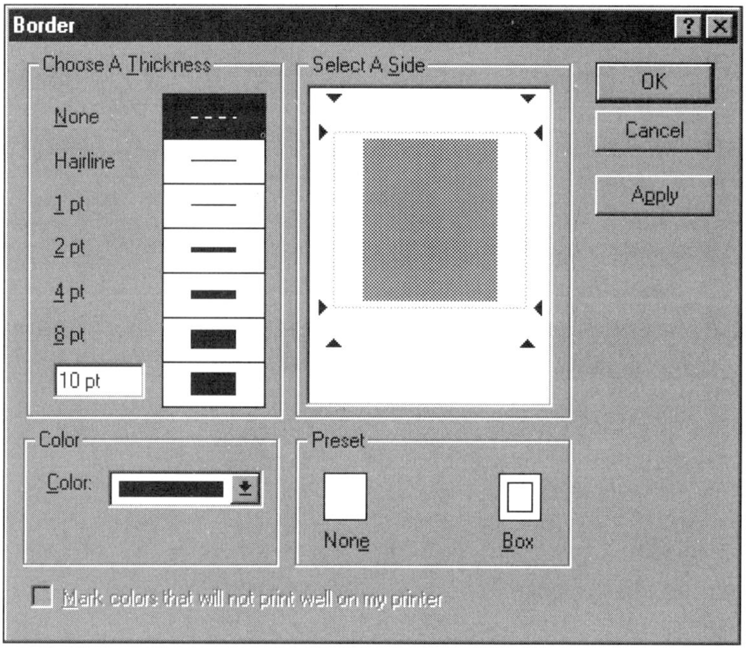

FIGURE 3.22 THE BORDERS DIALOG WINDOW.

In the middle of the dialog window is a section called **Select A Side**. When you click on **4 pt**, Publisher assumes that you want the border on all four sides of the frame. But you have a choice, and you can construct your border one side at a time. Notice the four pairs of arrow-heads? When you click on a side, all the arrow pairs disappear except for the pair marking the side you clicked on. Once you specify a side, you can set the line width (point size). You can also use the drop-down list box to select a color for the line. Click on **OK** to keep the 4 pt border.

TIP

If you want to work on two or three lines at the same time, hold down the **Shift** key while you click on the second and third sides.

Adding and Removing Shadows

When you are working with picture objects, adding or removing shadows refers to adding or removing a frame shadow. First make sure that you have selected the picture frame, then click on the last speedbutton in the Format toolbar. That's all there is to it. When you use this speedbutton, Publisher applies its standard shadow. It is always one quarter inch wide, gray in color, and placed along the right and bottom sides of the frame.

If you can't see the shadow, zoom in to get a closer look. Figure 3.23 shows the picture frame and a little bit of the surrounding page.

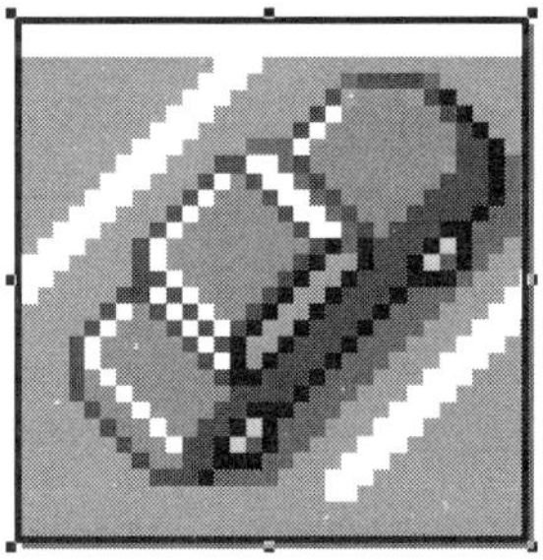

FIGURE 3.23 AN ENLARGED VIEW OF THE CAR PICTURE WITH A SHADOWED FRAME.

The **Shadow** option on the Format menu produces exactly the same results, as does pressing **Ctrl-D**. All three methods (button, menu, and keyboard) work as a toggle switch. Either **Shadow** is on or off. So if you use the speedbutton to add a shadow and then select the **Shadow** menu option, Publisher removes the shadow.

If you want a wider shadow or a more colorful shadow, you'll have to create your own. The technique is simple, and it does not involve the **Add/Remove Shadow** button or menu option. You create a box the same size as the frame, fill it with whatever color you want, drag it so that it overlaps the picture frame on two sides (usually right and bottom), and then place the box behind the picture frame. The degree to which the box peeks out from behind the picture frame determines the width of the shadow. (I'll walk you through these steps in more detail when you get to Chapter 5.)

PICTURE OBJECT MENU

Before we move on to our next sample publication, this seems like a good time to take a quick look at the picture object menu. In the last chapter, I showed you the text object menu that appears when you click on a text frame with your right mouse button. I also mentioned that Publisher has a pop-up menu for all object types.

To see the picture object menu as shown in Figure 3.24, use your right mouse button to click on the picture frame.

The first group of options—**Cut Picture Frame**, **Copy Picture Frame**, **Delete Picture Frame**—are identical to the options on the Edit menu. The second group of options has to do with the size of the display. The **Full Page** and **Actual Size** options are identical to the options on the View menu. **Zoom to Selection** enlarges the selected frame.

The third group consists of the **Scale Picture...** and **Recolor Picture...** options, both of which function identically to their counterparts on the Format menu.

The fourth group of options deals with the image file within the picture frame. The **Insert Picture File...** option is the one you used earlier to replace the handicapped image with the bitmap picture of the car. This option allows you to insert an external picture file of any type. You can even use it to insert the handicapped image. The main point is that this option brings up that Insert File dialog window from which you can choose your folder, file type, and file.

FIGURE 3.24 DISPLAY THE PICTURE OBJECT MENU BY RIGHT-CLICKING ON A PICTURE FRAME.

The **Insert ClipArt...** option brings up the ClipArt Gallery dialog window that you'll examine later in this chapter. You can use the **Insert Object...** option to insert objects of all types, provided that they are available on your system. In addition to the bitmap images and clipart files, other objects might include a Microsoft Graph or Word 6.0 Document file. I'll talk more about objects when I discuss program compatibility in Chapter 8.

The fifth group of options relates to formatting and frame properties. The **Pick Up Formatting** option is identical to the one on the Format menu and works the same as discussed earlier in this chapter. The **Picture Frame Properties...** option brings up a dialog window as shown in Figure 3.25. As you can see, the picture frame properties consist of margins and the two wrap options (**Wrap to Frame** and **Wrap to Picture**) discussed earlier in this chapter. The margins apply to the wrap options.

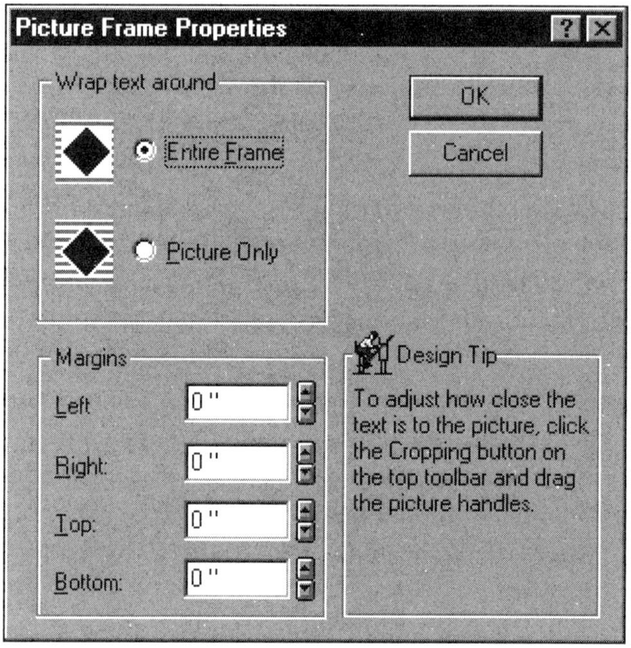

FIGURE 3.25 THE PICTURE PROPERTIES DIALOG WINDOW.

The last option on the picture object menu, **Help on this Picture Frame**, opens the Help panel to the Picture Frame subject. Here you can get help on adding and replacing pictures, changing their look and size, wrapping text around pictures, hiding pictures, and other image-related topics.

SAMPLE CHANGE OF ADDRESS CARD

Most people will move their home or office at least once or twice in their lives and will probably spend a fortune on cute change of address notices. Now you can print out your own postcards using the Specialty PageWizard. By now you know that selecting **Create New Publication** from the File menu allows you to start a new publication. And once you select the page layout (either a PageWizard, Existing Publication, or Blank Page), Publisher asks whether you want to save your previous work. If Publisher is not running, launch it now.

When the Specialty PageWizard asks *What do you want to make?*, select **Address Postcard**, click on **Next>**, and then on **Create It!** Publisher saves your name, address, and telephone information, and this is displayed when the PageWizard prompts you to type in your information. If Publisher already has your new information, just click **OK**. Otherwise, enter the new data. Figure 3.26 shows the Change of Address postcard that the PageWizard created for me.

FIGURE 3.26 THE CHANGE OF ADDRESS POSTCARD CREATED BY THE SPECIALTY PAGEWIZARD.

Now this is certainly a fine-looking card, but I would like to make a few changes. Before I do, however, I would like to have a little more room on my screen in which to work. I find that I seldom if ever use the standard toolbar and hiding it would give me a little more space. Also, I have no real need for the ruler right now because the PageWizard created the layout for me. So I can hide that bar too.

In Chapter 1, you learned a couple of ways to hide and show the toolbars. You can use the **Toolbars and Rulers...** option on the View menu, or you can simply right-click on either the vertical or horizontal toolbar to bring up the pop-up menu. Figure 3.27 shows my screen with the Change of Address postcard displayed at 100%. The two toolbars are hidden, and you can see the toolbar pop-up menu with check marks next to the Format toolbar and the status line indicating that they are visible.

FIGURE 3.27 MY SCREEN, WITH THE CHANGE OF ADDRESS PUBLICATION, AFTER HIDING TWO TOOLBARS

Now, let's get back to the postcard. What do I want to change? Well, the image is a little too clever for my taste. The house is a nice touch because it gives people a visual clue as to the meaning of the card—and visual clues are important to effective communication. But perching the house atop a weather vane is a bit much. What I'd really like to do is cut out the weather vane portion and leave the house. No problem.

Cropping Pictures

Cropping a picture means to cut away outer parts of the image. You can cut off the right or left sides, or the top or bottom sides, as much as you want. You just can't cut a portion out of the middle. Earlier in this chapter, you worked with the concept of resizing picture frames. Cropping works almost the same way, except that when you move the edges of the frame, the picture does not resize to fit.

Select the picture frame containing the image you want to crop. In our sample, this is the house/weather vane image. Then click on the **Crop Picture** speedbutton—it's the first one on the left of the Format toolbar, and it looks like two pairs of scissors. Now move your mouse over the bottom middle frame handle and watch your cursor change shape. The **Crop Picture** option is a toggle switch, and when it is selected, your cursor will change to its dueling scissors shape instead of the Resize cursor whenever you pass over a picture frame handle.

Now with your scissors cursor over the bottom middle handle, click and drag the bottom of the frame upward. As you are doing this, you will see the edge of the frame move upward, while the image remains in place (see Figure 3.28). Try it.

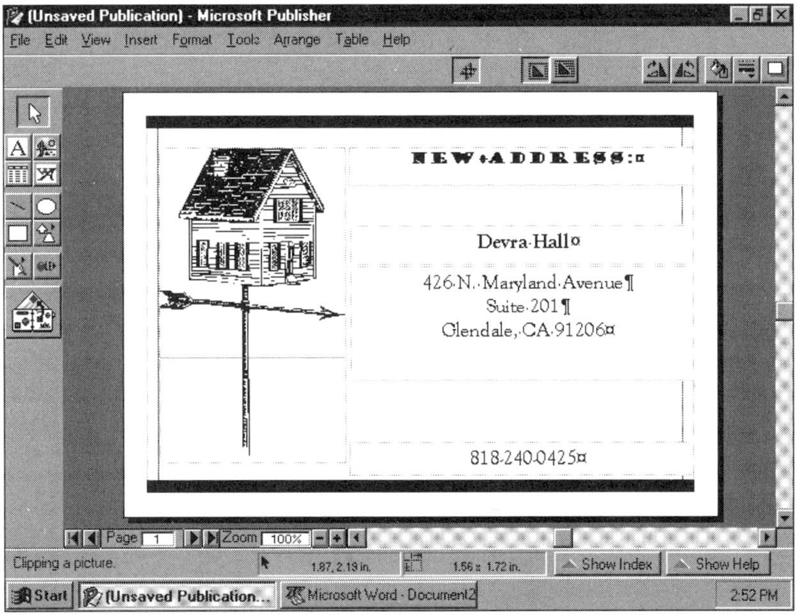

FIGURE 3.28 IN THE PROCESS OF CROPPING THE IMAGE ON THE CHANGE OF ADDRESS POSTCARD.

Cut off the weather vane portion of the image, leaving only the house. Once you let go of the mouse button, Publisher redraws the picture and the part you cut disappears, as shown in Figure 3.29. If you don't like it, you can drag the frame back down, and the cropped portion of the image will reappear. Alternatively, you can select the **Undo Crop Object** option from the Edit menu.

NOTE

If you look at the Edit and Format menus while the house image is selected, you'll find that several of the options refer to *Object* instead of *Picture*. Just like the Handicapped image from earlier in this chapter, the house image is a draw-type image from the ClipArt Gallery and considered to be an object.

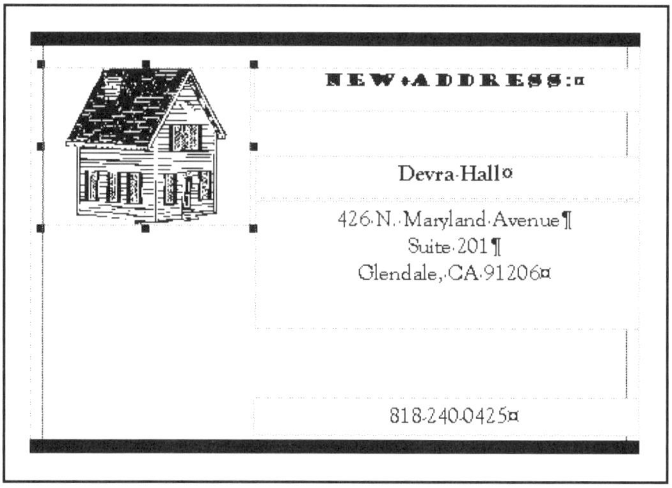

FIGURE 3.29 THE CHANGE OF ADDRESS CARD AFTER CROPPING THE IMAGE.

Now that the picture takes up only the top-left portion of the card, I have room below it to add more information. Frequently, companies with whom you do business want to know your previous address. This is especially true of magazine publishers and mailing houses. Also, it's often useful to include the date when your new address becomes effective. So, if you want, you can add one or more text frames for this information. Or you may decide that rather than cropping the house image, you'd rather substitute some other image from the ClipArt Gallery.

Hiding Pictures

If you have complex pictures, or even several simple pictures on a page, redrawing can be time consuming. Did you mind the time it took Publisher to redraw the house image when you experimented with cropping? If you are working on your pictures at the time, you'll have to live with it, but it you are finished placing and sizing your images and are ready to work on other parts of a publication, you can hide the images so that Publisher will not have to redraw them.

The **Picture Display...** option is on the View menu. When you select it, the Picture Display dialog window appears, as shown in Figure 3.30. You have three choices. You can allow all pictures to be displayed in all their glorious complexity (**Detailed Display**) and wait patiently while Publisher redraws. You can choose **Fast Resize and Zoom** to continue displaying images, but with a low level of detail so that redraws are faster.

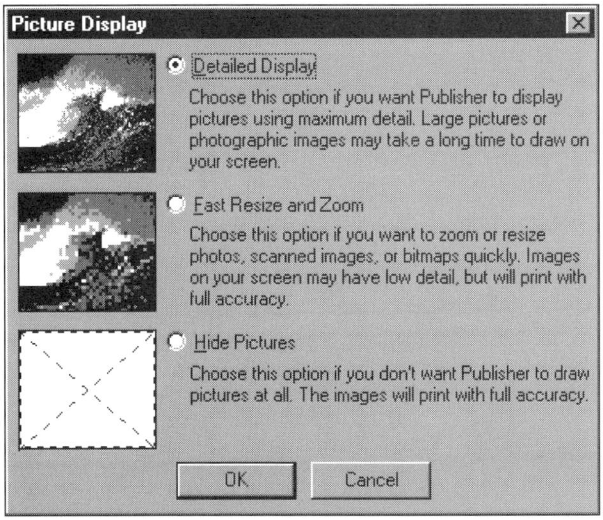

FIGURE 3.30 THE PICTURE DISPLAY DIALOG WINDOW.

Your third option is to **Hide Pictures**, leaving only an X to mark the spot of picture frames containing a hidden image. **Hide Picture** will hide the content of all Picture, WordArt, and embedded Objects, leaving only the frames in view. These three options relate only to the display on your screen. No matter which option you choose, your images will print in full detail.

The ClipArt Gallery

If you have the Deluxe Edition of Microsoft Publisher, you have access to more than 1,000 images. If you don't have the Deluxe Edition, you still have plenty of images to work with. The ClipArt Gallery comes with a minimum of 164 images.

When you double-click on a frame containing a ClipArt image, the Microsoft ClipArt Gallery window appears, as shown in Figure 3.31 (If you don't like double-clicking, you can select **ClipArt...** from the Insert menu or use your right mouse menu to access the Picture Object menu and select the **ClipArt Gallery** option from there.)

The instructions in the Gallery dialog window say *Choose a category, then select a picture.* When the window first appears, little thumbnail versions of all the images can be seen by scrolling down the center section. However, when you have hundreds, or even thousands, of images, this can be time consuming. That's why each image is assigned to one or more categories.

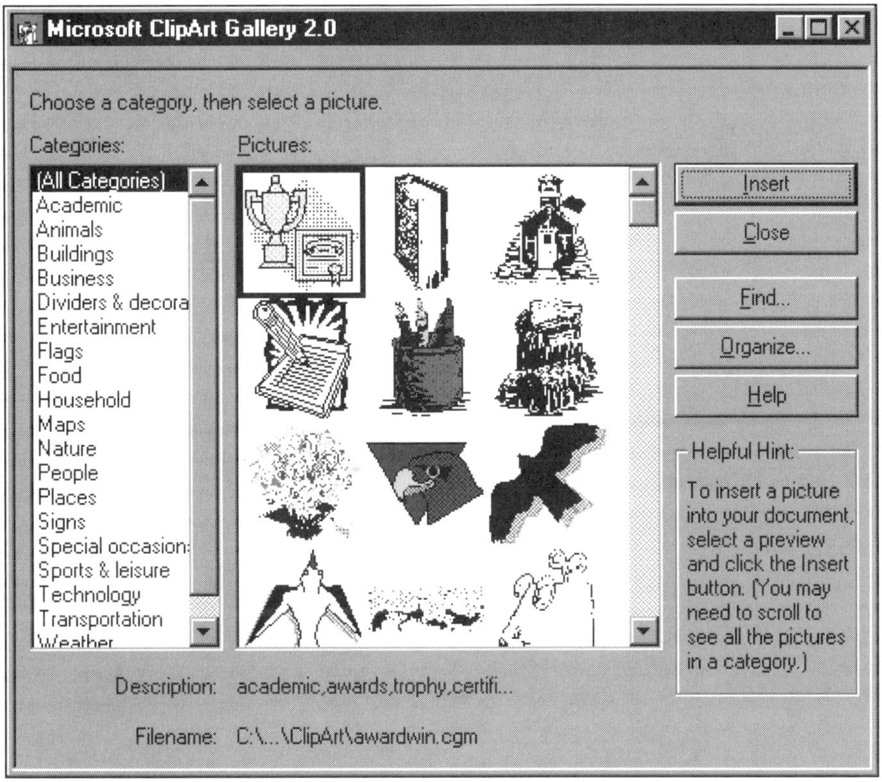

FIGURE 3.31 THE MICROSOFT CLIPART GALLERY DIALOG WINDOW.

The scrolling list of categories is located along the left side of the dialog window. When you select a category, your image options become fewer and easier to navigate. Click on **Buildings** in the *Categories* list; then find the image from the Change of Address postcard and click on it. Your Gallery dialog window should now look like the one in Figure 3.32. The word **Building** should be highlighted, and there should be a box around the picture.

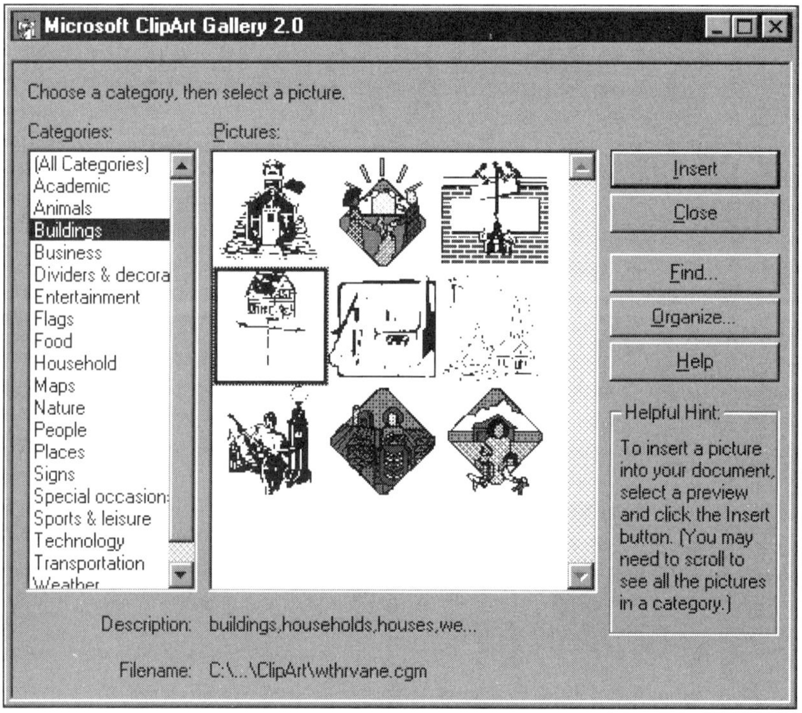

FIGURE 3.32 THE CLIPART GALLERY DIALOG WINDOW SHOWING THE IMAGES ASSIGNED TO THE BUILDINGS CATEGORY. THE WTHRVANE.CGM FILE HAS BEEN SELECTED.

Notice the two lines of text at the bottom of the window. The first line provides a description of the selected image by listing a few key words. The second line tells you the name of the file and where it is located on your system. In the description for the selected image—buildings, households, houses, weathervanes—the first two words are also categories, and the second two are not. So not all keywords are categories.

NOTE

The Gallery dialog window only shows the first 30 characters of the description. The full description is visible in the Picture Properties dialog window, as you'll see shortly.

In the Buildings category, our image is one of nine. If you click on the **Household** category, you'll find that our image is one of 29 assigned to that category. Click on it, and you'll see that the *Description* and *Filename* remain unchanged.

The **Helpful Hint** on the lower-right portion of the dialog window reminds you that once you have selected a picture, all you have to do is click on **Insert** to place it in your frame. But before you select a new picture to replace the PageWizard's choice, let's look at some of the other features of the Gallery.

Finding Images

The purpose of the keywords in the description is to help you find an image. If you click on the **Find...** button, the Find ClipArt dialog window appears as shown in Figure 3.33. The Find function bases its search on three criteria and only searches for files that are a part of the ClipArt Gallery.

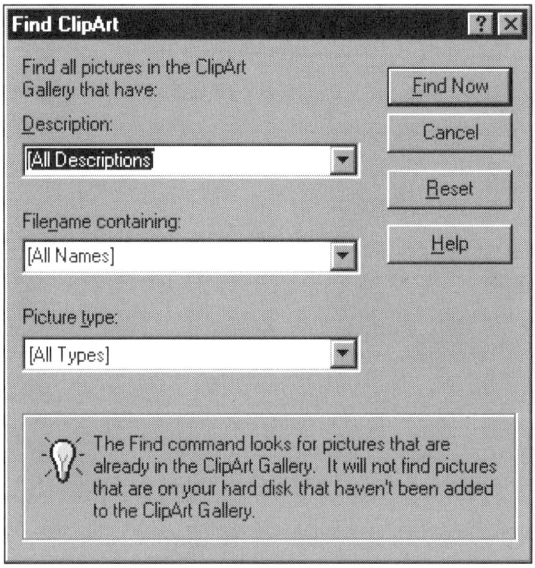

FIGURE 3.33 THE FIND CLIPART DIALOG WINDOW.

The first criteria is the description This is where you enter a keyword. Publisher includes partial matches. For example, enter the word **weather** and click **Find Now**. The results are shown in Figure 3.34. The first image found is our weathervane, because weather was a partial match to the key word *weathervanes*. The other five images all have the word *weather* in their descriptions as well.

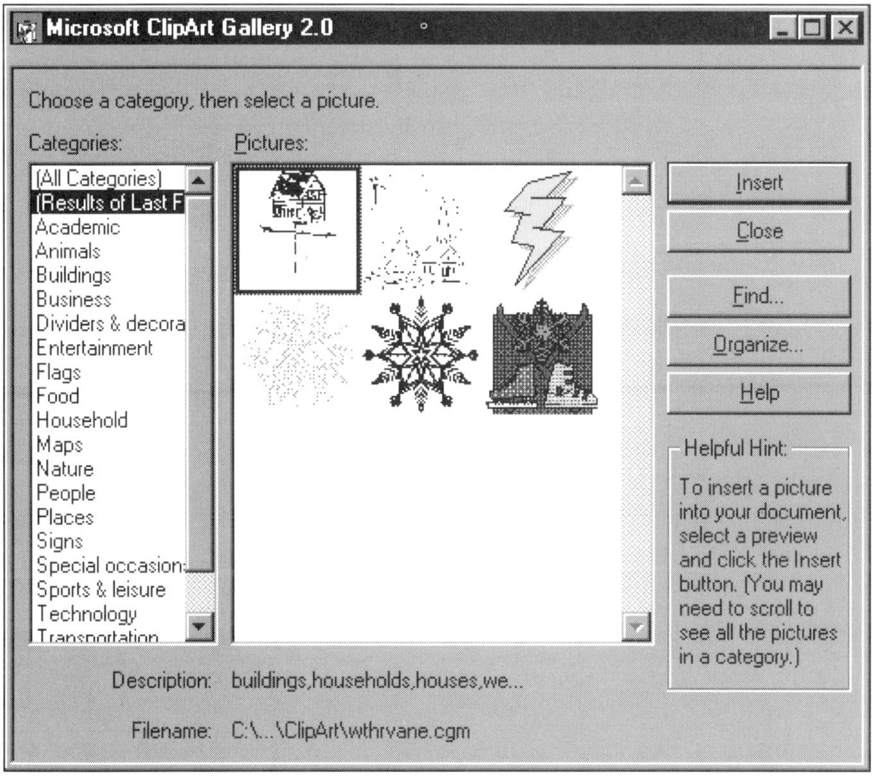

FIGURE 3.34 THE RESULTS OF A CLIPART GALLERY SEARCH FOR IMAGES CONTAINING THE WORD *WEATHER* IN THEIR DESCRIPTIONS.

If you click on the **Weather** category, you will find the same five images there as well. In the Weather category, you will also find a sixth image, the wedding shower image, that while assigned to the Weather category does not include the word *weather* in its description. This is a good illustration of how category assignment and descriptions are used independently of one another.

The other two search criteria for finding images are filenames and picture types. You can limit your searches to only those files that contain certain words or letters as part of the filename. For example, the filename for the weathervane image is wthrvane.cgm, so you could search for files with **wthr** as part of the filename. If you try this, you'll find that it is the only one in the Gallery.

You can also limit your search to a specific picture type, such as Windows Bitmaps, Computer Graphic Metafile (the type of all the clipart that comes with the Gallery when you install Publisher), Kodak Photo CD, and all the other types discussed in he beginning of this chapter.

When you first install Publisher, the ClipArt Gallery contains only computer graphic metafile images, and as I mentioned earlier, these are draw-type images. But as you may have just inferred, the Gallery can contain all image types. So let's take a look at how you can organize your Gallery and add other images. Start by clicking on the **Organize** button to bring up the Organize ClipArt dialog window shown in Figure 3.35. Organizing your Gallery involves four activities: adding pictures, updating preview images, changing picture properties, and editing the category list.

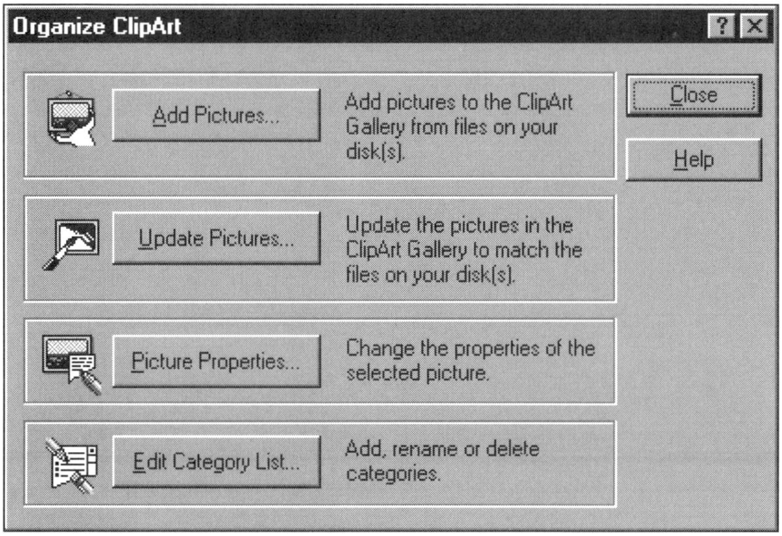

FIGURE 3.35 THE ORGANIZE CLIPART DIALOG WINDOW.

Adding Pictures

When you click on **Add Pictures...**, the dialog window shown in Figure 3.36 appears. It looks just like the Insert Picture dialog window you saw earlier in this chapter, only with a different title bar. For practice, let's add that bitmap car image you found in the Windows folder. When you find it again, select it and click on **Open**, as shown in Figure 3.37.

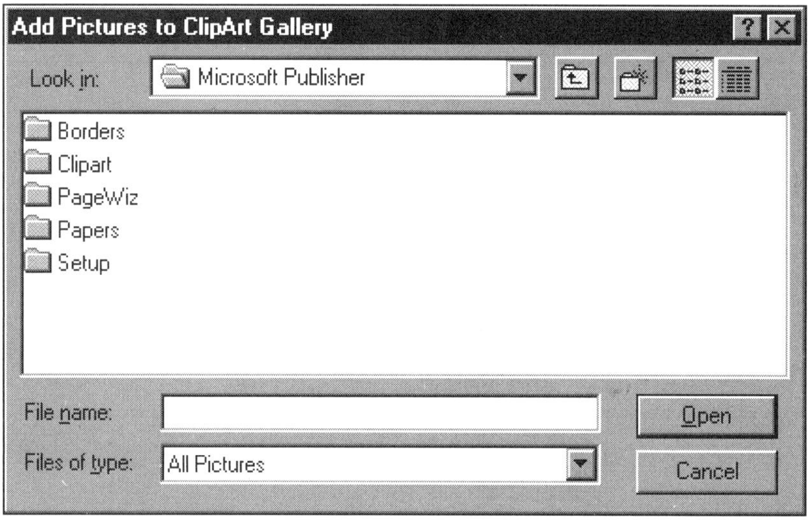

FIGURE 3.36 THE ADD PICTURES TO CLIPART GALLERY DIALOG WINDOW AS IT FIRST APPEARS.

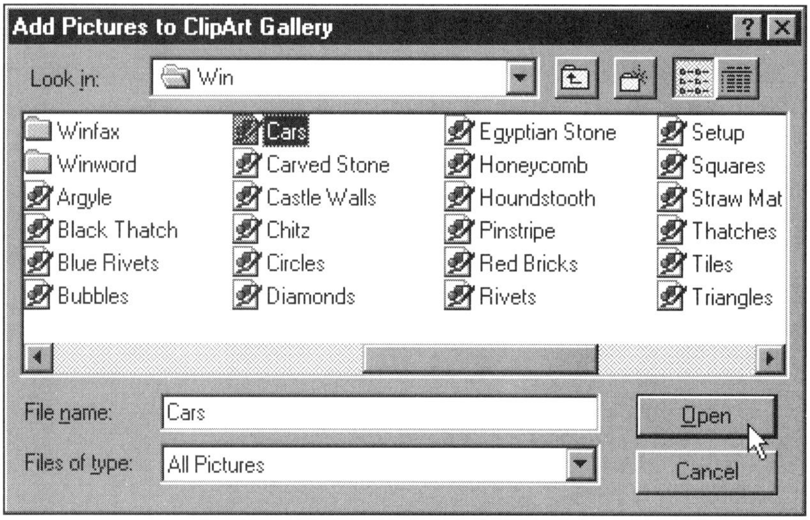

FIGURE 3.37 THE ADD PICTURES TO CLIPART GALLERY DIALOG WINDOW WITH THE CARS BITMAP SELECTED FROM THE WINDOWS FOLDER.

This brings up the Picture Properties dialog window shown in Figure 3.38. You can see a thumbnail version of the image in the top-left corner, along with the filename and type. Initially the **Description** field is blank, and this is where you type in the keywords. I entered five keywords, separated by commas, as you can see in the figure. You can use my keywords, or choose your own.

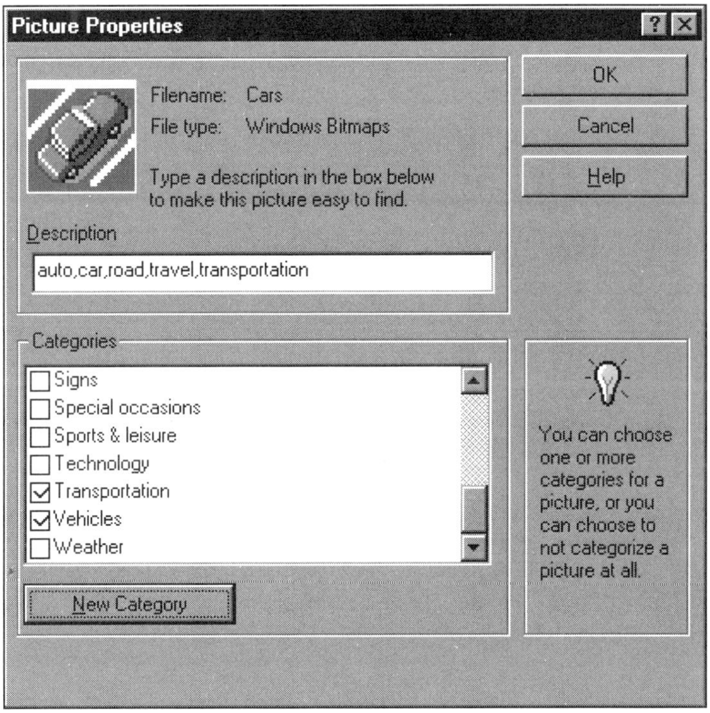

FIGURE 3.38 THE PICTURE PROPERTIES DIALOG WINDOW FOR THE CARS IMAGE AFTER ENTERING KEYWORDS FOR THE DESCRIPTION AND ASSIGNING THE IMAGE TO TWO CATEGORIES.

Next you get to assign the image to one or more of the existing categories. I thought **Transportation** to be the only one appropriate, so I clicked on the checkbox to select it. Now you could stop there and click on **OK**, but I wanted to add a new category for this image—one called Vehicles.

To add a category, click on **New Category** and a little tiny dialog window appears. Type in the new category name and click on **OK**. Publisher automatically adds the new category to the Categories list, and marks the checkbox for you. Now we're done, so click on **OK**. You should be back at our Gallery dialog window now, and the new category should be on the list. When you do a **Find** using any of the keywords for the car, Publisher will find the car image for you.

Updating Picture Previews

You saw how when you added the cars image to the ClipArt Gallery, it created a little preview image to display in the Gallery dialog window. The purpose of the preview image is to let you see an image before you decide to place it in your publication—in other words, to preview the picture to make sure that you are selecting the right file. But what happens if after you add an image to the gallery, you or someone else makes changes to the file? You could think you were inserting a picture of a coupe and end up with a convertible because someone erased the roof, but your preview picture still shows the coupe.

The **Update Pictures...** function takes care of that problem by updating the preview images to match the actual files. If you want Publisher to match up files residing on network and/or removable drives, select the appropriate checkboxes before clicking on **Update** (see Figure 3.39). Once you click on **Update**, Publisher does the rest.

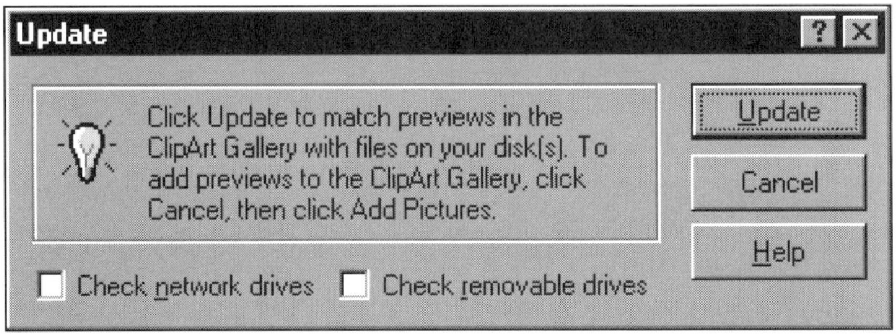

FIGURE 3.39 THE UPDATE DIALOG WINDOW FOR UPDATING CLIPART PREVIEW IMAGES.

Changing Picture Properties

When you added the Cars image, you entered the keywords and selected categories in the Picture Properties dialog window. This is the same dialog window that appears when you click on the **Picture Properties...** button. The information shown in the dialog window will be the data for whichever picture you have selected in the Gallery dialog window. Once the Picture Properties dialog window appears, you can change the description and/or category assignments.

Editing the Category List

The **Edit Category List...** button brings up the Edit Category List dialog window, shown in Figure 3.40. From here you can add a new category by clicking **New Category...** just as before. If you want to rename an existing category, select the category name from the list, click on the **Rename Category...** button, enter the new name in the dialog window that appears, and click on **OK**.

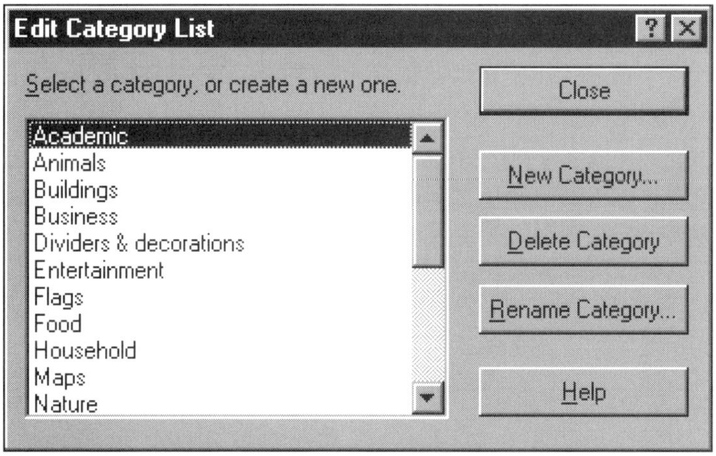

FIGURE 3.40 THE EDIT CATEGORY LIST DIALOG WINDOW.

You can also delete a category, so if you were just humoring me earlier by adding a Vehicles category, now is your chance to delete it.

Highlight it and click on the **Delete Category** button. When you are done editing categories, click on **Close** to make the Edit Category List dialog window disappear.

NOTE

Deleting a category will not delete an image assigned to the category unless it is the only category to which the image is assigned.

SAMPLE LOST & FOUND FLYER

The last sample publication you'll examine in this chapter is the Lost & Found Flyer created by the Flyer PageWizard. The **Flyer** icon is on the first row, second from the left. The PageWizard considers the Lost or Found flyer to be for personal use, so select **Personal** when asked *What's the flyer for?* Click on **Next>**, select **Lost or Found**, click on **Next>** again, and finally click on **Create It!** PageWizard asks you to type in a title for your flyer (I used **Lost Dog**), and prompts you for your name and telephone number. This is the name and number you want someone to call if they have any information.

Figure 3.41 shows the PageWizard's creation. The two text boxes contain text that is illegible unless viewed at 50% zoom or higher, and at that point it is unintelligible unless you can read Latin. Of course, if you plan to use this flyer you will replace that text with the description of your lost dog in whatever language is appropriate.

FIGURE 3.41 THE LOST OR FOUND FLYER, CREATED BY THE PAGEWIZARD, AND VIEWED AT 33% ZOOM.

You'll have to change the image as well, unless of course, you have lost your alligator. You could choose to replace the gator image with one of the two dog images in the ClipArt Gallery, but that wouldn't be nearly as effective as using a picture of your own Rex or Fluffy. As mentioned at the beginning of this chapter, you could leave a blank space for the picture, and then paste the original photo on a printout and photocopy your flyers. But if you have a scanner, you can scan your photo directly into your publication.

NOTE

If you have been making Photo CDs of your snapshots, you may already have a digitized photo of your dog. In that case, you can use the **Insert Picture** option, and don't have to use the scanner to import a photo image.

Scanning a Photo

The process of scanning a photo directly into Publisher is really quite simple. The only catch is that your scanner and scanning software must be properly installed, and your scanning software must be TWAIN32 compliant. Support of the TWAIN32 standard makes it possible to scan directly into your Publisher document. If your scanning software does not support this standard, you will have to scan your image independently of the Publisher program, save it as a file, and then import it into Publisher using **Insert Picture File**.

You can scan your image in six easy steps:

1. Place the picture on your scanner (make sure that your scanner is turned on).
2. Create a picture frame, or select an existing one. If you forget, Publisher will create a frame for your scanned image and place it smack in the middle of your page. Then you can move or resize it as desired.
3. Select **Scanner Image...** from the Insert menu. This menu option is only available if you have a scanner. If you happen to have more than one scanner available on your system, you will also need to choose **Select Scanner** and indicate which one you want to use.

NOTE

If you have a scanner, but don't see this option on your menu, try reinstalling your scanner software.

4. Select **Acquire Scanned Image**. This calls up your scanner program.
5. Use your scanner software to make any adjustments to the image and start the scan.
6. Exit scanner program when scan is completed.

That's all there is to the procedure. However, you may hit a glitch or two along the way. Usually, when problems occur it has something to do with memory or the resolution and number of colors you choose when you scanned the image.

Choosing Resolution and Color

Publisher uses system memory when importing bitmaps, and if your image is compressed on your disk, Publisher uncompresses it in memory. Depending on your resources, this could cause a problem (such as an *Out of Memory* error message). The image in the Lost or Found flyer is 4.75 x 2.25 inches. Assuming 300 dpi (dots per inch), Publisher needs to use almost 250K of memory for a black-and-white bitmap image, 2MB for a 256-color bitmap (also referred to as 8-bit color), and close to 6MB for a 16-million color bitmap (also referred to as 24-bit color).

Memory will also be a factor when printing color images. If your system has barely enough memory, your images will take a long time to print. If your system does not have enough memory to do the job, the image will not print at all. You may need to scan at a lower resolution or with fewer colors.

SUMMARY

- Although Wingdings may look like pictures, they are actually text characters.
- Publisher supports five types of bitmap files: plain bitmaps (BMP), JPEG files, Kodak Photo CD pictures (PCD), pictures created in PC Paintbrush (PCX), and Tagged Image Format files (TIF). Publisher also supports six draw-type image files: images from CorelDraw!

(CDR), Micrografx Designer/Draw (DRW), and Draw Perfect (WPG), plus Encapsulated Postscript files (EPS), and Computer Graphics Metafiles (CGM).

- ✷ You can place any image type in a picture frame using the **Picture File...** option on the Insert menu.
- ✷ Click-and-drag any handle on a picture frame to resize the frame and image inside it. To resize the image proportionally, use a corner frame handle and hold down the **Shift** key while resizing. To maintain the picture's center, use a corner handle and hold down the **Ctrl** key while resizing.
- ✷ The **Scale Picture...** option on the Format menu resizes images based on a percentage of the original height and width. When you scale a picture, the top-left corner position coordinates remain the same.
- ✷ To crop a picture, click on the **Crop** speedbutton or select **Crop Picture...** from the Format menu, and resize the frame. Publisher redraws the image displaying only the portion that fits within the resized frame. The cropped portion of the picture is still available should you wish to restore the image by selecting the **Crop** button again and resizing the frame in the opposite direction.
- ✷ When a picture frame appears inside a text frame, you can choose to have the text wrap around the edges of the picture frame, or around the picture itself.
- ✷ You can rotate a picture, to the right or left, 90 degrees at a time, by selecting the frame and clicking on the **Rotate Right** or **Rotate Left** speedbuttons on the Format toolbar. To rotate a picture frame manually, select the frame, hold down the **Alt** key (cursor changes to the rotate symbol), and drag the image around to the position you desire.
- ✷ To recolor the space between a picture and its frame (the picture canvas), select the frame, use the **Recolor Object** speedbutton on the Format toolbar, and select a color from the drop-down palette. To use a **Tint**, **Fill Pattern**, or **Gradient** on the canvas of a picture frame, click on the **Patterns and Shading...** button on the palette.

- To recolor a picture, select that option from the Format menu. If the picture is a multicolor bitmap, Publisher recolors the whole picture using various shades of whichever color you select. To use a **Tint**, **Fill Pattern**, or **Gradient** in a picture of a picture frame, click on the **Patterns and Shading...** button in the Colors dialog window.
- To create a border around a picture frame, select the picture frame and use the **Border** speedbutton or the **Border...** option on the Format menu to bring up the Border dialog window.
- To create a standard, gray, .25-inch shadow, select the picture frame and use the **Add/Remove Shadow** speedbutton or the **Shadow** option on the Format menu. To create your own custom shadow, use a shape object as discussed in Chapter 5.
- If you want to save time spent on redrawing pictures, use the **Picture Display...** option on the View menu to bring up the dialog window. Select **Fast Resize and Zoom** to display pictures with less detail, or **Hide Pictures** to show only an X inside every picture, WordArt, and embedded object frame except those that remain empty.
- To access the ClipArt Gallery dialog window, select **ClipArt...** from the Insert menu or double-click on a ClipArt picture frame. Publisher displays preview images in the center section of the window. To narrow your selection, click on a category from the list on the left. You can see descriptive keywords and the file's name and location at the bottom of the Gallery dialog window.
- To add pictures of any type to the ClipArt Gallery, update Gallery preview images, change a picture's properties (description and category assignments), or edit the Category list, access the ClipArt Gallery dialog window and click on **Organize...**.
- To scan a picture directly into a publication, you must first successfully install your scanner and scanner software. Also, your scanner software must be TWAIN32 compliant. Choose **Scan Image** from the Insert menu. If you have more than one scanner, you also need to choose **Select Scanner** to specify the one you want to use.

- When scanning a picture directly, you should create or select a picture frame before beginning to scan. If you forget, Publisher creates a frame for you.
- The resolution and number of colors at which you scan impacts system memory resources. If you run out of memory, try scanning again at a lower resolution and/or with fewer colors.

CHAPTER 4

WORKING WITH TABLES

* Examining tables
* Selecting columns and rows
* Resizing tables, columns, and rows
* Using Grow to Fit
* Navigating tables
* Inserting and deleting columns and rows
* Merging and splitting cells
* Shading and coloring cells
* Picking up and applying formatting
* Adding borders and gridlines
* Filling down and right
* Setting cell margins
* Viewing the table and cell object menus
* Creating tables from scratch
* AutoFormatting tables
* Selecting border art

The main difference between table objects and text objects is formatting. A table is little more than text data placed in columns and rows. But it is the formatting of those columns and rows that make a table not only useful, but visually pleasing. Instead of making users create their own columns and rows by adding lines or borders, Publisher created the Table object to make your life easier.

The Business Form PageWizard creates 11 different publications, all of which use a table design. Let's begin our examination with the Expense Report. At the end of the chapter, I'll show you how to create your own table objects using the Table tool and AutoFormat.

EXPENSE REPORT

Once you choose Business Form on the PageWizard tab page and select Expense Report, the PageWizard prompts you to select a style. If you have created other documents using a particular style (such as Basic), the PageWizard asks if you want to use that same style. Select **Yes** and click on **Next>**.

NOTE

If you want to select a different style, select **No**. You can then choose **Basic**, **Classic**, **Modern**, or **Jazzy**.

The PageWizard then asks if you want the publication to include a logo picture or initials and asks you to choose between the portrait (vertical) and landscape (horizontal) layout. Chose landscape. You can also include your Company Address if desired. Then you get to specify the columns that you want to include in your expense report. For this example, I selected all the suggested columns: **Date**, **Description**, **Trans** (transportation), **Lodging**, **Meals**, **Other**, and **Total**.

Finally, the PageWizard wants to know which language you want to use, so that it can enter the headings for you in the language of your choice. I use the **English** setting for all the sample publications in this book, and Figure 4.1 shows the Expense Report as created by the PageWizard. For comparison, Figure 4.2 shows you just the top portion of the Expense Report using the **Portrait** layout with **Swedish** as the selected language. Go ahead and select whichever language you prefer to use.

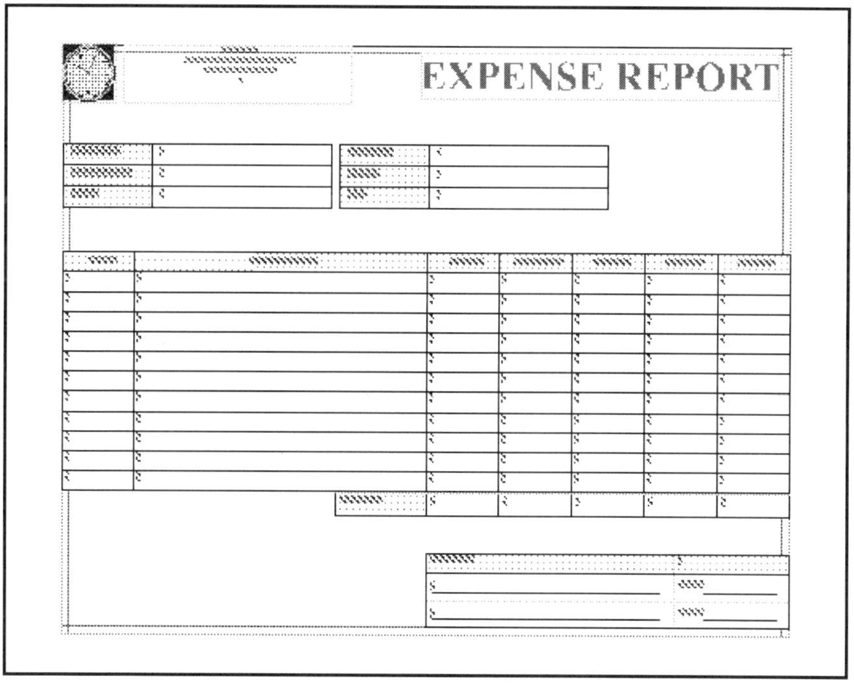

FIGURE 4.1 THE EXPENSE REPORT AS CREATED BY THE BUSINESS FORM PAGEWIZARD

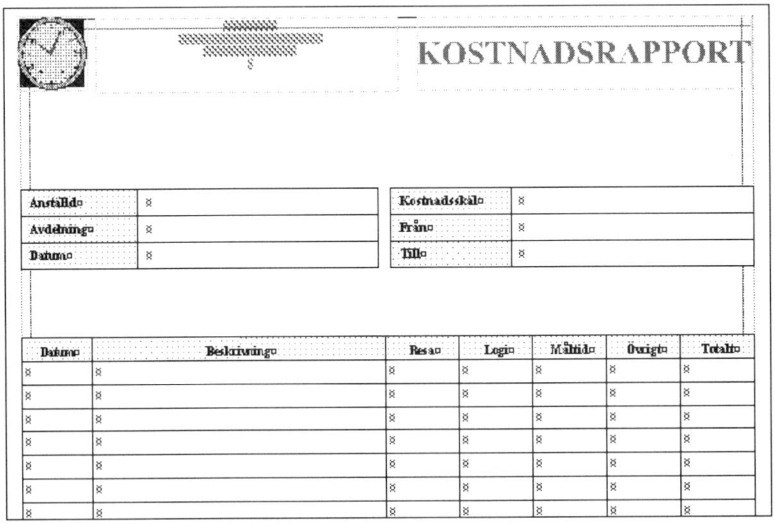

FIGURE 4.2 THE TOP PORTION OF AN EXPENSE REPORT CREATED IN SWEDISH WITH A PORTRAIT FORMAT.

At first glance it looks like this form might contain four tables, two at the top, one larger one that takes up most of the page, and one at the bottom. But the two blocks of boxes at the top are not tables. What you are looking at are 12 individual text frames, six with text and six blank, placed in two groups that look like tables. If you click on **Employee** or **Department** or **From**, you'll see that each is a text frame. And if you right-click on one, the Text Object menu appears.

Now click anywhere in the middle section below. Not only do the frame handles appear, but also a series of column selectors appears across the top and row selectors down the left side (see Figure 4.3). These selectors are sort of like buttons. To highlight or select an entire row, you click on a row selector. Similarly, to select an entire column, just click on the column selector. And to select the entire table, click the selector button in the top-left corner.

NOTE

If you prefer menu options, you can choose **Highlight Entire Table** from the Table menu. No menu options exist for selecting specific columns or rows.

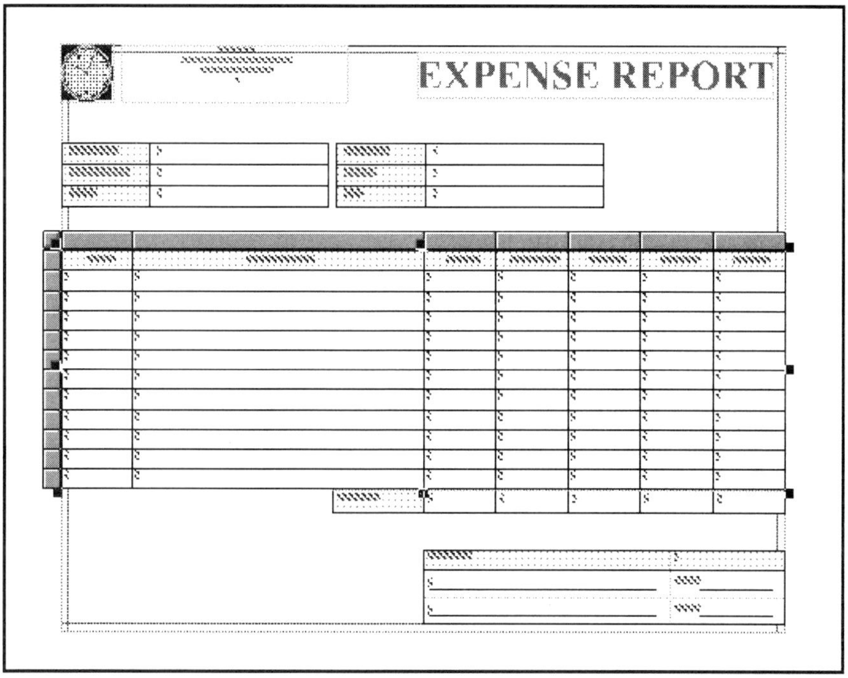

FIGURE 4.3 WHEN YOU CLICK ON THE MAIN TABLE OBJECT, ROW AND COLUMN SELECTORS APPEAR.

Take a good look at the frame handles around the table. Did you notice that the bottom handles do not encompass the last row. The last row used for Totals is actually a separate single-row table. How can you tell that it's a table and not a series of individual text frames? Click on it, and you'll see the column and row selectors appear. Same with the bottom section used for signature and dates. So now we know that the Expense Report consists of three tables, 14 text frames (12 plus the two for the report title and company address), and a picture frame for the logo.

As with the other objects you have examined, whenever you click on an object, specific speedbuttons appear on the Format toolbar. In the case of table objects, the toolbar is identical to the one for text objects. Tables are composed of cells, and although certain functions relate to the table as a whole (such as adding and deleting rows), there are also functions that relate to individual cells and their contents.

Individual cells act just like a text frames. If you want to enter or edit text in a cell, all you have to do is place your cursor in that cell by clicking on it. When you want to format the text, change its font or color, or make it bold, you use the same procedures you would use for any text frame. Because each cell is like a frame, changes you make to the text style in one cell, have no relationship to the text style in another cell.

Resizing Tables

Because you are already familiar with frame handles and the concept of resizing, let's start there. You can resize a table by clicking-and-dragging a table frame handle. Try making the table narrower, something like the one shown in Figure 4.4. Notice that all the columns and rows are still there, but each column is proportionally narrower. Now use the **Undo Resize Object** option on the Edit menu, or press **Ctrl-Z**, to restore the table to its original size.

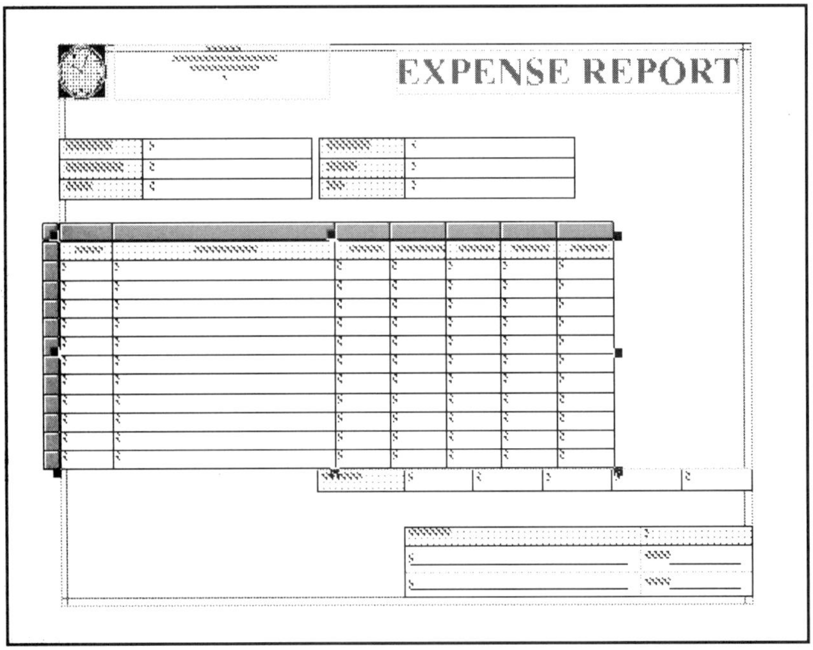

FIGURE 4.4 EXPENSE REPORT AFTER RESIZING THE MAIN TABLE TO MAKE IT NARROWER.

Resizing Columns and Rows

The lines separating the column selectors from one another are called *column boundaries*. And the lines separating the row selectors from one another are called *row boundaries*. You can move these boundary lines in the same way that you resize frames—by clicking-and-dragging. When you place your mouse over a boundary line, and the cursor changes from a pointer to the Adjust shape, you can click on the line and drag it in either direction: left or right for columns, and up or down for rows.

Here's the catch. If you simply drag a boundary line, it impacts the size of the entire table. Try it. Expand the Description column by dragging the right boundary line to the right. When I did this I ended up pushing columns right off the page as shown in Figure 4.5. I got more space in my Description column, but running off the page is not an acceptable solution. There must be another way to do this. Time to press **Ctrl-Z** (Undo) and try again.

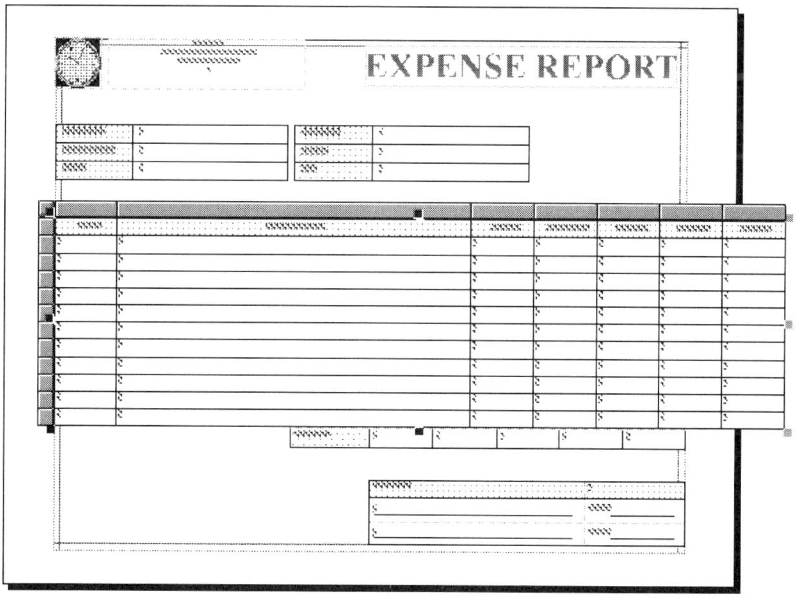

FIGURE 4.5 THE EXPENSE REPORT AFTER ENLARGING THE DESCRIPTION COLUMN BY DRAGGING THE BOUNDARY LINE TO THE RIGHT.

One way to get more space for the Description column without pushing everything off the page is to balance the increase of that column with the decrease of another column. If you hold down the **Shift** key while you adjust the boundary line, the adjacent column will adjust to compensate. Try the same move again, this time using the **Shift** key. Your Expense Report should look something like the one shown in Figure 4.6.

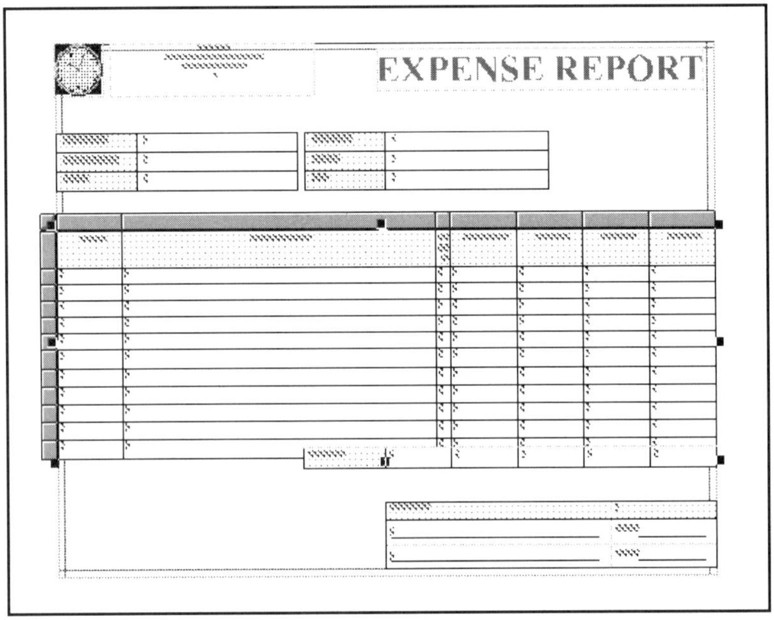

FIGURE 4.6 THE EXPENSE REPORT AFTER ENLARGING THE DESCRIPTION COLUMN BY HOLDING DOWN THE **SHIFT** KEY WHILE DRAGGING THE BOUNDARY LINE TO THE RIGHT.

Needless to say, this won't do either. Now there is not enough room in the Transportation column to enter more than 99 cents, and we all know that you can't even go around the block for that amount. So let's **Undo** it again, and come up with a different solution.

The only other solution I can think of is to increase the height of each cell. I already mentioned the row boundary lines, and you've probably guessed that you can adjust them the same way you adjust the column boundaries. If you drag a row boundary line downward, the following rows get pushed down too. In Figure 4.7 you can see how they end up colliding with the Totals row.

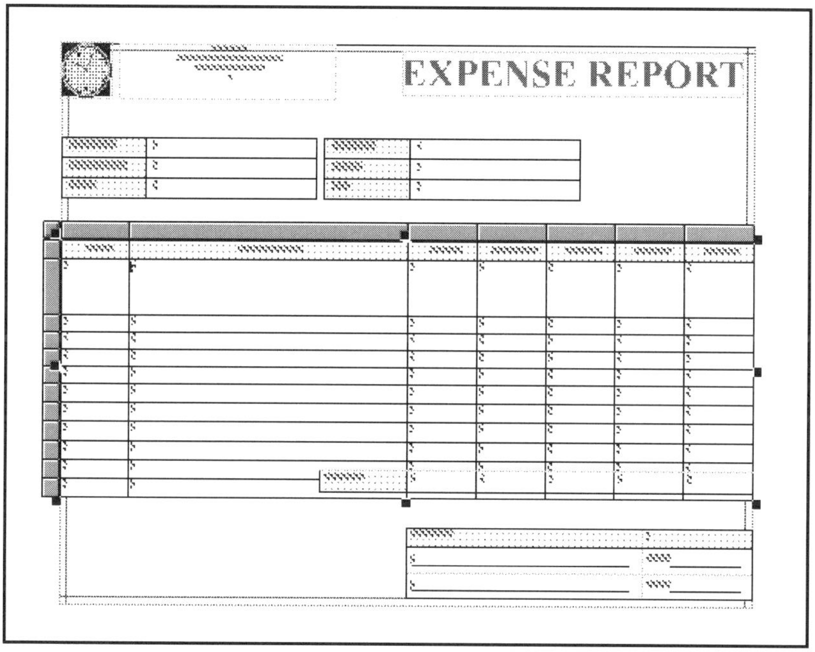

FIGURE 4.7 THE EXPENSE REPORT AFTER INCREASING THE HEIGHT OF THE FIRST ROW BY DRAGGING THE BOUNDARY LINE DOWNWARD.

If you hold the **Shift** key while dragging a row boundary downward, the row immediately beneath adjusts to compensate, while the rest of the rows remain unchanged, as shown in Figure 4.8.

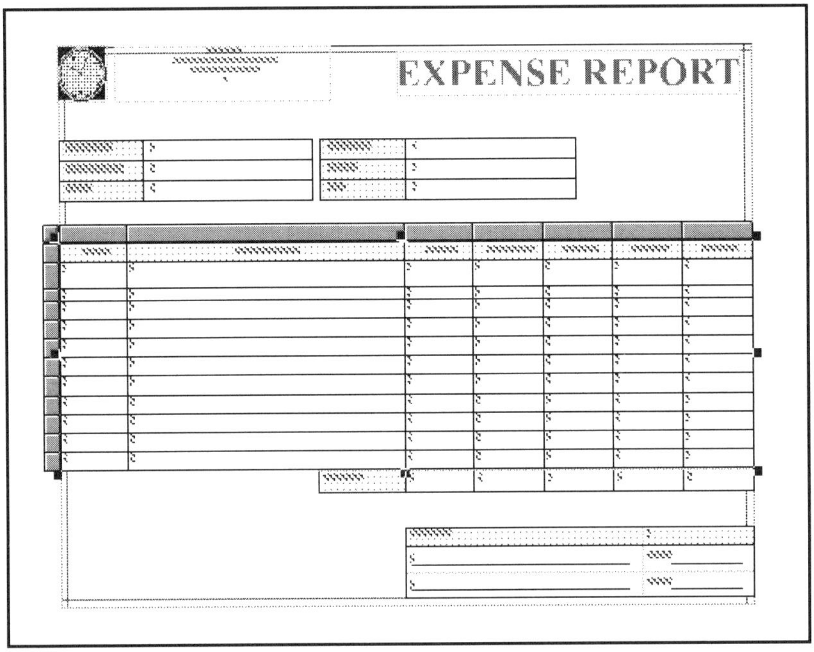

FIGURE 4.8 THE EXPENSE REPORT AFTER INCREASING THE HEIGHT OF THE FIRST ROW BY HOLDING DOWN THE **SHIFT** KEY WHILE DRAGGING THE BOUNDARY LINE DOWNWARD.

Now that's all well and good if you want to adjust the height of a single row. However, you want to adjust the amount of space available in the Description cell for every row. That means that you have to adjust each row. Luckily, you do not have to adjust them one at a time. Instead, you can highlight multiple rows and make the adjustment just once.

NOTE

To highlight a row, click on the row selector. To highlight multiple rows, click-and-drag your mouse across the selectors for the desired rows.

Growing to Fit

If you do not need the extra space in every row, then resizing rows as you did above, is not always the best solution. Suppose that your expense report has six entries, and of those six, only two require a second line in the Description column. If you resize the rows to hold two lines of text, your table will expand to the size of 22 lines (not including the heading row), and push everything down and on to a second page. That would be fine if you needed to use all that space, but our premise is that you only need the extra line occasionally.

Okay, obviously you could resize the individual rows as and when needed. But Publisher has a feature that makes that unnecessary. It's called Grow to Fit, where the height of a row expands automatically to fit all the text you enter in a cell. The **Grow to Fit** option is on the Table menu, and it is one of those options that is either turned on or turned off. Using Grow to Fit is the default setting.

In a Description cell, type something long enough to require more than one line and watch the row expand. If you can't think of anything to type, use this quote from the American Library Association's statement about the Univac computer on exhibit at the New York World's Fair in 1964:

```
The computer is only a fast idiot, it has no
imagination; it cannot originate action. It is,
and will remain, only a tool to man.
```

Then try typing that same text into the space provided for the name of the person to whom you send the report. Again there is more text than will fit, but because that is a text frame, and not cell, the space will not expand. Instead, you will see the text frame button with the three dots indicating overflow text, as shown in Figure 4.9.

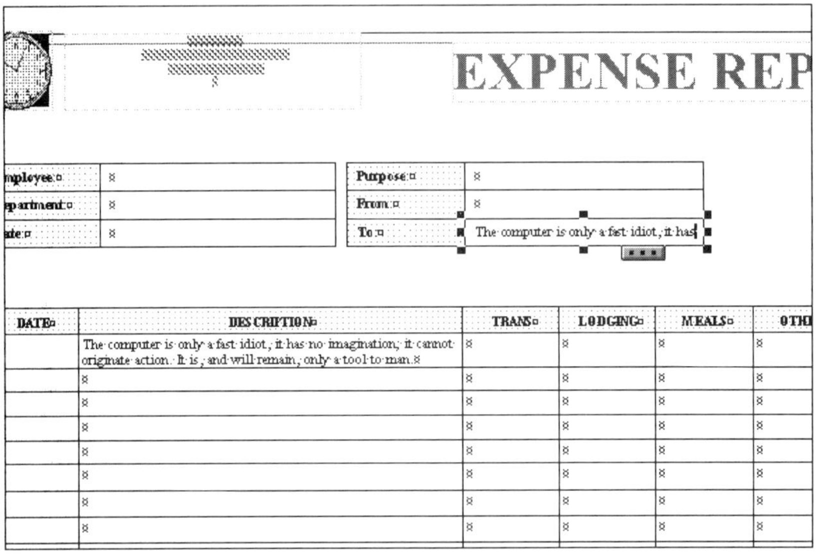

FIGURE 4.9 AN EXCERPT FROM AN EXPENSE REPORT ILLUSTRATING TEXT FRAME OVERFLOW AND GROW TO FIT EXPANSION OF A TABLE CELL.

Sometimes Publisher tries to be useful by providing helpful tips and offers of assistance. When you enter the quote in the text frame, causing it to overflow, you might see the message shown in Figures 4.10.

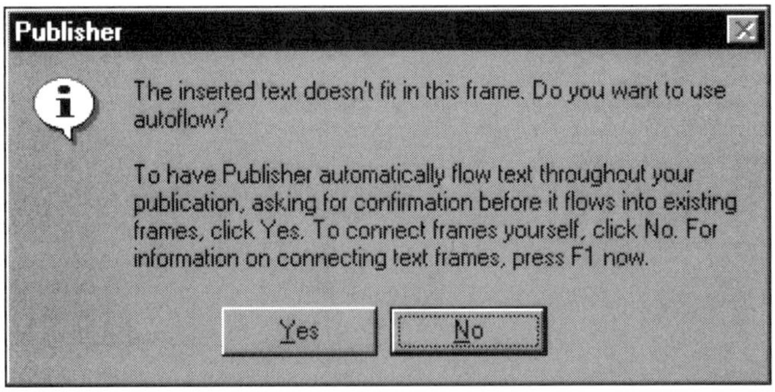

FIGURE 4.10 A PUBLISHER TIP POINTING OUT THAT TEXT HAS OVERFLOWED THE FRAME AND OFFERING THE USE OF AUTOFLOW.

When Publisher reminded me that I could flow text from one frame to another, either manually or automatically by using Autoflow, I wondered whether I could flow that text from its frame into a table cell. After all, the cells do hold text. Try it. Click on the **Text Frame** button to turn your cursor into a bucket full of text, and then click on one of the table cells. You should get the error message shown in Figure 4.11.

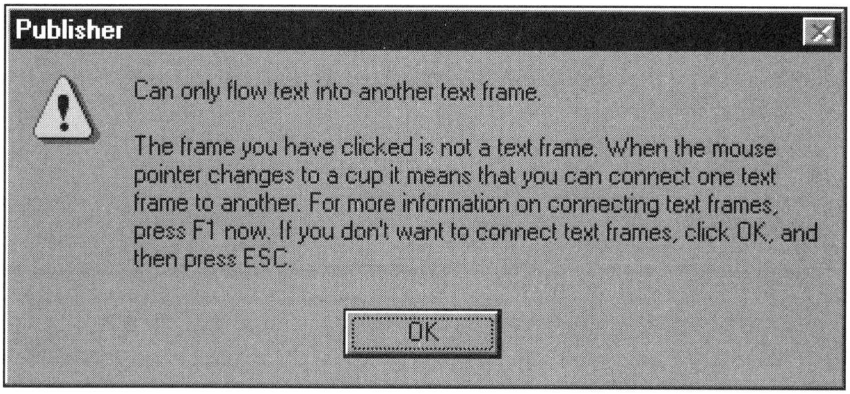

FIGURE 4.11 PUBLISHER DISPLAYS THIS ERROR MESSAGE WHEN YOU TRY TO POUR OVERFLOW TEXT FROM A TEXT FRAME INTO A TABLE CELL.

Then I wondered what happens if you place too much text in a table cell and the **Grow to Fit** option is off. The answer is nothing. There is no visible indication that your text has overflowed its cell boundaries. Unless you have reason to think that there is more text in a cell than is visible, you'd never know. Publisher does not provide a way to connect cells in the same way that you can connect text frames, so you cannot flow text from one cell to another. The only way to see the hidden text is to enlarge the cell, either manually or by selecting **Grow to Fit**.

Let's continue our discussion of tables by examining a different PageWizard publication. There's really no difference between the tables in the various publications, but I thought you might like so see some of the other Business Forms.

TIME BILLING FORM

You know the routine. Select **Create New Publication...** from the File menu, and click on the **Business Form** icon on the PageWizard tab page. When asked *What form would you like?* select **Time Billing**. Then choose the **Basic** style, include a **Picture**, specify the **Landscape** format, and include the **Address** to match the Expense Report design. Figure 4.12 shows the Time Billing form created by the PageWizard

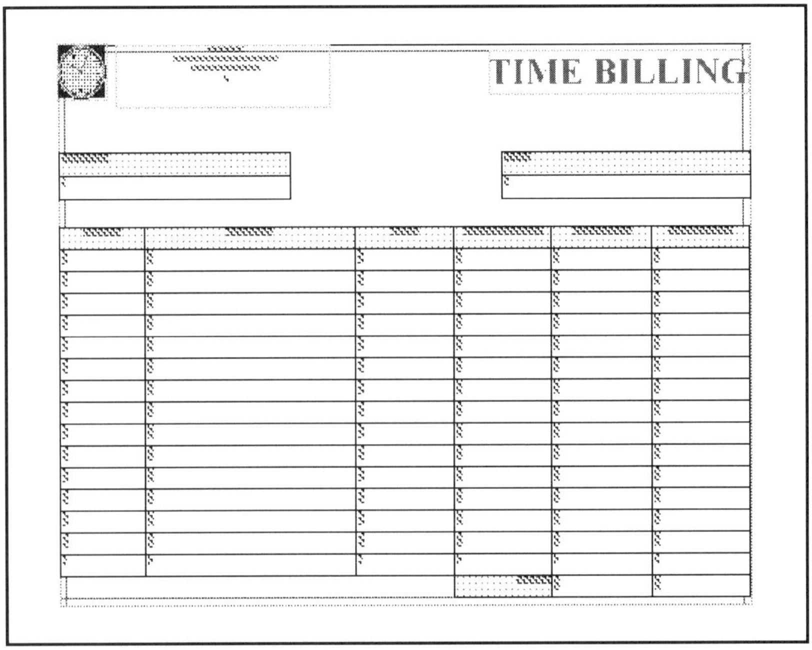

FIGURE 4.12 THE TIME BILLING FORM CREATED BY THE BUSINESS FORM PAGEWIZARD.

This business form publication contains two text frames, a picture frame, and four tables. Can you find them all? Unlike the Expense Report, the two top sections are tables, not individual text frames. Why this difference in the design approach I can't tell you, but it seems much easier to create a table than to create individual text frames and line them up so precisely. Then there is the large table with six columns (Client, Activity, Rate, Overtime Rate, Time Spent, and Total), and the one-row table for the total.

Navigating Tables

We haven't talked at all yet about how you move from cell to cell to input your data. Of course you can use your mouse to click in each cell, but that involves more hand action than necessary when you're typing. The simplest way to move from cell to cell is to use the **Tab** and/or arrow keys.

The **Tab** key moves your cursor to the next cell on the right. If your cursor is already in the last cell of a row, **Tab** moves to the first cell on the next row. If you hold down the **Shift** key when you press **Tab**, your cursor moves to the left. And if your cursor is already in the first cell of a row, **Shift-Tab** moves to the last cell of the previous row.

The arrow keys are even more direct. The **Up** arrow moves your cursor to the cell directly above. The **Down** arrow moves your cursor to the cell below. The **Left** arrow moves to the left, and the **Right** arrow moves to the right. Again, moving right from the last cell in a row takes you to the first cell of the next row.

If you hold down the **Shift** key while using the arrow keys, you will end up highlighting the cell or cells. But if you hold down the **Alt** key while using the arrow keys you will find your entire table moving to the right or left, up or down. Publisher calls this *nudging an object,* and I'll talk more about it later in this chapter. If you hold down the **Alt** key while pressing **Tab**, Windows 95 displays a task window that you can use to switch to other running applications. This is a Windows 95 feature and not a function of the Publisher program.

Now you know how to move around a table (and how to move a table around), so you can enter your time billing data if you want to use this form. Unfortunately, there's no way that this PageWizard's design will suit everyone. In order for my company to use this form, I need to make some changes. First, I like to keep separate sheets for each client, so I don't need a client column in my main table. Also, I charge clients different rates for different services, but I do not charge overtime rates per se. So I don't need that column either. Here's what I did to customize this form for my own use and the use of those who work for me.

1. Change the Date heading in the top mini-table to **Client**.

2. Change two headings in the main table: Client becomes **Date**, and Activity becomes **Task & Time**.
3. Insert a column before the Activity column and call it **Project**.
4. Delete the **Overtime Rate** column.
5. Change the Description heading to **Amount Charged**.

Go ahead and start by changing the headings as specified in items 1 and 2. Just place your cursor in the cell and treat it like any text frame.

Inserting a Column

When you select the **Insert Rows Or Columns...** option from the Table menu, or right-click on the table and select the same option from the Table Object menu, Publisher looks to see whether you have selected an existing column. If you have not, Publisher takes note of the column in which your cursor is currently located. Then the Insert dialog window appears as shown in Figure 4.13. Here you specify whether you are inserting rows or columns, how many, and whether you want the insertion placed before or after the selected cells or current position.

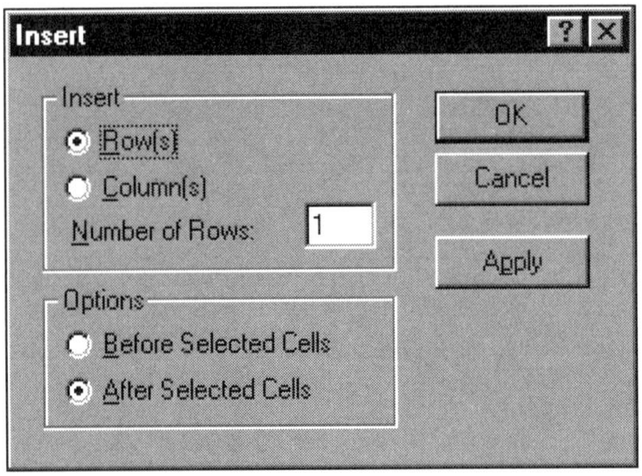

FIGURE 4.13 THE INSERT DIALOG WINDOW.

To continue customizing the sample Time Billing form, the next step is to insert a column between the Date and Activity columns. First you need to identify your position in one of four ways. You can select the **Date** column by clicking on the column selector; you can select the **Activity** column by clicking on its selector; you can place your cursor in one of the cells in the Date column; or you can place your cursor in one of the cells of the Activity column. Once you are in position, select the **Insert Rows or Columns...** option from the Table menu.

When the Insert dialog window appears, make sure that you select **Column(s)** and leave the **Number of Rows** set to 1. (By the way, if you selected a column before using the menu, the **Column(s)** indicator should already be selected. If you only positioned your cursor, then **Row(s)** is preselected.) Finally, choose your option. If you selected the **Date** column, or placed your cursor in a cell within that column, then choose the **After Selected Cells** option. If you selected the **Activity** column, or placed your cursor in a cell within the Activity column, choose the **Before Selected Cells** option. Then click on **OK**.

Is there a difference between the **Before** or **After** methods? Yes! If you select a column, and then choose the **Before** option, the width of the new column will be the same as the width of the selected column. However, if you use the **After** option, the width of the new column will be the same as the width of the column to the right.

If you've been following along, you should now have a new column. Type in the word PROJECT in the top cell used for headings. You've probably noticed that when you inserted this column, it caused the other columns to move to the right and off the page. So we've got some adjusting to do. For my purposes, this column is too wide anyway. So let's adjust it so that it's only about half as wide. Click on the boundary line between the Project and Activity column selectors and drag it to the left.

Okay, that takes care of item number three. Next you need to delete a column.

Deleting a Column

Deleting a column is really simple. Select the column and delete. Well....maybe not that simple. Did you try to use the **Delete** key after selecting the column? If you did, you found out that all you deleted was the text in the column, but not the column itself. Once you select the column(s) you want to delete, use the **Delete Columns** option on the Table menu, and poof, its gone.

If you want to delete the current column—the column in which your cursor is currently located—without first selecting it, you can still use the **Delete** menu option. This time the Delete dialog window appears to ask whether you want to delete the current column or the current row, as shown in Figure 4.14

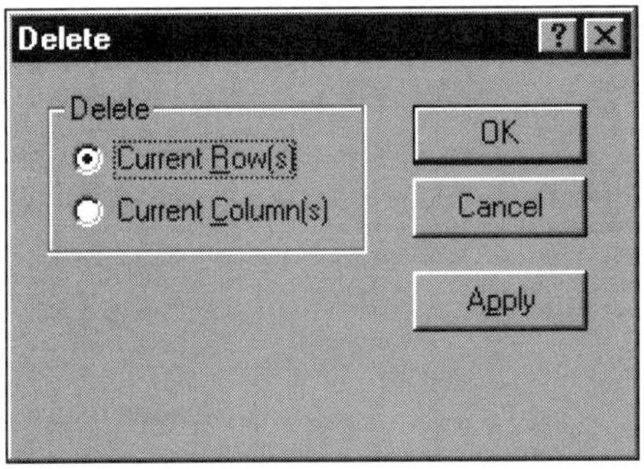

FIGURE 4.14 THE DELETE DIALOG WINDOW.

NOTE

Publisher menus seem to change the wording of their options from time to time. Sometimes I think I'm losing my mind. Then I remember that the Publisher program is smart. If you select a column, the Table menu option reads **Delete Columns**. It already knows what you want to delete. If you do not select a column, the menu option reads **Delete Rows** or **Columns...** because the program does not yet know what you want to do.

If you haven't done so already, go ahead and delete the Overtime Rate column. After resizing the Project column and deleting the Overtime Rate column, all the remaining columns fit on the page. Item number four is now complete, and all that remains is to change the last column heading from DESCRIPTION to AMOUNT BILLED.

When you're all done, reduce **Zoom out** so that you can see the entire form on your screen. (Probably between 33% and 66%, depending on the size of your screen and resolution.) The form looks pretty good, except for one tiny detail. The single-row table for Totals is slightly out of alignment with the columns in the table above it. The degree to which it is out of sync depends on how much you resized the new Project column.

You can use various methods to move it over. One method is to click on the table object, move your cursor over the edge of the table until it (the cursor) changes from a pointer into the moving van, and then click-and-drag the table into position. An alternative method is to nudge it into position by holding down the **Alt** key and using your arrow to move the object in the desired direction.

I like to use the nudging method, but sometimes the object moves too far. When this happens, I change the distance control by selecting **Nudge Objects...** from the Arrange menu. When the Nudge Objects dialog window appears (see Figure 4.15), I can specify whatever distance I want.

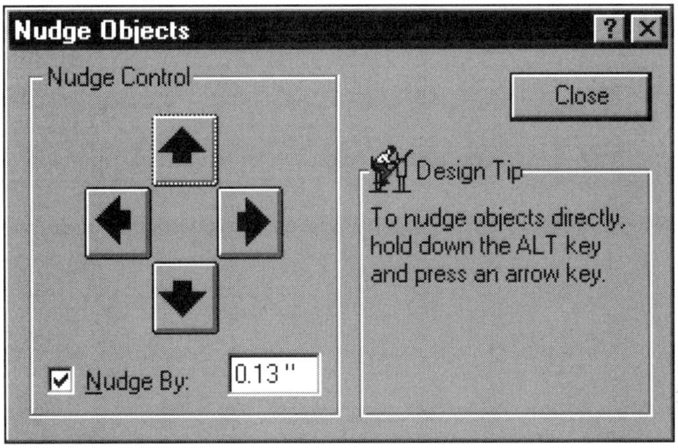

FIGURE 4.15 THE NUDGE OBJECTS DIALOG WINDOW ALLOWS YOU TO SPECIFY THE DISTANCE COVERED BY EACH NUDGE.

If you like the changes I made to the Billing form, you might want to save this sample. Or, better yet, customize it for your own use and then save it. I have a few more table functions to show you, and I want to show you yet another PageWizard publication.

EMPLOYEE TIME SHEET

Use the Business Form PageWizard to create an Employee Time Sheet. Again I am using the **Basic** style, with a **Picture**, in a **Landscape** format, and including the address. You know what to do, and so does the PageWizard. Figure 4.16 shows the PageWizard's creation.

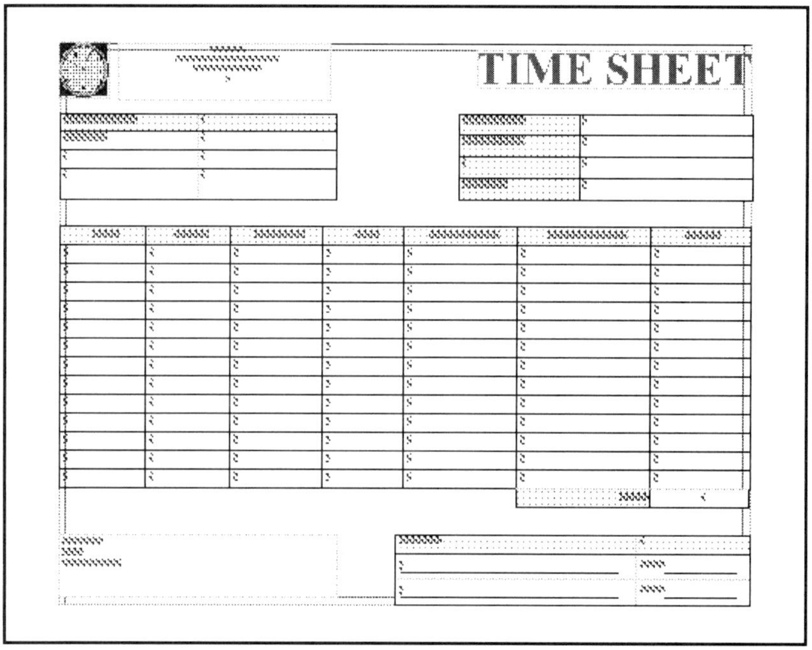

FIGURE 4.16 AN EMPLOYEE TIME SHEET CREATED BY THE BUSINESS FORM PAGEWIZARD.

This form consists of a picture frame for the logo, three text frames (address, form title, and account number), and five tables. I'm not sure why the PageWizard used a table for the Employee Name and Address section. I can understand using multiple rows for an address, but not multiple columns.

Looking at the current design, I'm not exactly sure where to enter the data. The words *Employee Name* are in a cell with a textured background that usually indicates a heading or title. But the cell containing the word *Address* does not have a textured background even though it is obviously a heading. Later in this chapter, I'll show you how to add texture or color to cells, but for now what I propose to do is merge some of those cells together.

Merging and Splitting Cells

I want you to merge the cell containing the words *Employee Name* with the cell on the right, creating a single cell on the first row. To merge these two cells you must first highlight or select them. Because they are the only two cells in the row, you can simply select the row. If there were other cells in the row, you would have to click-and-drag your mouse across the desired cells.

After you select the cells you want to merge, choose the **Merge Cells** option from the Table menu, or right-click on the table and select that same option from the Table Object menu. When you are finished merging those two cells, the table should look like the one shown in Figure 4.17

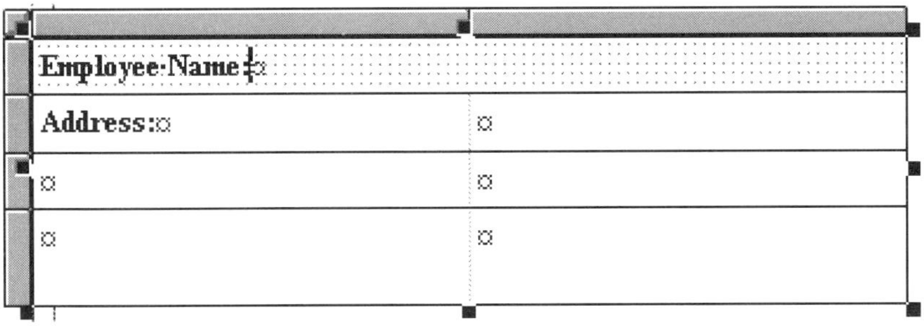

FIGURE 4.17 THE SMALL TABLE FROM THE EMPLOYEE TIME SHEET AFTER MERGING THE CELLS IN THE FIRST ROW.

Next, I'd like you to create one large cell for the address by merging the other six cells. Unfortunately, Publisher won't let us do that. If you select all six cells and use the **Merge Cells** option on either menu, Publisher will merge the two cells on each row, but it will not merge the rows in each column. Merge only works horizontally, so the cells must be in the same row.

Perhaps I should rethink my design plan and start over again. It's too late to use the **Undo** option to reverse the merging of the Employee Name cells. However, if you select that row, or even place your cursor in that cell and then look at the Table menu, you'll find a new option—**Split Cells**. Click on the option and your merged cell becomes two again.

Now you can start over again. This time, I'd like you to resize the first column so that it is just big enough for the Employee Name heading. Click on the column separator and drag it to the left. Then I want you to delete the last row (use the **Delete** option on the Table menu), and enter **Home Phone** in the left cell of the new last row. Now the top-left section of your form should look like the one shown in Figure 4.18

Are you wondering how you are going to fit an entire address in that one little cell? Or did you remember the **Grow To Fit** option? As long as the **Grow To Fit** option remains selected (it's the last option on the Table menu), the cell will expand to fit the address. And you can enter multiple lines either by allowing the text to wrap around as it did with the example earlier in this chapter, or by using your **Enter** key to force line breaks as you would normally in your word processing software.

Enter a two- or three-line address to see how it looks. To balance out the top of the form, you should also delete the Home Phone row from the table on the right. Now the only thing that still looks sort of odd, is the shading behind the employee's name and the lack of shading behind the Address and Home Phone headings.

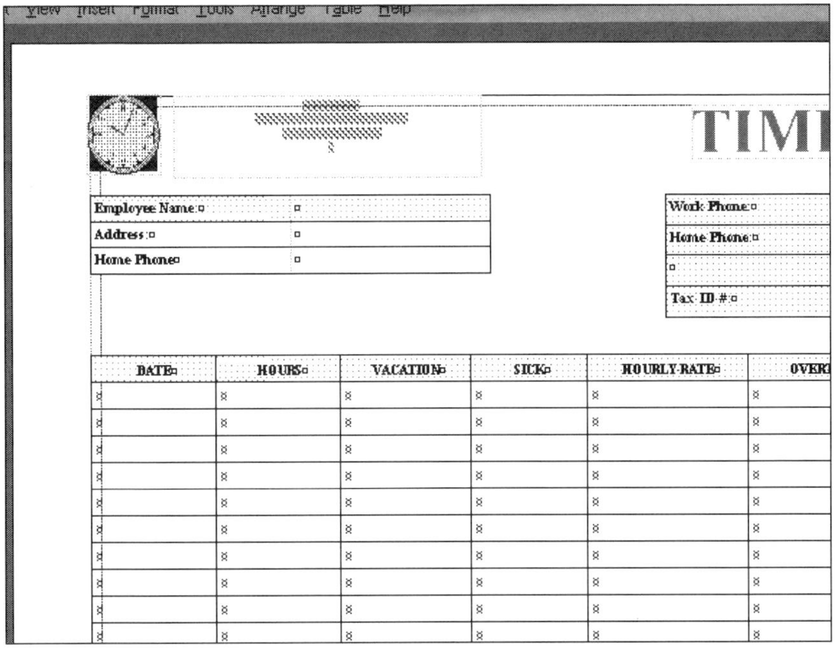

FIGURE 4.18 A PORTION FROM THE TOP OF THE EMPLOYEE TIME SHEET AFTER DELETING A ROW AND ADDING SOME TEXT TO THE TOP LEFT TABLE.

Shading and Coloring Cells

Although most of the speedbuttons on the Format toolbar relate to the text inside the table cells, the last three buttons—**Object Color**, **Border**, and **Add/Remove Shadow**—relate to selected cells or the table as a whole.

Place your cursor in the cell containing the employee's name. Not the cell with the heading, but the cell where you enter the name itself. Then select the **Object Color** speedbutton on the toolbar and click on **Patterns & Shading**. When the Fill Patterns and Shading dialog window appears, select the box on the far left of the style section, as shown in Figure 4.19. This represents 0% tint as indicated in the Sample section, bottom-left corner of the dialog window. Then click on **OK**.

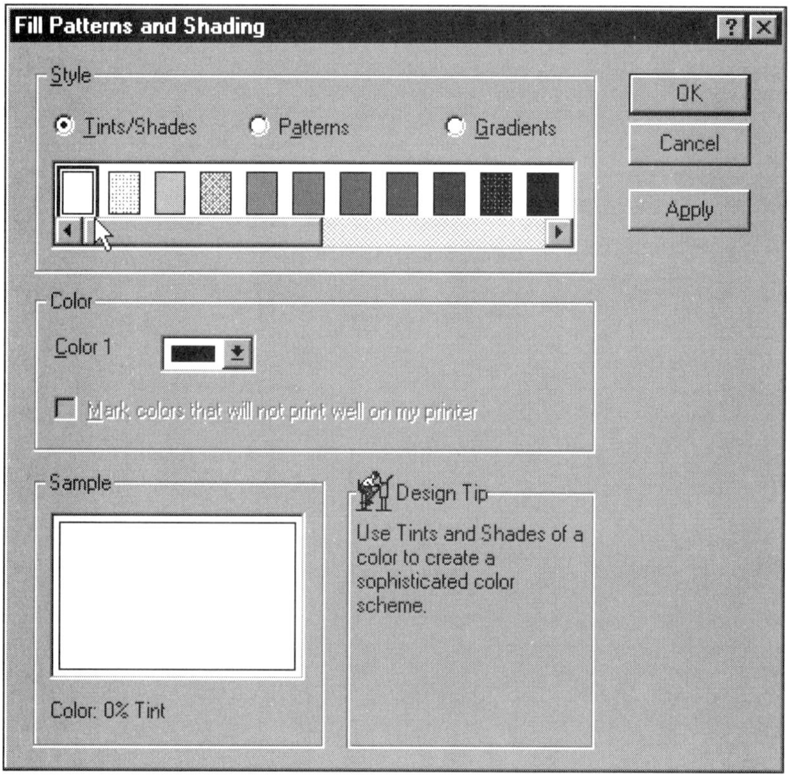

FIGURE 4.19 THE FILL PATTERNS AND SHADING DIALOG WINDOW.

Oh well. Not only did we remove the shading from the current cell, but from the whole row. Not exactly what I had in mind. Use the **Undo Shading** option (**Ctrl-Z**) on the Edit menu, and then we'll try again. From this exercise, you can see that unless you highlight or select the specific elements you want to modify, Publisher assumes that you intend to change the whole row.

This time, highlight the cell by clicking-and-dragging your cursor across the cell's contents. If the cell is empty, highlight the end-of-file character. Then use the **Object Color** button again, or select **Fill Patterns & Shading...** from the Format menu. Again, scroll left and select the first box (same one as before), and click on **OK**. This time, the shading disappears only from the selected cell.

Picking Up and Applying Formatting

Finally, before moving on, you really should add shading to the Address and Home Phone heading cells. Click-and-drag your mouse to select both cells; then select the **Fill Patterns & Shading...** option from the Format menu again. This time when the dialog window appears, the color white is shown as the current color selection. This could be a problem.

You could select any shading you want, but the intention here was to match the other shaded headings, and they are a very, very light gray. You could try clicking on the arrow button in the **Color** section to display the mini color palette, but they gray you want is not there. You could even click on **More Colors...** to bring up the Colors dialog window you saw in the last chapter. But the gray you want is not one of the 84 Basic colors shown.

You could then switch to the **All Colors** model, but you'd have to know the **Red**, **Green**, and **Blue** settings for the color you want. But how would you know? I could tell you that the gray you want is made of Red 247, Green 247, and Blue 247, but there is a much easier way to handle this.

If you still have open dialog windows, make them disappear by clicking on **Cancel**. When you can see your form again, highlight the cell containing the words *Employee Name*. This cell already contains the shading you want. Then click on the **Pick Up Formatting** option toward the bottom of the Format menu. Next, highlight the **Address** and **Home Phone** heading cells again. And finally, select the **Apply Formatting** option from the Format menu. All three of the heading cells should now have identical shading.

NOTE

You can also use this method to remove the shading from a cell by picking up the formatting from a cell without shading and applying it to the cell with the shading you want to remove.

Adding Borders and Grids

Take another look at the two small tables at the top of the Time Sheet. In the process of merging and then splitting cells in the left table, we lost the vertical border line between the columns. The table on the right still has a vertical border. When a table has both horizontal and vertical borders, separating each individual cell, it is called a *grid.* I like grid lines on large tables, but it seems unnecessary on these little ones. So instead of adding one to the left table, let's remove the vertical line from the right table.

Select the right table object (just click anywhere in the table); then click on the **Border** speedbutton on the Format toolbar (second from the right) and select **More...** to bring up the Border dialog window shown in Figure 4.20. Even though you can only see four pairs of arrow heads in the Select A Side section, you can see that the current setting is for a black hairline not only on all four sides, but also across the middle both horizontally and vertically.

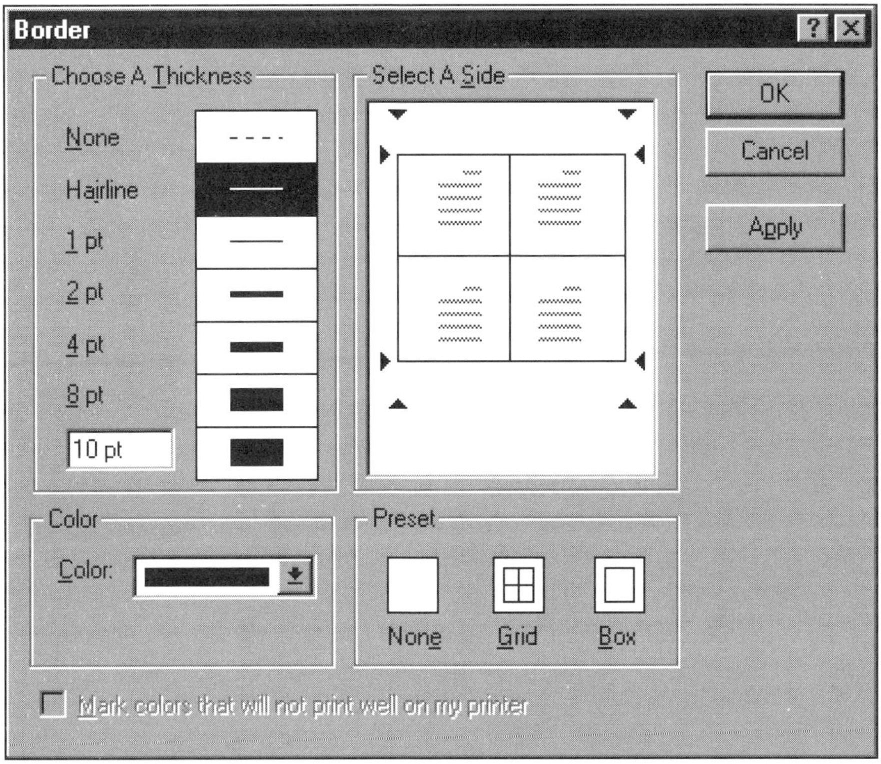

FIGURE 4.20 THE BORDER DIALOG WINDOW REFLECTING THE STATE OF THE TOP RIGHT-TABLE. GRID LINES APPEAR EVEN THOUGH **GRID** IS NOT SELECTED IN THE PRESET SECTION.

Click on the middle box in the Preset section, the one that says **Grid**. Now the other two pairs of arrow heads appear. Click on the vertical line running down the center of the box. When you click on a specific line, all the arrow heads disappear, except for the pair that define the line you selected. Publisher will now apply whatever settings you choose only to that selected line. Click on **None** in the Choose A Thickness section, and the vertical line disappears, as shown in Figure 4.21. You should also notice that Publisher automatically deselected the **Grid** box because once you remove that center line you no longer have a grid. Click on **OK** to accept your changes.

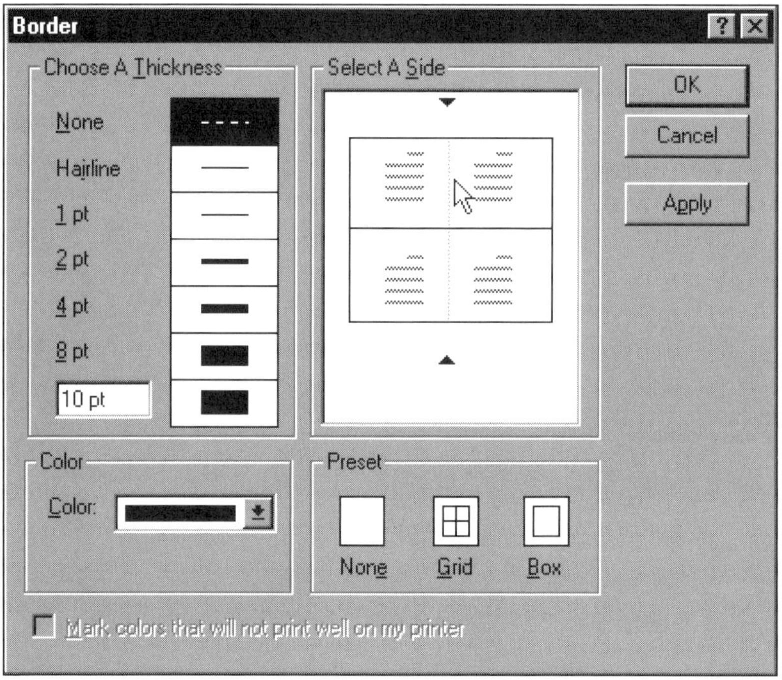

FIGURE 4.21 THE BORDER DIALOG WINDOW AFTER CLICKING ON THE VERTICAL GRIDLINE AND SELECTING A THICKNESS OF **NONE**.

Using Fill

Tables often contain a lot of repetitive data. Take the Time Sheet for example. Chances are that if you work in the corporate world, you probably report eight straight-time hours each day, except when you take vacation or sick time. Rather than type in the number **8** in every row, you can enter it in the first row and let the **Fill Down** option do the rest.

To use this option, first enter the number; then select the entire column and click on the **Fill Down** option on the Table menu. Oops. I goofed again. If you followed my instructions, you should now see the word *HOURS* in every row. Why did that happen? Because Publisher takes the contents of the top row of the selected column, which in our example is the heading HOURS, and copies that content into all the following rows. It even replaced the **8** you entered in the first data row.

Select **Undo Fill Down** (**Ctrl-Z**) from the Edit menu, and I'll give you better instructions this time. Instead of clicking on the column selector button, use your mouse (click-and-drag) to select all the hour cells starting with the row where you entered the **8**. Then select the **Fill Down** option from the Table menu. Success!

Because you actually select the cells to be filled, **Fill Down** does not have to extend all the way to the bottom of the table. Try entering a zero in any row of the Vacation column. Then select that cell and the five cells below it, and use the **Fill Down** option. Your Time Sheet should now show 0 in six rows of the Vacation column.

The same functionality is available to fill in values to the right of a cell, and the same rules apply. Select the cell with the value you want to copy and the cells to the right that you want to fill; then use the **Fill Right** option on the Table menu.

You can **Fill Down** more than one column at a time, provided that there is a value in each of the cells in the top row. For example, if you have an **8** in the top data cell of the hours column, and a **0** in the top data cell of the Vacation column, you can select both groups of cells and use the **Fill Down** option. The result will be an Hours column full of **8**s, and a Vacation column full of **0**s. And the same applies to **Fill Right**.

Setting Cell Margins

Let's spend another moment looking at those 8s and 0s. These text characters are all left justified in their cells. You can double-check this by placing your cursor in one of those cells and looking at the Format toolbar. Then click on the **Center** or **Right Justify** speedbuttons and watch the character realign.

When left justified, how far away do you suppose those characters are from the left edge of their cells? Let's find out. Select the contents of one of those cells and then click on the **Table Cell Properties** option on the Format menu. When the Table Cell Properties dialog window appears (see Figure 4.22), you'll see that all four margins—Left, Right, Top, and Bottom—are set to .04 inches.

NOTE

If your Table Cell Properties dialog window appeared with blank settings, you did not select the contents of a cell, or Publisher realized that different cells had different margin settings and didn't know which to show you.

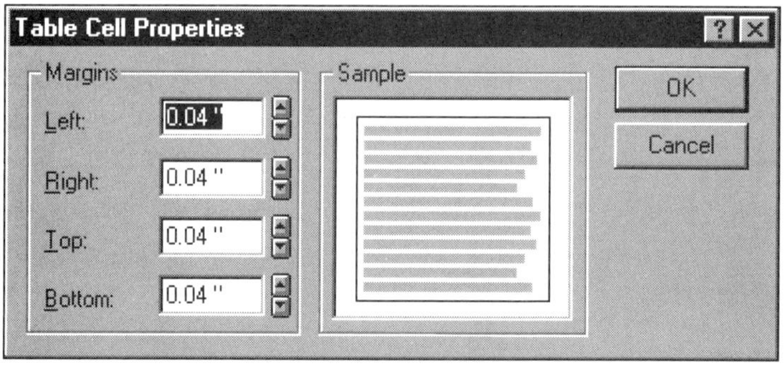

FIGURE 4.22 SET CELL MARGINS IN THE TABLE CELL PROPERTIES DIALOG WINDOW.

You can change these settings by using the up and down increment arrows or type in the desired margin. Click on **OK** to accept the changes, or **Cancel** to close the dialog window. Assuming that you selected one or more specific cells, Publisher applies the margin settings to only those cells. If, however, you did not select specific cells, Publisher applies the margin settings to all the cells in the table.

In a moment, I'll show you how to create your own table without the PageWizard. But first I want to talk about object menus as they relate to tables.

TABLE AND CELL OBJECT MENUS

In Chapters 2 and 3 you learned about the Text Object menu and the Picture Object menu, each available by right-clicking on the object. And in this chapter I've made several passing references to various options on the Table Object menu, available by right-clicking on a table object. Figure 4.23 shows the options on a Table Object menu.

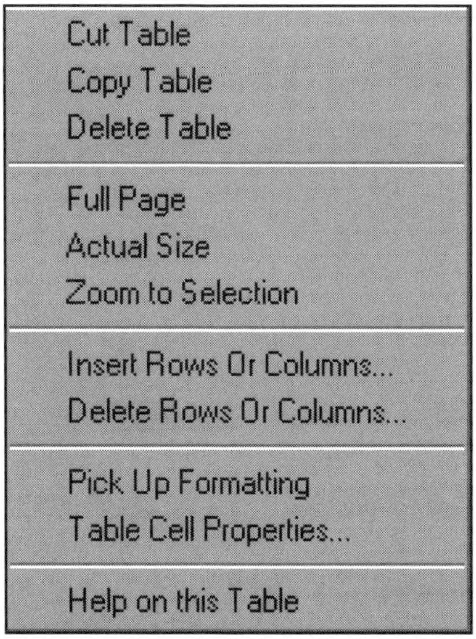

FIGURE 4.23 A TABLE OBJECT MENU.

If you like working with these pop-up object menus that appear with the click of the right-mouse button, you should know that Cell Objects also have their own menu (see Figure 4.24). And that is the menu that appears if you right-click on a table where you have selected one or more cells.

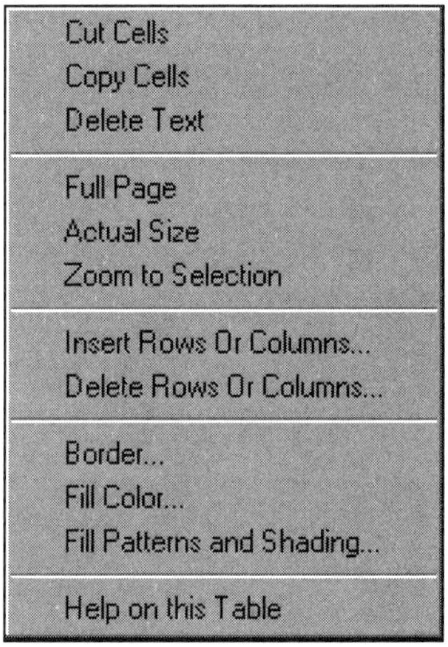

FIGURE 4.24 A CELL OBJECT MENU.

Most of the options in the Cell Object menu are similar to those on Table Object menu. For example, **Cut Cell** instead of **Cut Table**. In the fourth section however, the Cell Object menu has completely different options. From the Cell Object menu you can access **Border...**, **Fill Color...**, and **Fill Patterns and Shading...** options that are not available on the Table Object menu. And from the Table Object menu you can Pick Up Formatting and access the **Table Cell Properties** option.

Creating a Table

Now it's time to create an object from scratch. You should have an empty page to work on. You can either use the **Create New Publication** option, and select a **Blank Page** instead of a PageWizard, or you can click on the right arrow next to the **Page** number at the bottom of your screen.

Because the current publication does not have a second page, a dialog window appears to verify that you want to insert a new page. Click on **OK**. You could also select **Page...** from the Insert menu. I'll talk more about that option in Chapter 7.

As described in Chapter 1, you can create an object by selecting an object tool from the vertical toolbar and either clicking on your workspace or clicking-and-dragging out the area for the object frame. When you do this using a Table object tool button, the Create Table dialog window appears, as shown in Figure 4.25. Here you need to specify how many columns and rows you want your table to contain, and you get to pick a format if you want one.

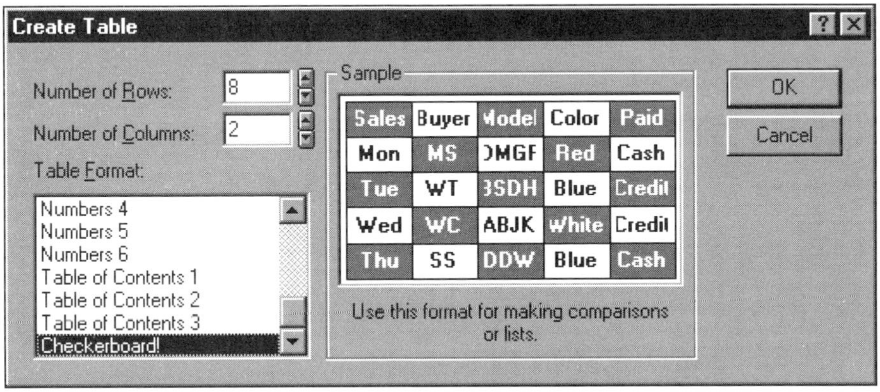

FIGURE 4.25 THE CREATE TABLE DIALOG WINDOW SHOWING THE **CHECKERBOARD** FORMAT IN THE SAMPLE SECTION.

In addition to **Default** and **None**, there are 21 other formats from which to choose. They include: Checkbook Register, seven list formats, three lists with titles, six number formats, three tables of contents, and a Checkerboard format. To get an idea of what each format looks like, you can select each one from the scrolling Table Format list and see a Sample in the window. When you find one you like, select it and click on **OK**. I'm going to use the Numbers 5 format for our sample.

Now that I can see the table on my page, I don't really care much for the yellow shading. So let's change it.

AutoFormatting

Earlier in this chapter, I showed you how to change the patterns and shading in cells, but now I am going to show you a much easier solution. Select **AutoFormat...** from the Table menu to bring up the dialog window shown in Figure 4.26. If the option is not available on your menu, you haven't selected the table object. Once you select the table, options on the Table menu become available.

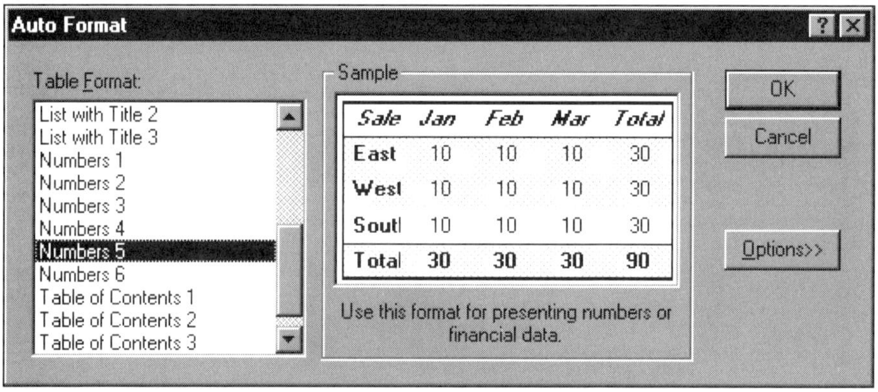

FIGURE 4.26 THE AUTOFORMAT DIALOG WINDOW.

So far, this dialog window looks a lot like the Create Table dialog window you saw a few minutes ago. But wait. Click on the **Options>>** button. The AutoFormat dialog window expands, as shown in Figure 4.27. Now you have the option of accepting one or more of the four types of formatting applied to the Auto Format type called Numbers 5. At the moment, all four options are selected. Let's look at each one.

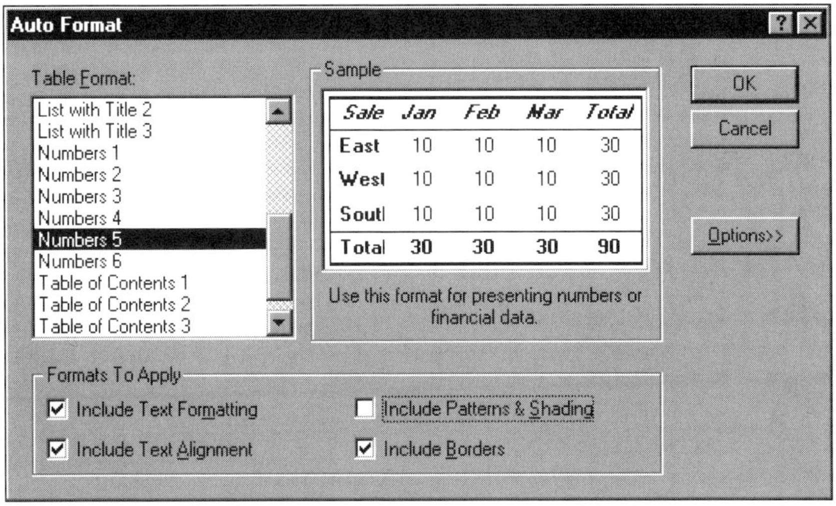

FIGURE 4.27 THE AUTOFORMAT DIALOG WINDOW WITH OPTIONS DISPLAYED.

Text formatting includes such things as bold text. If you remove the check mark by clicking on **Include Text Formatting**, the headings and total amounts in the Numbers 5 sample will no longer be bold. Try it. Personally, I think we should keep the text formatting, so select it again.

The next option is **Include Text Alignment**. In the Numbers 5 format, the numbers are aligned on the right. If you deselect this option, you'll see these numbers move to the left in the Sample area. Try it. I think we should keep the text alignment, so make sure that the check mark is there before you move on.

The third option is **Include Patterns & Shading**. This is the part I wanted to change. Click on the checkbox to deselect this option and watch the color shading disappear from the Sample. Let's leave it that way.

The last option is **Include Borders**. Let's see what it looks like without the borders. Pretty boring. Let's keep them. When you are satisfied with the look of the Sample, click on **OK**.

Selecting Border Art

To make a table stand out on your page, you could add a shadow—either the standard shadow created by Publisher when you use the **Add/Remove Shadow** speedbutton or Format menu option, or a custom shadow of your own creation. Or you might want to use Border Art.

Publisher comes with a variety of border art designs (more than 100 of them), ranging from simple, to elegant, to outright zany. To apply border art to your table, select the table (you do not have to highlight the table, just make sure that the selector buttons are visible) and click on the **BorderArt** option on the Format menu to bring up the dialog window shown in Figure 4.28.

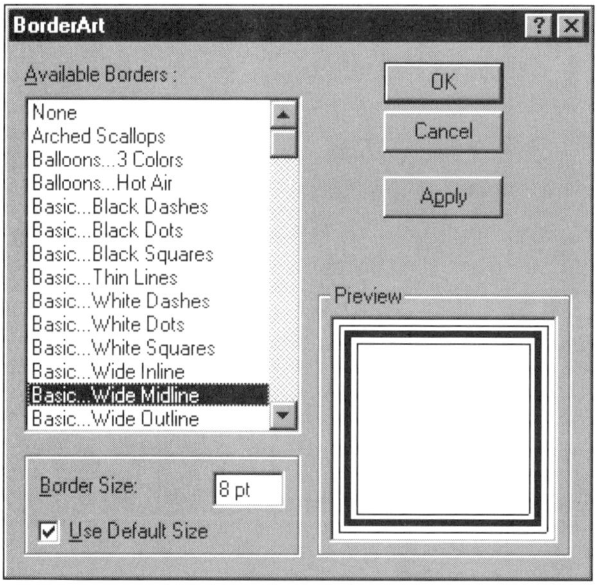

FIGURE 4.28 THE BORDERART DIALOG WINDOW WITH THE **BASIC...WIDE MIDLINE** DESIGN DISPLAYED IN THE PREVIEW SECTION.

Scroll through the Available Borders list and single-click on any one that you want to see. Publisher automatically displays a sample in the Preview section of the dialog window. You'll find more than 100 BorderArt designs. Check out the Classical Wave, one of the many flower border designs, and the Zig Zag Stitch. Select one you like and click on **Apply** or **OK** to add the border to your table.

NOTE

You can apply BorderArt to any Text, Picture, Table, or WordArt frame.

SUMMARY

- Groups of text frames can be positioned to look like tables. When you click on a table object, column and row selector buttons appear along with the frame. To highlight a column or row, click on its selector button.
- Resizing a table adjusts all columns and rows proportionally.
- Resizing individual columns or rows by simply dragging a column or row boundary line will impact the position of the rest of the table, but will not alter size of the other cells or rows.
- Resizing individual columns or rows by holding down the **Shift** key while dragging the boundary line forces the adjacent cell or row to compensate accordingly. For example, adding a half-inch to one column will decrease the adjacent column by the same amount.
- When you select the **Fit to Grow** option, rows automatically expand their depth to fit all text entered into a cell. If you do not use the **Grow to Fit** option, you may never know if a cell contains undisplayed text because, unlike text frames, Publisher does not indicate cell overflow.
- Use the **Tab** and/or arrow keys to navigate a table. The **Tab** key and the **Left** and **Right** arrow keys, move your cursor from column

to column. **Up** and **Down** arrow keys move your cursor from row to row.

✷ Pressing the **Alt** key simultaneously with an arrow key nudges an object in the direction of the arrow. You can control the distance of a nudge by selecting the **Nudge Objects...** option from the Arrange menu and setting the desired distance.

✷ The Insert dialog window allows you to indicate whether you want to insert columns or rows, and whether you want the insertion to appear **Before** or **After** the current column or row. If you have not highlighted a column or row, Publisher identifies the current position by the location of your cursor.

✷ When inserting a column **Before**, the width of the new column will be the same as that of the current column. When inserting a column **After**, the width of the new column will be the same as that of the column to the right of the current column.

✷ To delete one or more columns, highlight the column(s) and use the **Delete Columns** option on the Table menu.

✷ To merge two or more cells in a row, select the cells and click on the **Merge Cells** option on the Table menu. If you use a row selector to highlight an entire row, **Merge Cells** will merge all the cells in that row.

✷ If you select more than one row and use the **Merge Cells** option, Publisher will merge the cells of each row, but will not merge rows. You can only merge cells that are adjacent and part of the same row.

✷ Because Publisher remembers its merged cells, you can use the **Split Cells** option at any time to separate them again.

✷ To specify fill patterns, shading, and colors for individual cells, select the cell(s) and use the options on the Format menu or the Cell Object menu. If you do not highlight specific cells, Publisher applies your selections to the entire current row.

✷ If you want to apply the shading or color of one cell to another, you can use the **Pick Up Formatting** and **Apply Formatting** options on the Format menu.

✷ To modify borders and gridlines on a Table, select the table and use the **Border** option on the Format menu. Publisher applies your thickness and color settings to whichever lines you have selected in the Select A Side section.

✷ The **Fill Right** and **Fill Down** options on the Table menu copy the content in the first cell selected and paste it in all the following selected cells. If a subsequent cell already contains content, Publisher replaces it with the copied content.

✷ To set the margins within a cell or cells, highlight the cell(s) and use the **Table Cell Properties...** option on the Format or Cell Object menu. If you do not select specific cells, Publisher applies your margin settings to all the cells in the table.

✷ When you right-click on a table, the Table Object menu appears, unless you have highlighted specific cells, in which case the Cell Object menu appears. The Table Object menu has some options that the Cell menu does not have and vice versa.

✷ When you use a Table object tool from the vertical toolbar, the Create Table dialog window appears so that you can specify the number of columns and rows you want. You can also select a predefined table format.

✷ The Table menu's **AutoFormat...** option brings up a dialog window from which you can select a predefined table format. You also have the option of using a predefined format without accepting the **Text Formatting**, **Text Alignment**, **Patterns & Shading**, or **Border** specifications.

✷ A shadow is one way to make a table stand out. BorderArt is another. Use the **BorderArt** option on the Format menu to bring up a dialog window with a Preview section and a scrolling list of more than 100 border art designs.

CHAPTER 5

WORKING WITH OTHER OBJECTS

- ✷ Manipulating WordArt
- ✷ Working with transparent objects
- ✷ Using Wingdings in WordArt
- ✷ Adding arrows to lines
- ✷ Placing shape objects
- ✷ Arranging layers
- ✷ Creating custom shadows
- ✷ Incorporating PageWizard elements

So far you have examined text, picture, and table objects. In this chapter you'll learn about WordArt objects, which are a cross between text and image; Lines and Shape objects that are great for adding artistic touches; and internal PageWizards that create special elements that you might want to include in a publication.

SAMPLE HALLOWEEN CARD

The Card & Invitation Wizard (second row, farthest right) is one of my favorites, both because you can create fun cards and because it saves me a lot of money. This Wizard has designs for six types of cards: Holiday, Everyday, Special Occasion, Invitation, Business Event, and card designs for use with Special Paper.

Select **Holiday** and then **Halloween**. Publisher provides suggested card greetings, both serious and humorous, for those who do not feel poetic. I often use the suggested greetings, and then customize them by adding the person's name. When you opt to see the suggestions, the next window displays a scrolling list with the first few words of each greeting. When you click on one, you can see the full greeting text on the left side of the window, as shown in Figure 5.1.

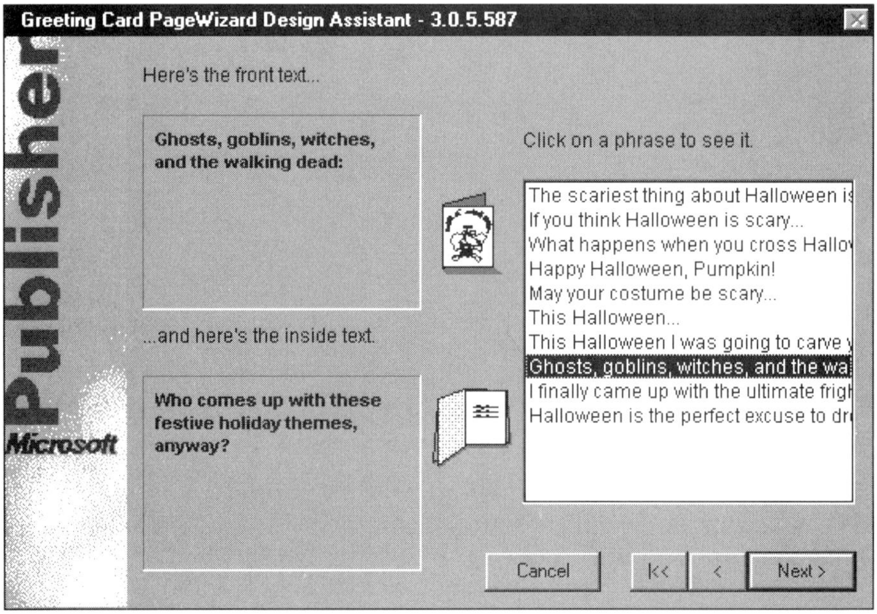

FIGURE 5.1 THE CARD & INVITATION PAGEWIZARD PROVIDES SUGGESTED GREETINGS.

I chose the one that begins "This Halloween..." Select a greeting you like and click on **Next>**. Then, just like a Hallmark card, you can put your name or a short message on the back of the card as well. Finally, let the PageWizard **CreateIt!**. Figure 5.2 shows the card's cover page.

NOTE

Publisher displays cards and invitations on four separate pages, even though it prints on a single page that you then fold.

FIGURE 5.2 THE COVER OF A HALLOWEEN CARD AS CREATED BY THE CARD & INVITATION PAGEWIZARD.

Examining WordArt Frames and Tools

You can probably guess that the words "This Halloween..." are not plain text. When you examined text frames and text formatting options in Chapter 2 you did not find anything that allowed you to curve or arc text in this fashion. When you click on the frame containing those words, you'll see that no text frame button appears at the bottom of the frame. Nor do the text formatting options appear on the Format toolbar. What you do find on the Format toolbar are the same eight speedbuttons (see Figure 5.3) that you used in Chapter 3 for working with pictures.

FIGURE 5.3 WHEN YOU SELECT A WORDART FRAME, EIGHT SPEEDBUTTONS APPEAR ON THE FORMAT TOOLBAR: **CROP**, **WRAP TO FRAME**, **WRAP TO PICTURE**, **ROTATE RIGHT**, **ROTATE LEFT**, **OBJECT COLOR**, **BORDER**, AND **ADD/REMOVE SHADOW**.

Working with the WordArt Application

WordArt is a type of picture object created by a separate program that Publisher calls upon when requested. The WordArt program works from inside the Publisher program, altering the menu bar, placing the WordArt tools on the Format toolbar, and displaying a small window in which you edit your text. To bring up the WordArt program, double-click on the WordArt frame.

NOTE

When you create a new WordArt frame by selecting the WordArt object tool on the vertical toolbar and dragging out an area on your page or workspace, control automatically passes to the WordArt application, and a small dialog window appears prompting you to *Enter Your Text Here.*

As you can see from Figure 5.4, Publisher's menu bar now contains only four menus. If you click on the File menu, control moves from the small editing window (the one that says *Enter Your Text Here)* to the main screen, and you can see that the File menu options remain unchanged. The Edit menu contains only one option, **Edit WordArt Text....** Use this option to transfer control back to the small editing window. The Format menu now contains six options, each of which corresponds to a speedbutton on WordArt's Format toolbar, and the Help menu only contains help that relates to WordArt.

Also shown in Figure 5.4 is the Format toolbar with the selection boxes and speedbuttons that apply to WordArt. From left to right you find three drop-down selection boxes for **Shape**, **Font**, and **Font Size**, followed by 11 speedbuttons: **Bold**, **Italic**, **Even Height**, **Flip**, **Stretch**, **Alignment**, **Character Spacing**, **Special Effects**, **Shading**, **Shadow**, and **Line Thickness**.

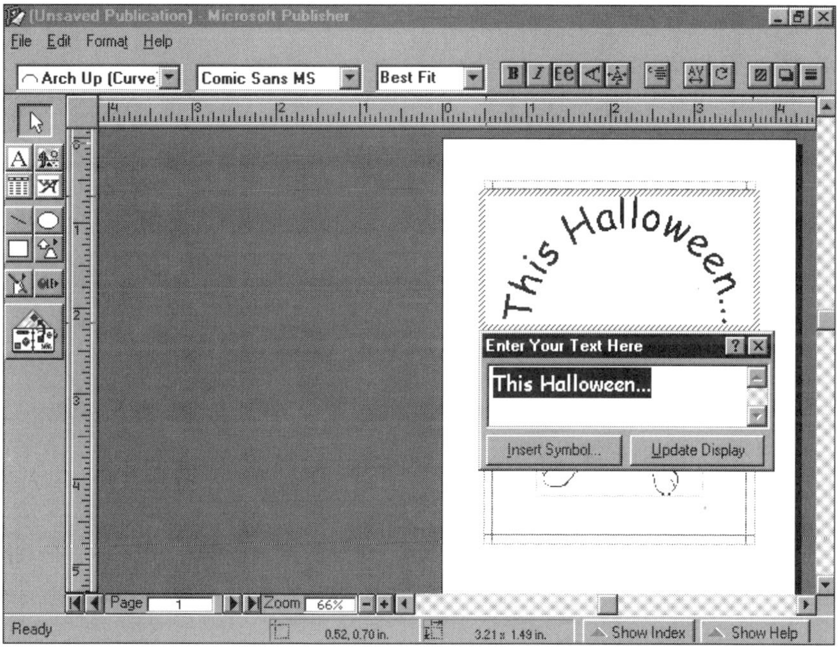

FIGURE 5.4 THE PUBLISHER SCREEN WHEN WORDART TAKES CONTROL.

The drop-down box for **Shape** provides the 36 choices shown in Figure 5.5. The list of **Fonts** is the same as those available on your system, and the only surprise on the list of **Font Sizes** is the **Best Fit** option that allows WordArt to fit all the text into the frame using the largest font size possible.

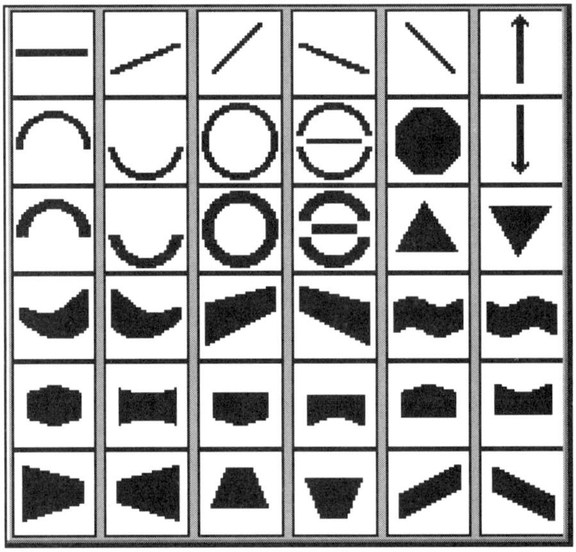

FIGURE 5.5 SHAPES AVAILABLE WHEN YOU CLICK ON THE **SHAPES** DROP-DOWN SELECTION BOX.

The **Bold** and **Italic** buttons are self-explanatory. The **Even Height** option makes all letters, whether lowercase or capital, the same height. **Flip** turns letters on their side. And **Stretch to Fit** enlarges the letters so that they touch all four sides of the frame. You can also turn the **Stretch to Fit** option on and off using the Format menu.

Alignment provides the standard options, left, center and right, but not flush on both sides. For that you could use **Stretch** or **Character Spacing**. **Character Spacing** brings up the dialog window where your choices range from **Very Loose** to **Very Tight**, and include **Custom** spacing as shown in Figure 5.6. You can access this same dialog window by selecting the **Spacing Between Characters...** option on the Format menu.

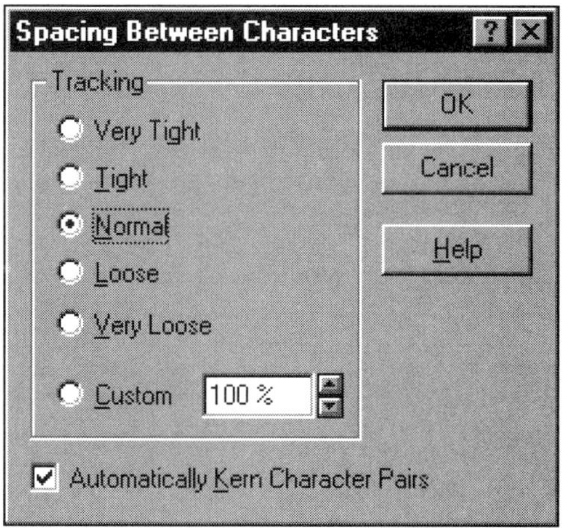

FIGURE 5.6 THE SPACING BETWEEN CHARACTERS DIALOG WINDOW FOR WORDART.

Clicking on the **Special Effects** speedbutton, or selecting the **Rotation and Effects...** option on the Format menu, brings up the dialog windows shown in Figure 5.7. Using this dialog window you can rotate your WordArt or alter its arc by a specific number of degrees. You can also reduce letter height by a specific percentage.

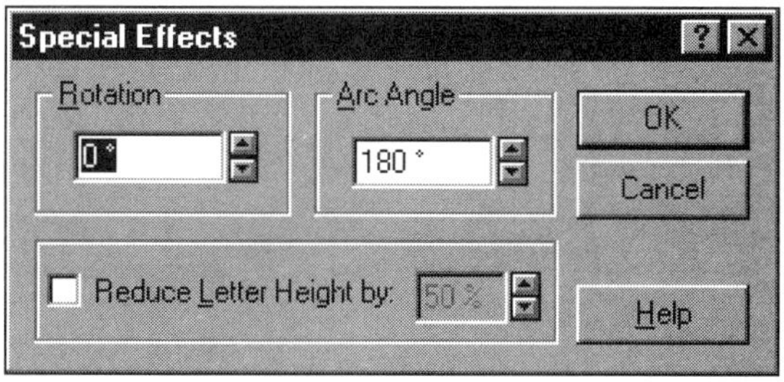

FIGURE 5.7 THE SPECIAL EFFECTS DIALOG WINDOW FOR WORDART.

When working with WordArt, you can choose foreground and background colors, and select a pattern or shading style all from within the same Shading dialog window shown in Figure 5.8. Although the shading option is not new to you, its application in WordArt is different. The other instances of shading you have seen thus far all applied to the space within the object frame. In WordArt, shading applies to the look of the characters. This is how you create effects such as striped text. To bring up this dialog window, select the **Shading...** option from the Format menu, or click on the **Shading** speedbutton.

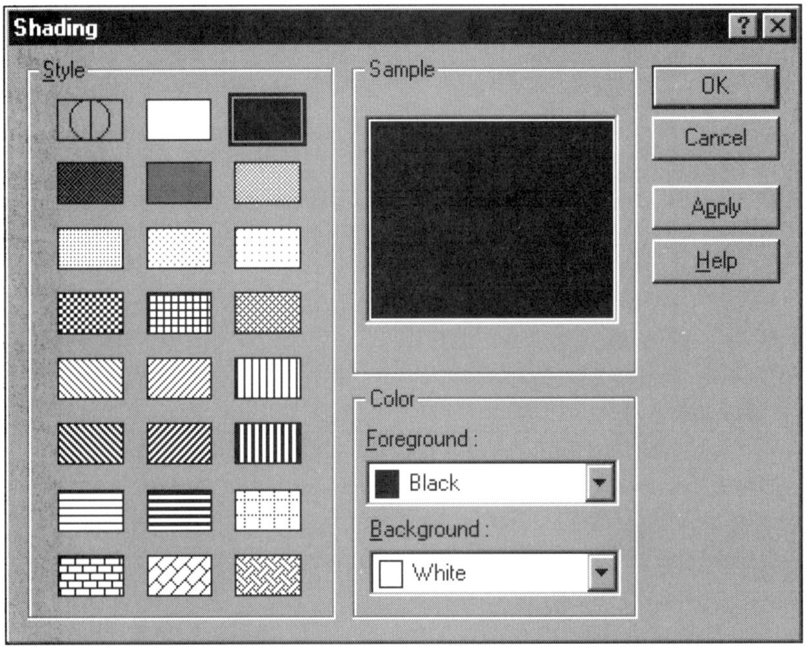

FIGURE 5.8 THE SHADING DIALOG WINDOW USED TO CREATE SHADED WORDART CHARACTERS.

Another effect that WordArt applies to the characters instead of the frame is the Shadow effect. When you select **Shadow...** from the Format menu, or click on the **Shadow** speedbutton, the dialog window shown in Figure 5.9 appears. Character shadows can fall in seven different ways, and you can select whatever shadow color you want.

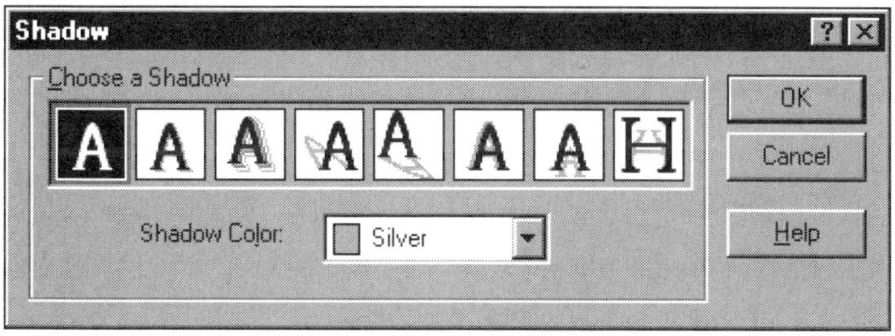

FIGURE 5.9 THE SHADOW DIALOG WINDOW FOR ADDING COLORFUL SHADOWS TO WORDART CHARACTERS.

The Format menu's **Border...** option brings up the dialog window shown in Figure 5.10. This is something of a misnomer, because the thickness and color settings apply to the actual text, not the frame as is the case with other objects. The corresponding speedbutton, **Line Thickness**, is more aptly named.

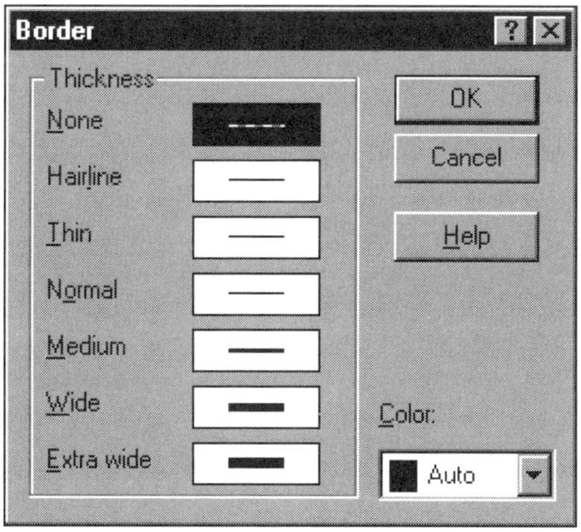

FIGURE 5.10 THE BORDER DIALOG WINDOW USED TO SET THE THICKNESS AND COLOR OF WORDART CHARACTERS.

To see your changes applied to the publication without leaving the WordArt program, click on the **Update Display** button in the editing dialog window. When you close the editing dialog window, Publisher applies your changes regardless of whether you use **Update Display**. There is no way to cancel your changes. The WordArt Edit menu does not include an **Undo** option, and when you leave WordArt, returning control to the Publisher program, Publisher is not aware of your WordArt actions, so **Undo** does not apply.

The easiest way to leave the WordArt application is to simply click somewhere on your publication page (but not in the WordArt frame) or in your workspace. If instead you close the WordArt editing dialog window, control still remains with the WordArt program. You would then have to click on your publication (again, not in the WordArt frame), or press the **Esc** key.

SAMPLE GENERAL PARTY INVITATION

Let's look at another publication that uses WordArt. Use the Card & Invitation PageWizard again, only this time select **Invitation** as the type of card. Then select the first of the two **General Party** choices (bottom left) and opt for the suggested greeting that begins "Special occasions...."

The PageWizard then prompts you to enter text describing the occasion and specifying the date, time, and party location, as well as an RSVP request. As with the previous card, you can put your name on the back. Figure 5.11 shows the first page of a General Party invitation as created by the Card & Invitation PageWizard.

The front of the card contains two elements: text and a graphic design. Because the text is not curved in shape, it could have been created in a text frame and then rotated into a slanting position. However, it's much easier to create such things using WordArt, and that's what the PageWizard did here. If you double-click on the words, the WordArt application takes control, and you can see the settings for the **Slant Up (More)** shape, **Impact** font, and **Best Fit** font size.

FIGURE 5.11 A GENERAL PARTY INVITATION AS CREATED BY THE CARD & INVITATION PAGEWIZARD. THE POINTER CURSOR POINTS TO THE OUTLINES OF TWO DIFFERENT FRAMES.

You can't really tell by looking whether the graphic design is a fill pattern or a picture. Of course, I tipped you off in the caption to Figure 5.11 when I pointed out two different frames. Also, once you get familiar with the various fill patterns, you'll know that this is not one of them. The confetti turns out to be an image from the ClipArt Gallery.

Working with Transparent Objects

So now you know that this card has two objects, one on top of the other. This is called *layering*, and you'll see more and more examples of layering when you look at shapes later in this chapter. Take another look and notice how the words look as if they are floating on top of the confetti. And you can see through the WordArt object to the confetti image behind it. To see through a frame, it has to be transparent. Now click on the WordArt and press **Ctrl-T**. Suddenly the WordArt frame is no longer transparent. Press **Ctrl-T** once more, and the frame becomes transparent again.

You can control transparency in two ways. The first is by pressing **Ctrl-T** as just described. Using **Object Color** is the second method for controlling transparency. Make sure that your WordArt frame is still selected; then click on the **Object Color** speedbutton. The drop-down palette appears as shown in Figure 5.12. Notice how the **Clear** button appears depressed. Click on a color, perhaps lime green, and watch the WordArt frame fill in with that color, obscuring the view of the confetti in the frame below. Then use the **Object Color** button again. This time the **Clear** button does not appear to be selected. Click on it and watch the WordArt frame become transparent (clear) once again.

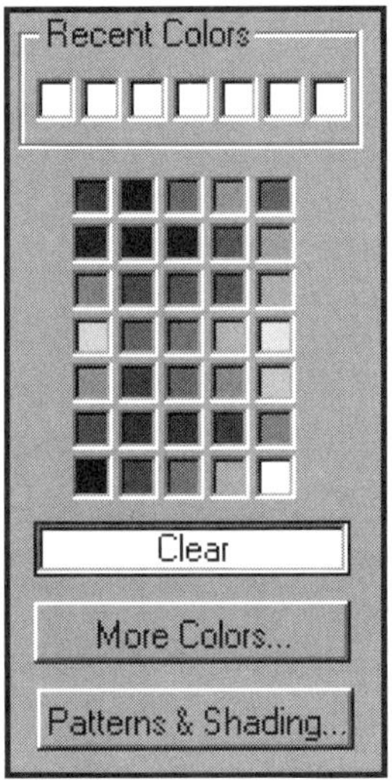

FIGURE 5.12 THE OBJECT COLOR DROP-DOWN PALETTE CAN BE USED TO MAKE OBJECT FRAMES TRANSPARENT (CLEAR) OR OPAQUE (ANY COLOR).

SAMPLE FORMAL SIGN

Before we move on to Line objects, let's look at one more sign that uses WordArt. Use the Sign PageWizard and select **Other** for type and **Formal** for style. Make it 8.5 x 11 with a **Landscape** format. We're not interested in pictures right now, so answer **No** to using a picture. Figure 5.13 shows the PageWizard's creation. Both the words and the embellishment characters are WordArt.

FIGURE 5.13 THE FORMAL SIGN AS CREATED BY THE PAGEWIZARD.

Before you double-click on the embellishment characters to invoke the WordArt application, let's take a look at the WordArt Object menu. A single right-click on either object will do the trick. Figure 5.14 shows the WordArt Object menu.

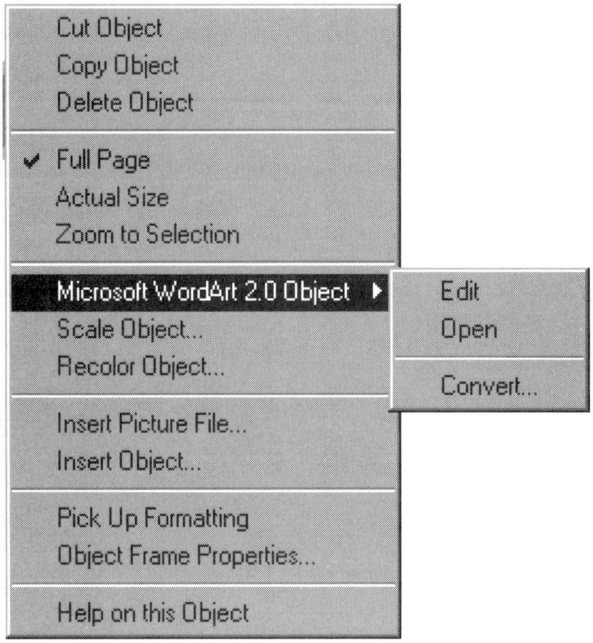

FIGURE 5.14 THE WORDART OBJECT MENU.

Many of these options are already familiar to you, and several of them bring up the same dialog windows that you saw in Chapter 3 when working with Picture objects. The first section of the Object menu contains the **Cut**, **Copy**, and **Delete Object** options. **Full Page**, **Actual Size**, and **Zoom to Selection** are the viewing options that comprise section two. Section three contains the options that allow you to manipulate the look of the WordArt object.

The first of these section three options is the **Microsoft WordArt 2.0 Object** option that leads to a submenu with three options: **Edit**, **Open**, and **Convert**. **Edit**, which has the same effect as double-clicking on the WordArt object, allows WordArt to take control. **Open**, on the other hand, brings up WordArt in is own separate application window (see Figure 5.15) where you have all of the same options. The third submenu item is **Convert**, and I'll talk more about that in Chapter 8 when we get to the subject of OLE objects.

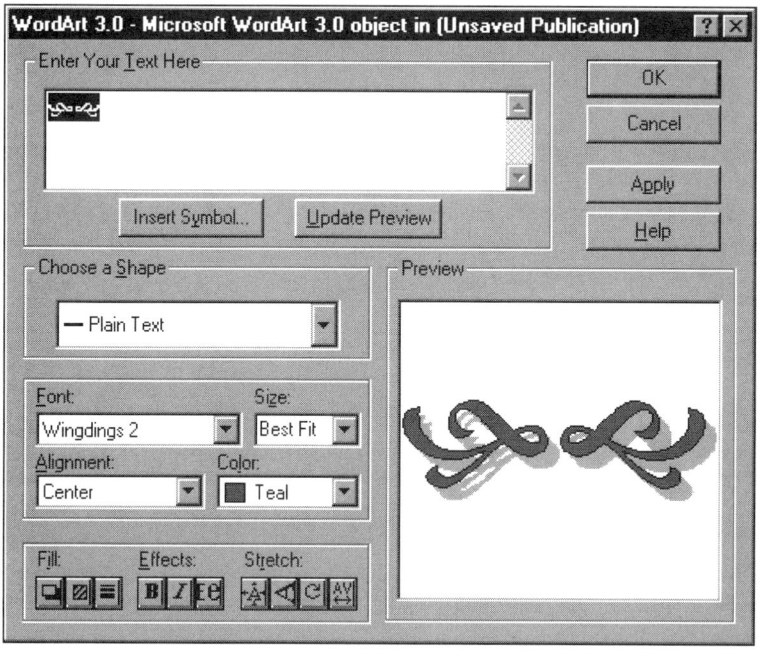

FIGURE 5.15 THE WORDART 3.0 APPLICATION WINDOW.

Also in section three are the **Scale Object...** and **Recolor Object...** options. **Scale Object...** brings up the same dialog window you used in Chapter 3 when scaling Picture objects. Enter the percentage of the object's original height and width and click on **OK**. The **Recolor Object...** option also brings up a familiar dialog window from Chapter 3. This is the dialog window that has a preview section so that you can see how the colors and patterns look before you apply them to the object.

The section four options, **Insert Picture File...** and **Insert Object...**, allow you to insert a picture or object into the selected frame. The Insert Picture dialog window is the same as the one you examined in Chapter 3. This is the one where you can search your system for any type of picture file, preview the image in the dialog window, and insert it into the selected frame. Similarly, you can use the **Insert Object...** option to insert objects of all types, providing that they are available on your system. In addition to the bitmap images and clipart files, other objects might include a Microsoft Graph or Word 6.0 Document file. I'll talk more about objects when I discuss program compatibility in Chapter 8.

You can use the **Pickup Formatting** option to copy the format settings so that you can apply them to another object. The **Object Frame Properties...** option, which is the same as the **Picture Frame Properties...**, consists of margins and the two wrap options (**Wrap to Frame** and **Wrap to Picture**). The margins apply to the wrap options. And as usual, the last option on the Object menu is a **Help** option.

Using Wingdings in WordArt

In Chapters 2 and 3 I showed you wingdings used in text frames. Like any other character set, wingdings can also be used in WordArt frames. The wingding characters used in this WordArt have a shadow, as shown in Figure 5.16. If you remove the shadow, the wingding characters look like those shown in Figure 5.17.

FIGURE 5.16 WINGDING CHARACTERS IN THE FORMAL SIGN AS THEY APPEAR WITH A SHADOW.

FIGURE 5.17 WINGDING CHARACTERS IN THE FORMAL SIGN WITH THE SHADOW REMOVED.

One of the nice things about WordArt is that if you use **Best Fit**, you don't have to figure out which font size to use. But don't confuse **Best Fit** with the **Stretch to Fit** option. Figure 5.18 shows what the same wingding characters look like when you apply **Stretch to Fit**. Now let's move on to Line objects.

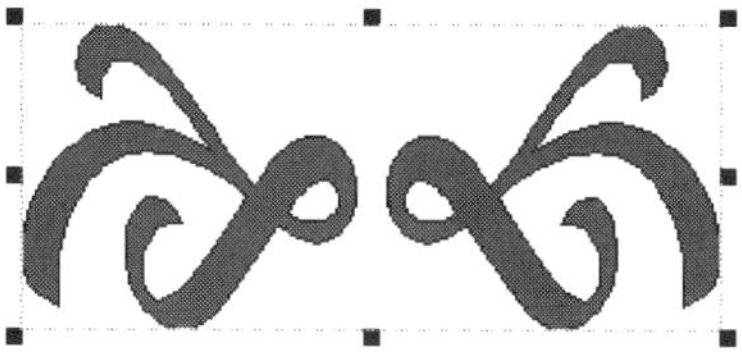

FIGURE 5.18 STRETCH TO FIT OPTION APPLIED TO THE WINGDING CHARACTERS IN THE FORMAL SIGN.

SAMPLE NO SMOKING SIGN

Using the Sign PageWizard, select the **Public Information** type, choose the **No Smoking** sign. Figure 5.19 shows the PageWizard's creation. The No Smoking graphic is actually two images; the red X is an image in a transparent frame so you can see through to the cigarette image beneath. When you use two separate objects as one, it makes sense to group them together. To see if the PageWizard grouped these two, click on the image.

FIGURE 5.19 THE NO SMOKING SIGN AS CREATED BY THE PAGEWIZARD.

Sure enough, there's a group. You can see multiple frame handles and a group button. But wait. Click on your workspace to make the handles all disappear; then click again on the page to the left or right of the image, but not on it. The same multiple frame handles and **Group** button appear. It turns out that the PageWizard made all the objects in this sign part of a single group. To prove it to myself, I moved the group right off the page, as shown in Figure 5.20. Use **Undo Move Object** to place the sign elements back on the page.

FIGURE 5.20 THE NO SMOKING SIGN OBJECTS MOVED IN UNISON OFF THE PAGE AND ONTO THE WORKSPACE.

Examining a Line Object

Break the group into its individual objects by clicking on the **Group/Ungroup** button. When you ungroup, your sign should look like the one shown in Figure 5.21, and you'll be able to select individual elements.

FIGURE 5.21 THE NO SMOKING SIGN WHEN THE OBJECTS ARE NO LONGER GROUPED.

See the black line near the top, and the second black line just above the images? Notice that these lines do not coincide with the edges of any frame. That means they can't be frame borders. Click on the line near the top of the page. This is a line object, and it has two handles, one at each end, defining the beginning and ending points of the line.

Now right-click on the line to bring up the Line Object menu, as shown in Figure 5.22. You've probably noticed by now that these pop-up Object menus are all quite similar. The first section has options to cut, copy and delete the object—in this case a line. The second section relates to the screen view. The third section of the Line Object menu has two options: **Line Properties...**, and **Pickup Formatting**. And the final section contains the **Help** option leading to help that relates to the specific object.

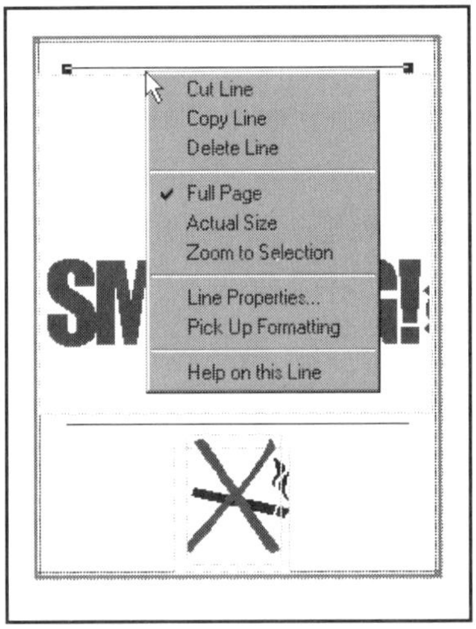

FIGURE 5.22 THE TOP LINE OBJECT ON THE NO SMOKING SIGN, WITH THE LINE OBJECT MENU DISPLAYED.

The Line Properties option brings up the Line dialog window shown in Figure 5.23. You can also access this dialog window by selecting the **Line** option from the Format menu. Here you can control the width or thickness or a line, and the color of the line, plus the type of arrowhead. Your current line does not have an arrowhead, so the **Arrowheads Type** option is not active. In a moment, I'll show you the arrowhead options, but first let's look at the Format toolbar. Click on **Cancel** to close this dialog window.

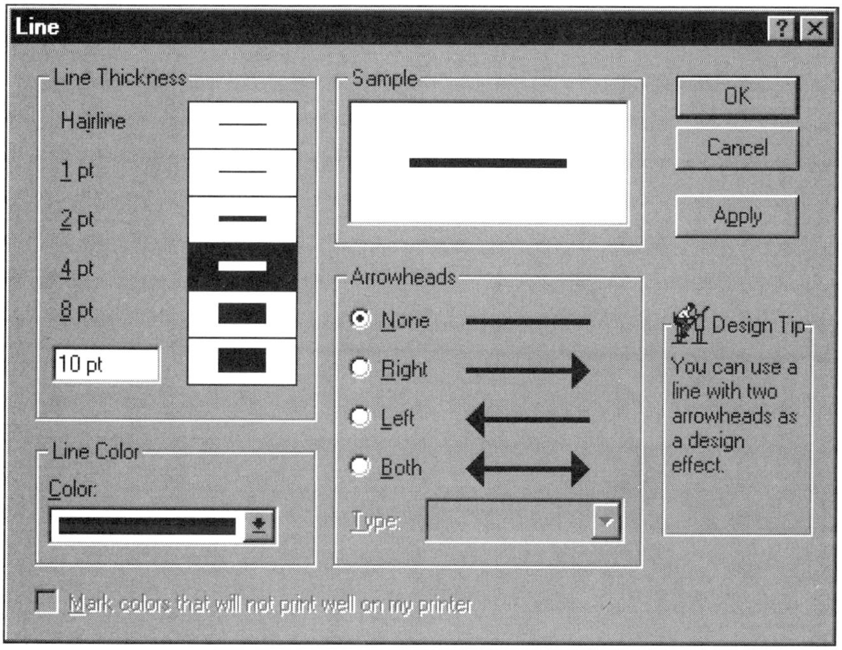

FIGURE 5.23 THE LINE DIALOG WINDOW APPEARS WHEN YOU SELECT LINE PROPERTIES FROM THE FORMAT OR LINE OBJECT MENU.

Flipping Lines and Adding Arrows

Now take a look at the Format toolbar. Once again, it has changed to provide tools that you might need when working with lines. You should be familiar with the four speedbuttons farthest to the right: **Rotate Right**, **Rotate Left**, **Border**, and **Shadow**. The others are new.

The two resembling the Rotate buttons are **Flip Horizontal** and **Flip Vertical**. The other three speedbuttons correspond to the Arrowheads section of the Line dialog window, adding or removing the right, left, or both arrowheads from the ends of a line.

Flip Horizontal flips the object so that the right is on the left, and the left is on the right. It's hard to spot any difference when horizontally flipping a plain line, so click on the **Add/Remove Right Arrow** button to place an arrowhead on the right end of the line. Now when you click on the **Flip Horizontal** speedbutton, you can see how the right arrow is now on the left. **Flip Horizontal** again, and you're back where you started.

Now that the line has an arrowhead, we can examine the arrowhead types. This time, instead of using the **Line** option on the Format menu, click on the **Border** speedbutton and select **More**. This brings up the exact same dialog window, but this time you can see the arrowhead in the **Type** box. Click on the selector button to display the drop-down list of types, as shown in Figure 5.24.

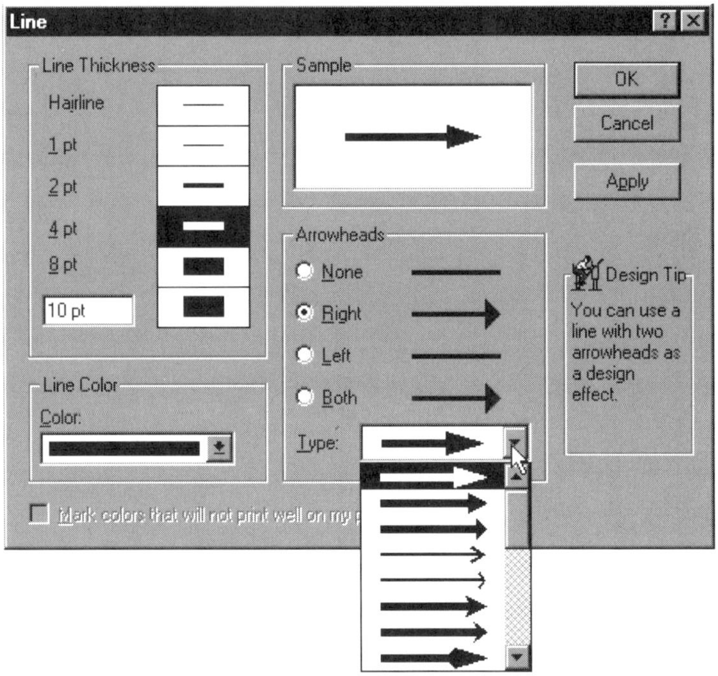

FIGURE 5.24 THE LINE DIALOG WINDOW WITH THE DROP-DOWN LIST OF ARROWHEAD TYPES DISPLAYED.

SAMPLE FUN SIGN

Now let's play with some shapes. Begin by examining one more Sign PageWizard. When asked what type of sign would you like, select **Other**. Then select the **Fun** sign. Make it 8.5 x 11 inches with a **Landscape** format. We've seen enough pictures for awhile, so answer **No** to using a picture. Figure 5.25 shows the PageWizard's creation.

FIGURE 5.25 THE GENERIC SIGN WITH A FUN STYLE AS CREATED BY THE PAGEWIZARD.

The PageWizard made this sign using the following objects: two yellow triangles, one blue rectangle, a text frame, a transparent box with a yellow border, and another transparent box with a gray 8-point border. Like the Special Occasions invitation, this sign uses layering. This time, however, not all of the layered objects are transparent.

Arranging Layers

As you've seen already, transparent objects allow you to see whatever is on the layer beneath. Objects that are not transparent obscure the view of any object on an underlying layer. If you select the blue rectangle and press **F6**, it will completely cover the yellow triangle. Press **Shift-F6** to make the yellow triangle reappear by moving the blue rectangle to the back again.

The **F6** and **Shift-F6** keystrokes are shortcuts for two of the four layering options on the Arrange menu: **Bring to Front** (**F6**), **Bring Closer**, **Send Farther**, and **Send to Back** (**Shift-F6**). **Bring to Front** and **Send to Back** correspond to the topmost and bottom-most layer. If you have five objects layered one atop another and you select the object on layer two, **Send to Back** moves that object to the bottom or fifth layer. However if you used the **Send Farther** option, the object on layer two would only move down to layer three. **Bring Closer** and **Send Farther** only move objects one layer at a time.

Working with Shapes

In addition to the circle and box, you also have access to 36 custom shapes. The triangle is one of these. Other custom shapes include other triangles, a star, a sunburst, curved arrows, a 3-D box, a crescent, a heart, and a lightning bolt. Create a few shapes of your own. You can place them on the sample Fun Sign page, or on the workspace. If you want to work with a clean page, you can insert a new page in the current publication by clicking on the arrow to the right of the page number at the bottom of the Publisher window. When the dialog window appears asking if you want to insert a new page, click on **OK**. If you prefer to create a new publication, select **Create New Publication...** from the File menu, and when the opening dialog window appears select **Full Page** from the **Blank Page** tab page.

NOTE

You can also use the **Page...** option from the Insert menu to create a new page.

Okay, it's time to create a shape. For the purposes of this discussion, I'm going to use the shape on the second-to-last row, third from the right, but you can create whatever shape takes your fancy. Click on the **Custom**

Shapes object tool on the vertical toolbar to display the custom shapes, as shown in Figure 5.26

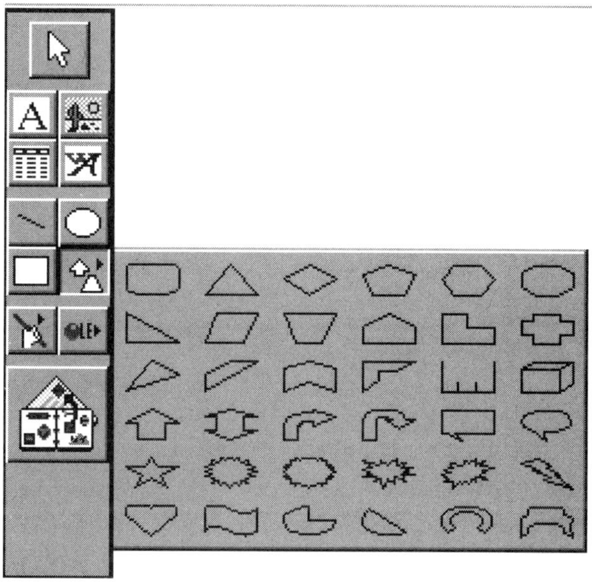

FIGURE 5.26 SELECT ONE OF 36 SHAPES WHEN YOU CLICK ON THE **CUSTOM SHAPES** OBJECT TOOL ON THE VERTICAL TOOLBAR.

When working with shapes, the **Border**, **Shadow**, and **Object Color** speedbuttons on the Format toolbar refer to the shape itself, not to the object frame.

I used the **Object Color** speedbutton to set the object color to a red cross- check pattern. If you prefer menu options over speedbuttons, you can use the **Fill Patterns and Shading...** option on Format menu to accomplish the same task. I also used the **Border** speedbutton to change the border width to 10 points, and the **Shadow** speedbutton to add a standard shadow. Finally, I enlarged its shape proportionally by holding down the **Shift** key and dragging on a corner handle. All of these settings are reflected in Figure 5.27.

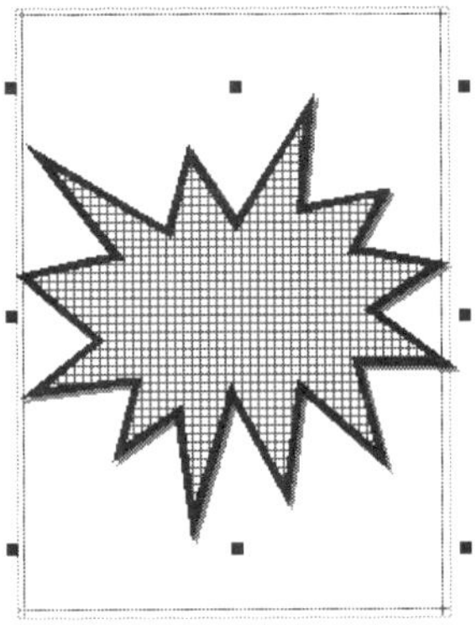

FIGURE 5.27 A PROPORTIONALLY ENLARGED CUSTOM SHAPE WITH A CHECKERED PATTERN, SURROUNDED BY A 10-POINT BORDER AND A STANDARD SHADOW.

Figure 5.28 shows the pop-up object menu for the custom shape. As usual, the first section contains the **Cut**, **Copy**, and **Delete** options. The second section relates to the view. Section three gives you easy access to the **Border...**, **Fill Color...**, **Fill Patterns and Shading...** options. The fourth section holds the **Pickup Formatting** option, and the last section is takes you to the object's **Help** topic.

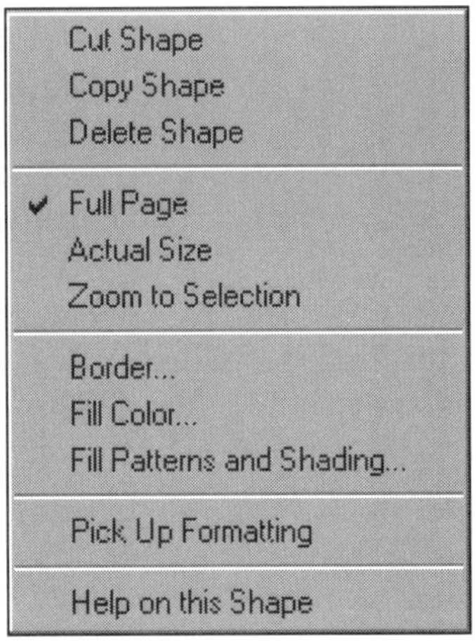

FIGURE 5.28 THE CUSTOM SHAPE OBJECT MENU.

Pick another shape and experiment with resizing. Then change the border and give it some color and a fill pattern. You might want to create several shapes and arrange them on different layers. Finally, add a standard shadow to various shapes to see what they look like.

Creating Custom Shadows

While we're on the subject of shadows again, this would be a good time for you to try making one of your own. For your first attempt I suggest you try using a simple shape, a box. So the first thing to do is create a box using the **Box** object tool. Then fill it in with a color or pattern and give it a border. Figure 5.29 shows my first box, filled with a blue diagonal check pattern and an 8-point border.

FIGURE 5.29 A BOX OBJECT, WITH A BLUE DIAGONAL CHECK PATTERN AND AN 8-POINT BORDER.

Next, create a second box and move it so that it hangs over the right and bottom edges of your first box (see Figure 5.30). The amount that hangs over the edge is the width of your shadow. Notice that the first box shows through. That is because all picture frames, WordArt, and shape objects are created transparent. If you press **Ctrl-T**, the box will become opaque, filled with white.

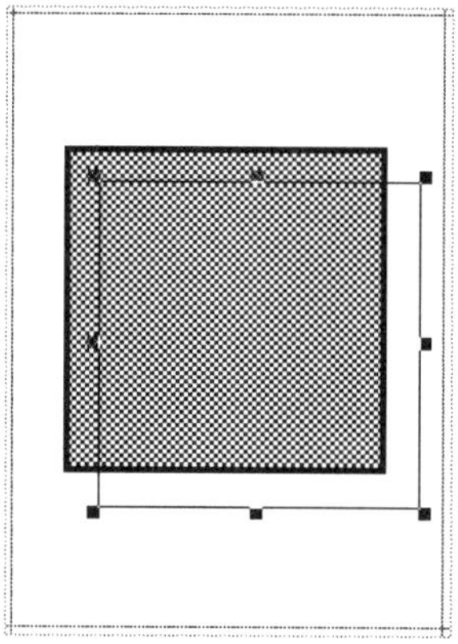

FIGURE 5.30 A NEW TRANSPARENT BOX OVERLAPPING THE BLUE BOX WITH THE DIAGONAL CHECK PATTERN.

Color this second box. I selected Navy Blue (column 4 in the Blue row of the Colors dialog window). As you can see in Figure 5.31, now that the second box is no longer transparent, it obscures most of the first box. For it to work as a shadow, the second box must be behind the first box. With the second box still selected, use either the **Send to Back** or **Send Farther** option on the Arrange menu. Because you are only working with two objects, either option will do the trick.

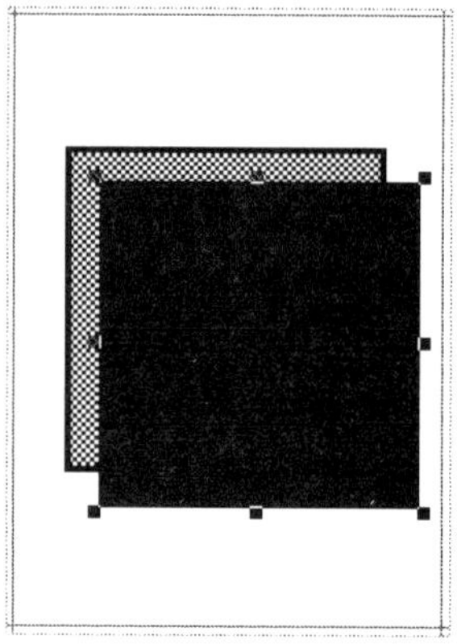

FIGURE 5.31 THE NEW BOX, NO LONGER TRANSPARENT, OBSCURES MOST OF THE FIRST BOX.

As Figure 5.32 shows, the solid navy blue box is now behind the checkered blue box much in the same way that the standard gray shadow appears on other objects. Frankly, this isn't a very good shadow. It's too wide. Figure 5.33 shows what it looks like when the shadow box is narrower. Better, isn't it?

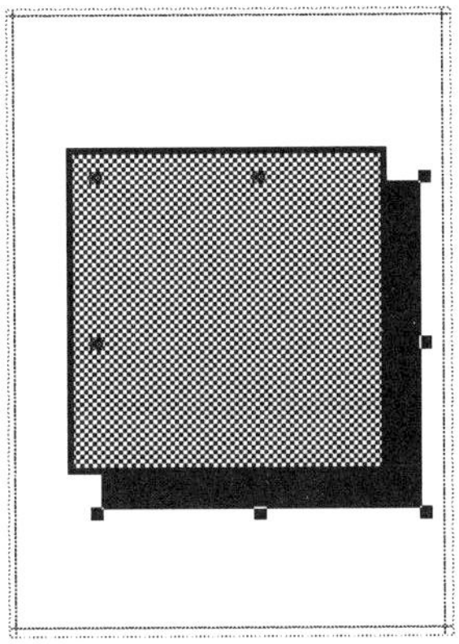

FIGURE 5.32 THE NEW BOX, WITH ITS DARK COLOR, CAN ACT AS A SHADOW WHEN MOVED BEHIND THE FIRST BOX.

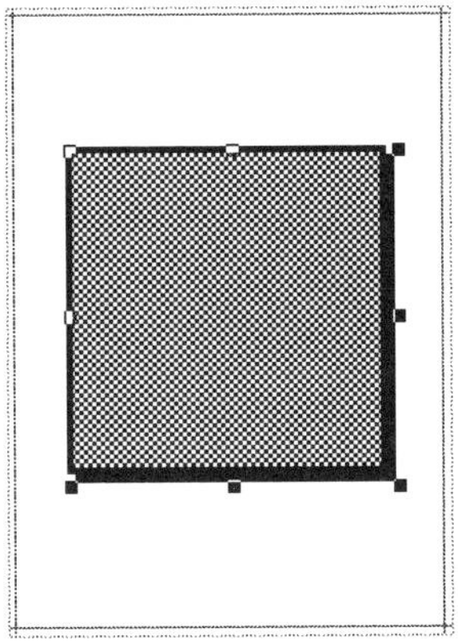

FIGURE 5.33 THE WIDTH OF A SHADOW IS AN IMPORTANT FACTOR IN ACHIEVING THE EFFECT YOU WANT. NARROWER IS USUALLY BETTER.

The procedure for creating a shadow on any shape object is the same. Simply create a second object of the same shape, place it behind but slightly overlapping the first object, and apply the desired color.

Now that you're familiar with that procedure and can use it on any shape object, I can tell you that there is a much easier way to create a shadow effect on box shapes. All you have to do is create a wider border on the right and bottom edges, and a narrower or nonexistent border on the top and left edges. Figure 5.34 shows the Border dialog window side by side with the resulting shadowed box. Notice the hairline settings for the top and left, and 10 point settings for the right and bottom edges. Not only does this method work for box shapes, but you can also use it with WordArt and text frames. Now let's move on to something new.

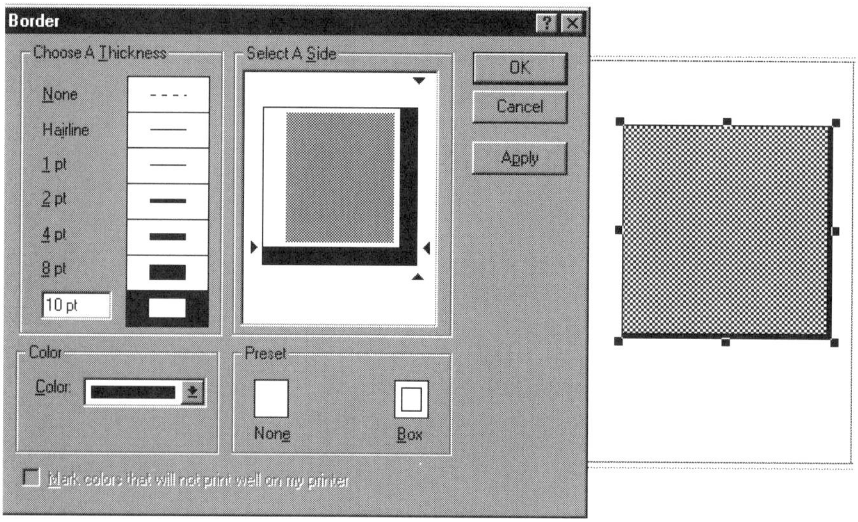

FIGURE 5.34 YOU CAN USE BORDER SETTINGS TO CREATE A SHADOW EFFECT.

FOUR SPECIAL PAGEWIZARDS

Examining PageWizards? That's what you've been doing for the last several chapters. You have already used 15 of PageWizard Design Assistants to create the sample publications discussed in Chapters 2-5. So what else is new? What's new is the fact that there are four more PageWizards that you can only access from the vertical toolbar (the tool button with the hand holding a magic wand). Unlike the other PageWizards that create whole publications, these PageWizards create four special objects or elements that you might want to include in a publication: Calendar, Ad, Coupon, and Logo. At one time, Microsoft referred to these special PageWizards as *Area Wizards*, a term that I find descriptively appropriate and useful in differentiating between the two types of PageWizards.

In the process of examining these Area Wizards, you're going to create a sample flyer. You will need a blank page to work with, so again, you have the choice of inserting a new page in your current publication, or creating a new publication.

To create an Area Wizard object, click on the **PageWizard** tool button on the vertical toolbar, select one of the elements, and drag out the area where you want the object to appear.

NOTE

In Chapter 1, I mentioned that if the **Single Click Object Creation** option is selected in the Options dialog window (which it is by default), you can create objects by selecting the tool and clicking on your page. This is not true for Area Wizards. Regardless of whether the option is on, you must drag out the area for an Area Wizard object. Logos must be no less than 1 x 1 inch in size, whereas Ads, Coupons, and Calendar elements must be at least 2 x 2 inches in size.

Logo

Start with the Logo object and place it in the top-left corner of the blank page. The area you drag out must be no less than 1 x 1 inch in size, or else you'll get the *Zikes!* message shown in Figure 5.35. Make the logo approximately 3.5 x 1.5 inches. As soon as you finish dragging out the area, the PageWizard dialog windows begin.

FIGURE 5.35 *ZIKES!* FOR THE LOGO OBJECT.

The PageWizard tool has three types of logos: small business, product identification, and corporate. For our sample, let's use a **Small Business** type of logo. When prompted for the style, select **Headline**. The PageWizard then wants you to pick a shape (round, square, or other great shape) and specify whether you want to use a picture or initials. Let's go with the **Other Great Shape** and a **Picture**. The PageWizard then gives you a choice between four fonts. For now, let's use **Copperplate Gothic Bold.** (You can always change a font later.) Finally, you get to enter the main text for your logo, followed by an optional tag line with a maximum of 40 characters. I used a dummy company name to match the PageWizard's choice of temporary clipart—Java Joe—with the tag line "savor the flavor."

This logo (see Figure 5.36) is fairly complex in that it's made up of nine separate objects. The most obvious are the two WordArt objects and the picture frame with the cup-of-coffee clipart. The WordArt frame containing the words "savor the flavor" is placed on top of a box object within another box object. (Both box objects are actually rectangular in shape.) The WordArt frame sits on top of a transparent box with a 1-point black border. And that box, in turn, rests on top of another box that is light gray (tenth column in the Black row of the Colors dialog window).

FIGURE 5.36 THE HEADLINE STYLE SMALL BUSINESS LOGO.

The coffee-cup picture frame sits on top of a diamond shape object of the same light gray color, with two very small ellipses of a darker shade of gray in the right and left tips. (The darker shade of gray is Column 7 in the Black row of the Colors dialog window.) This diamond sits on top of a second diamond shape, matching the darker gray of the ellipses. And all nine objects are grouped to function as one single object for the purposes of moving, resizing, and other manipulations.

Ad

Our sample flyer is going to advertise a special sale day. So next you need to create an Ad object. Select the Ad Wizard and drag out an area that begins about 1/4-inch below the logo. Make it stretch across the entire width of the page (excluding the .5-inch margins on either side) and 4.5 inches down.

In the first PageWizard dialog window you must specify the type of ad you want: **Classified**, **Event**, **Product**, **Sale**, or **Service**. As you click on each type, Publisher provides snippets of information. For example, when you click on **Classified**, Publisher tells you that it's *a text intensive design for smaller advertisements.* When you click on **Sale**, Publisher says *This advertisement features an eye-catching title.*, and so forth. For this sample, choose **Sale**.

Then you can select a style. Choose **Jazzy**. Next you can get help with your copy. I'm not much of an advertising copywriter, so let's opt to see Publisher's suggested slogans. They're pretty basic, ranging from **All Items Half Price!** to **Clearance**. Choose **One Day Only!**.

At a glance, you can see that the Ad element is composed of several objects. When you click on it, you can see the outer boundaries and the group button on the bottom, as shown in Figure 5.37. You can also see the outlines of the WordArt frame displaying the words *One Day Only!* in what WordArt calls a Bottom To Top shape. There are two text frames, one that says *Your text here,* and the other with a dummy phone number. The star-like shape in the back could have been made using a shape, except there is no way to crop a shape. This was made by cropping the starburst image from the signs category in the ClipArt Gallery.

FIGURE 5.37 A SALE AD WITH A JAZZY STYLE.

The only object I haven't mentioned yet is the Picture frame containing a clipart flag image. This picture really does nothing for our flyer, so let's get rid of it. If you click on it and press delete, you'll delete the entire group. Similarly, if you're thinking about the **Delete** option on the Object menu, you'll find that it too is a Group Object menu. So to get rid of the picture, first you have to ungroup by clicking on the **Group/Ungroup** button. When the group is split, right-click on the picture object and use the **Delete Object** option. Now you have more space in the Ad object, and I have just the object to fill in.

Calendar

Our flyer advertises a one-day-only sale, so let's add a calendar element to drive that point home. When you select the Calendar PageWizard tool, drag out an area inside the Ad object to replace the picture you just deleted.

The first PageWizard dialog window for Calendar elements asks you to select one of five different styles: **Basic**, **Bold**, **Formal**, **Retro**, or **Splashy**. Choose **Splashy**. Next you must specify whether you want to leave room for a picture. Select **No, thanks**. Then the PageWizard guesses that you want the current year, but checks with you first to be sure. You can type in a different year if you want. Once you select the year, you get to pick the month. Again, the PageWizard assumes the current month as the default.

The last three questions relate to how the calendar element will look. You must choose between initials and abbreviations such as Mon and Tue for days (choose initials), indicate whether you want your weeks to begin on Sunday or Monday (opt for Sunday), and pick a language.

NOTE This design element only creates a single-month calendar. If you want more comprehensive calendars, you probably want a calendar publication instead of a small calendar element in another publication. In that case you should use the PageWizard from the startup dialog window.

When the calendar element appears, click on a date. You can see that the PageWizard used a table for the days and dates, and grouped that together with the other components to create a group object that you can easily move around on the page. The other components include two WordArt objects for the year and the month and two line objects.

The only real problem I see with our flyer so far is that the year in the calendar appears to be almost the same color as the starburst image in the Ad group object. To make the year stand out a little better, without interfering with the other parts of the calendar, you can add a hairline border. Double click on the year to invoke WordArt. Then select **Border** and change the setting from **None** to **Hairline**.

Figure 5.38 shows what our flyer looks like so far. Now let's create a coupon object.

FIGURE 5.38 OUR SAMPLE ADVERTISING FLYER IN PROGRESS.

Coupon

Select the Coupon Wizard and drag out an area to fill the bottom portion of our flyer. When asked to select a coupon style, choose **Jazzy**. You can create coupons that are to be filled out and mailed back, but for now select **No**. And for our purposes in this sample, you will not need check boxes either, so select **No** there as well.

You also have a choice of including an expiration data, and Publisher tries to be helpful by entering the current date. Enter any date you choose, preferably a date within the same month you selected for the calendar element. PageWizard will create a dashed, dotted, or solid border, whichever you choose. I chose dotted for the sample. Next comes the text. You can enter your company name, a slogan, or whatever is appropriate. I used *One Day Only!* again to match the Ad portion of the flyer.

Figure 5.39 shows the sample coupon element. You can see that it is comprised of eight objects: the same starburst clipart, cropped differently, used in two separate frames; a third picture frame containing a musical clipart image; two text frames containing dummy text; two WordArt frames, one with the slogan One Day Only!, the other with the expiration date; and a box with a black dotted border, big enough to contain all these other objects. Again, these objects are bound together in a group.

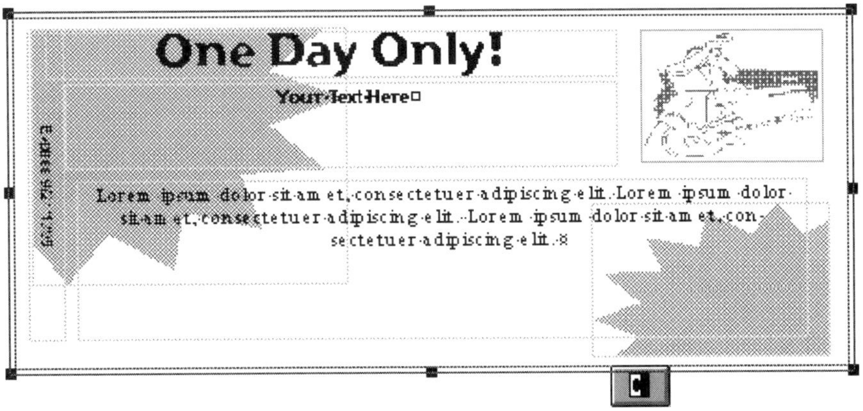

FIGURE 5.39 THE COUPON OBJECT CREATED BY THE PAGEWIZARD FOR YOUR SAMPLE FLYER.

The image in the picture frame on the coupon really doesn't go with the rest of the flyer, so go ahead and change the image. Double-click on the Picture frame to bring up the ClipArt Gallery dialog window. You can scroll around looking for a suitable image, or you can use the **Find...** feature. Click on **Find** and enter the word **coffee** in the description box. Then click on **Find Now**. The Gallery Organizer found three coffee images. Select one (I chose the middle one), and click on **Insert**.

In addition to filling in the text frames with pertinent copy, the last thing you might want to do to complete this sample flyer is add something to really make the sale date stand out. The flyer says One Day Only, but the calendar does not show which date that is. The only indication so far is the expiration date on the coupon, and that's hardly noticed.

My solution was to create another WordArt frame that says SALE DAY and draw lines pointing to the date on the calendar. I also circled the date in red. First select the WordArt tool and drag out a small area near the top of the flyer. When the WordArt editing dialog window appears, type in the words **SALE DAY** and use **Best Fit** for the font size. Then create the three lines. Mine are 4 points thick, and the last one has a left arrowhead. Finally create a small circle object on top of the date and specify a red border, 2 points thick. The final sample flyer is shown in Figure 5.40.

FIGURE 5.40 THE FINAL VERSION OF THE SAMPLE FLYER CONTAINING A LOGO, AD, CALENDAR, AND COUPON OBJECT, PLUS AN INDEPENDENT WORDART OBJECT, THREE LINES, AND A CIRCLE.

SUMMARY

- Speedbuttons on the Format toolbar for use with WordArt objects are the same as those used with Picture objects.
- WordArt is a separate application that can be run from within the Publisher program. When you double-click on a WordArt object, the WordArt program takes over the Publisher environment, changing its menu options and Format toolbar. WordArt can also be run in a separate window.
- WordArt's Format toolbar contains three drop-down selection boxes for **Shape**, **Font**, and **Font Size**, followed by 11 speedbuttons: **Bold**, **Italic**, **Even Height**, **Flip**, **Stretch**, **Alignment**, **Character Spacing**, **Special Effects**, **Shading**, **Shadow**, and **Line Thickness**.
- You can manipulate WordArt text into 36 different shapes, slants, and curves. You also have options for rotating WordArt and altering its arc by a specific number of degrees. You can use the **Best Fit** size option to allow WordArt to select the largest possible font size that will fit the frame. The **Stretch to Fit** option expands the text so that it touches all four sides of its frame.
- When working with WordArt, you can choose foreground and background colors and select a pattern or shading style all from within the same Shading dialog window.
- The **Shading**, **Shadow**, and **Border** options in WordArt apply to the WordArt text, not the WordArt frame.
- When you close the WordArt editing dialog window, Publisher applies your changes regardless of whether you use the **Update Display**. The easiest way to leave the WordArt application is to simply click somewhere on your publication page (but not in the WordArt frame) or in your workspace.
- To see through an object frame, it has to be transparent. You can control transparency in two ways: 1) press **Ctrl-T** to toggle transparency on and off and 2) set the **Object Color** option to **Clear** for transparent, or a color to make it opaque.

- The **WordArt** option on the Object menu contains three submenu items: **Edit**, **Open**, and **Convert**. **Edit** passes control over to the WordArt application; **Open** brings up WordArt in a separate window. **Convert** is discussed in Chapter 8.
- Access the Line dialog window to control the width or thickness of a line, the color of the line, and the application and style of line arrowheads.
- Objects that are not transparent obscure the view of any object on an underlying layer. The Arrange menu includes four layering options: **Bring to Front (F6)**, **Bring Closer**, **Send Farther**, and **Send to Back (Shift-F6)**. **Bring to Front** and **Send to Back** correspond to the topmost and bottom-most layer. **Bring Closer** and **Send Farther** only move objects one layer at a time.
- In addition to the circle and box, Publisher has 36 custom shape objects. When working with all shapes, the **Border**, **Shadow**, and **Object Color** speedbuttons on the Format toolbar apply to the shape itself, not to the object frame.
- You can create a custom shadow for any shape object by creating a second object of the same shape, placing it behind but slightly overlapping the first object and applying the desired color. You can also create a custom shadow by using the Border dialog window to make the right and bottom border edges wider and darker than the top and left edges. This second method only works for box shapes, WordArt, and text frames.
- The PageWizard object tool on the vertical toolbar can create four special objects or elements that you might want to include in a publication: The four special objects are: Calendar, Ad, Coupon, and Logo. These PageWizards are sometimes referred to as Area Wizards.
- Regardless of whether the **Single Click Object Creation** option is selected, you must drag out the area for a special PageWizard object. Logos must be no less than 1 x 1 inch in size, while Ads, Coupons, and Calendar elements must be at least 2 x 2 inches in size.
- Some objects may look like pieces of shapes. More likely, however, they are cropped clipart images. Shapes can not be cropped.

- Although it is not necessary to ungroup a group object to edit one of the individual objects within the group, you must separate the grouped objects if you want to cut, copy, paste, or delete an individual component.

CHAPTER 6

DESIGN OBJECTS AND ELEMENTS

- Working with BorderArt
- Manipulating objects to create custom-made borders
- Creating watermarks
- Using Wingdings to create custom borders
- Making fancy bullets out of wingdings and BorderArt
- Formatting Fancy First Letters in text frames
- Exploring the Design Gallery

In this chapter you'll see a few more PageWizard designs, and you'll also create a few designs from scratch.

One of the most important principles of good design is to creating a consistent look and feel throughout a publication. Design elements can promote instant recognition and a feeling of familiarity. Consistent use of design elements helps to create an image. It's not a good idea to use too many different font styles, and if you use Fancy First Letters, they should all be formatted alike. All of your design elements don't have to be identical, but they should be compatible. For example, you probably wouldn't want to mix very conservative design elements with splashy ones.

In today's world of snippets and sound bites, visual impact plays a major role. Elements such as titles, sidebars, and pullquotes can be used to enhance interest and focus the audience. And when you maintain consistency, you can use contrast to effectively add flair and focus. The contrast may be a spot of color or shades of gray. Or you can create contrast by adding an element so inconsistent that it startles the reader.

The placement of your objects and the formatting you apply to these objects constitutes *design*. In the last chapter we covered design effects created by applying shadows and shading, as well as by layering objects. In this chapter you'll examine some BorderArt, and create some custom-made borders. You'll also create some watermarks, and create custom bullet characters using wingdings and pieces of BorderArt. Then you'll take a look at designing Fancy First Letters, and in the last part of the chapter I'll show you the Design Gallery.

So let's get started. You've worked with Borders for several objects types, but the Border dialog window provides only plain options. BorderArt is where the fun is.

SAMPLE NO LOITERING SIGN

Use the Sign PageWizard to create a Public Information sign for No Loitering. This is a simple sign and the PageWizard doesn't require any input from you. The sign consists of a single text object. Click anywhere on the sign to display the frame handles, and notice the text button with the three diamonds at the bottom as shown in Figure 6.1. The PageWizard used the Impact font, size 16, for the lettering, and applied a yellow fill color to the text frame. The text frame is bordered by little people figures, but if you click on the **Border** speedbutton, or select **Border...** from the Format menu, the Border dialog window does not show any border (Thickness is set to None.) That's because Borders and BorderArt are two entirely separate things.

FIGURE 6.1 THE NO LOITERING SIGN AS CREATED BY THE PAGEWIZARD

Selecting BorderArt

There is no speedbutton for BorderArt, so you'll have to use the Format menu to bring up the BorderArt dialog window shown in Figure 6.2. This dialog window allows you to select one from a list of all of the available BorderArt styles. My list contains 132 choices, and the CD-ROM version of Microsoft Publisher contains more than 150 BorderArt styles. You can also specify the point size for the border or opt for the default size that is supposed to be the optimal size for that particular border style.

NOTE

You may only apply BorderArt to boxes and frames. BorderArt does not work with circles and custom shape objects.

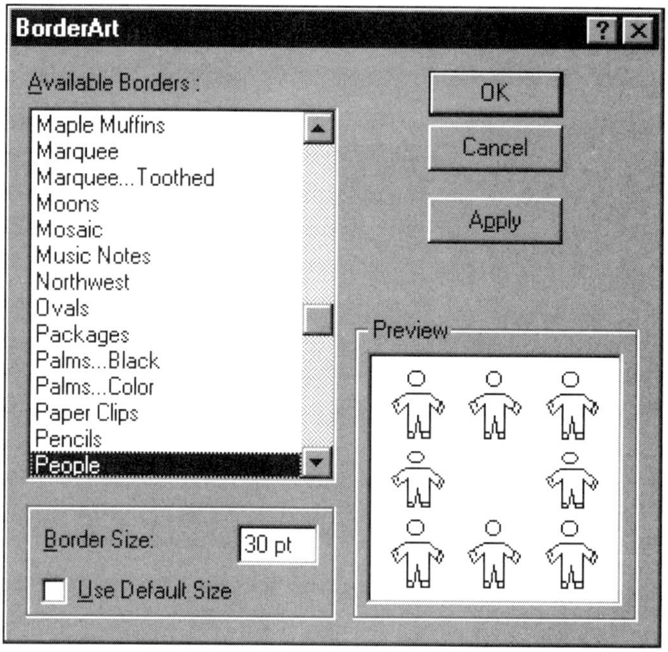

FIGURE 6.2 THE BORDERART DIALOG WINDOW, WITH THE PEOPLE BORDER SELECTED AND SHOWN IN THE PREVIEW SECTION.

The size of the BorderArt in the No Loitering Sign is 30 point, even though the optimal size is only 15 point. Apply the default size and see how it looks. The smaller size doesn't really look very good, but then again, I'm not sure that I'd pick this figure for a No Loitering Sign anyway. Let's take a look at another PageWizard sign.

SAMPLE BUSINESS OPEN SIGN

This time, select the **Business** type when prompted by the Sign PageWizard, and choose the **Open** sign. Figure 6.3 shows the sign as created by the PageWizard. This sign uses two objects: a WordArt object for the word OPEN (notice the dotted line indicating the frame boundaries), and a box object with BorderArt. This style BorderArt is called Corner Triangles. Access the BorderArt dialog window and use the **Preview** section to get a better look at it.

FIGURE 6.3 THE OPEN BUSINESS SIGN AS CREATED BY THE SIGN PAGEWIZARD.

The PageWizard could have assigned the same BorderArt to the WordArt frame, eliminating the box object all together, but it would have looked slightly different. Compare Figures 6.3 and 6.4. Can you see the difference? It has to do with WordArt's Stretch to Fit setting.

FIGURE 6.4 THE OPEN BUSINESS SIGN WITH BORDERART APPLIED TO THE WORDART FRAME, ELIMINATING THE NEED FOR THE BOX OBJECT.

Stretch to Fit is active in both versions, however the BorderArt has effectively changed the inside border. If you imagine a line connecting the inside corners of the corner triangles, you'll see that the WordArt text is stretched to touch that invisible line.

TIP

When you add BorderArt to a frame, Publisher places it just inside the frame, with the outer edge flush against the frame's boundary lines. So when you create a wide border, this leaves less space inside the frame for your content. If you need more space for content either reduce the border size or enlarge the frame. Alternatively, you can do as the PageWizard did and create two separate objects, one for the content, and a larger box around it for the BorderArt.

Presetting Object Borders

At the beginning of this chapter, I made a point about the importance of design consistency and repeating the same design elements. This could become tedious when constructing a publication. For example, every time you created a box, you would then have to go through the steps of applying the BorderArt to each box individually. Publisher will let you set a Border or BorderArt style for a tool object (i.e. a text frame, box, etc.) so that each time you use the tool to create another box, it will automatically have the desired border.

To pre-set the border for an object, click on the object tool and then click on the **Border...** or **BorderArt...** option on the Format menu without clicking on your page or workspace. Select the desired settings for your border and close the dialog window. Publisher will then apply this to all new objects created with that tool, and will not change any existing objects. The only bad news is that Publisher forgets all about your settings as soon as you close the Publisher program.

Now let's look at a brand new publication type.

SAMPLE BANNER

Select the Banner PageWizard (bottom row, first on the left) and choose the **Splashy** style. Make the banner 8.5" tall and allow the length to be determined by your text. Lots of banners do not have to have borders, but for this sample select **Yes**. When asked about pictures, select **No,**

thanks. Finally, you have to enter the text for your banner. Type in *Happy 30th Anniversary Mom and Dad!*

TIP

If your banner needs to be a specific length to fit in a particular location, it is better to set the length yourself.

Figure 6.5 shows the beginning section of the banner. This time the PageWizard used a plain text frame instead of WordArt for the text. If you click on the text frame and scroll right, you'll find the text frame button on the bottom edge of the frame between the words *Mom* and *and*. But like the Open sign, the PageWizard did assign the BorderArt to a separate box object. This BorderArt style is called Waveline, and the PageWizard used a 72 point size instead of the 20 point default size that would have been way too small for a banner.

FIGURE 6.5 THE BEGINNING OF THE SAMPLE BANNER CREATED BY THE PAGEWIZARD.

If you don't see any borders you like, you can always create your own. Start with a blank page, and you can create a design appropriate for love letters or a Valentine's Day card.

SAMPLE LOVE LETTER

Remember the Corner BorderArt style you saw a moment ago? You can create a similar effect by placing a shape and rotating it appropriately to embellish the corners. Start with a blank page, then select the heart shape and place the object on your page. You want it to be fairly small, so you'll need to resize it. Don't forget to hold down the **Shift** and **Control** keys while resizing so the shape doesn't get distorted. Move the object up into the top left corner.

Rotating and Flipping Objects

The shape would look much better in the corner if it was tilted at an angle. As you work more with the Publisher program you'll find that rotating and flipping objects is and important part of formatting design elements. You can rotate any object type, including text frames and tables.

Click on the heart object, then select **Rotate/Flip** option from the Arrange menu, and click on **Custom Rotate...** to bring up the Rotate Objects dialog window. Enter 25 in the Angle box and click on the Left Rotate button as shown in Figure 6.6. Close the dialog window.

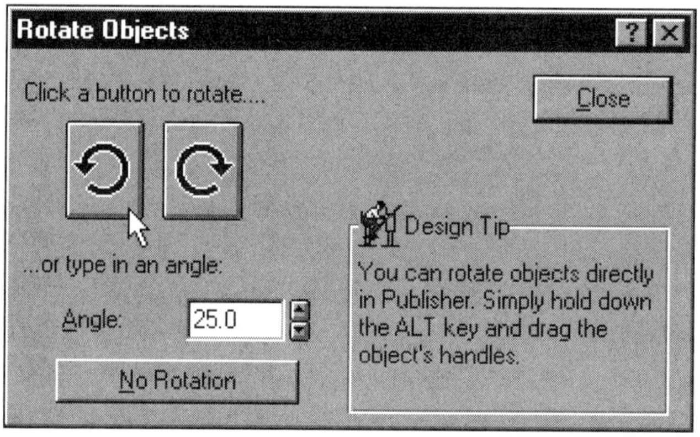

FIGURE 6.6 THE ROTATE OBJECTS DIALOG WINDOW.

Valentine hearts should be red, so select the **Object Color** speedbutton and make it red. Then copy the object and paste it three times so that you have four hearts. Move the top copy away from the original, select **Flip Horizontal** and place the object in the top right corner as shown in Figure 6.7.

FIGURE 6.7 IN THE PROCESS OF CREATING LOVE LETTER STATIONARY OR VALENTINE PUBLICATIONS.

Move the next copy away, use the **Flip Vertical** speedbutton, and move the object to the bottom left corner. Finally remove the remaining copy away from the original, use both the **Flip Horizontal** and **Flip Vertical** speedbuttons, then move it to the bottom left of the page.

NOTE

If you prefer, you can rotate an object manually by selecting the object, and holding down the **Alt** key while dragging the rotate pointer. If you hold both the **Shift** and **Alt** keys down together while dragging the object, it will rotate in 15-degree increments.

Finally, to pull the corners together, create a large box surrounding all four hearts, and apply an 8 point plain red border. Your finished page should look something like the one shown in Figure 6.8.

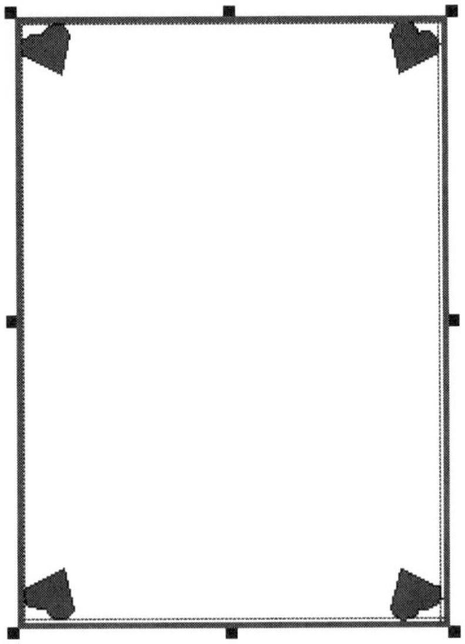

FIGURE 6.8 LOVE LETTER STATIONARY WITH A CUSTOM-MADE BORDER.

If you think you might ever want to use this custom border again, you can create a group object and save it in the Design Gallery. To create the group, hold down the **Shift** key and select each of the five objects. Then click on the group button that appears at the bottom of the group frame. Save this publication so that you can use it again later in this chapter when I show you how to add objects to the Design Gallery.

If you want to use this as the basic design for writing your love letters, all you have to do when you want to write another love letter is simply open the publication, add a text frame, and either import your text from a word processing file or type it directly into the publication. If you want to save each letter, use the **Save As** option on the file menu, leaving your original form unchanged.

If you're not much of a letter writer, you could add to this design, creating a Valentine for that someone special. Let's try adding a larger heart shape in the center with a gradient fill.

Gradient Fills

Make sure your heart shaped object has no border, then select **Object Color**, set the color to Red. Then choose **Fill Patterns and Shading...** from the Format menu to bring up the dialog shown in Figure 6.9.

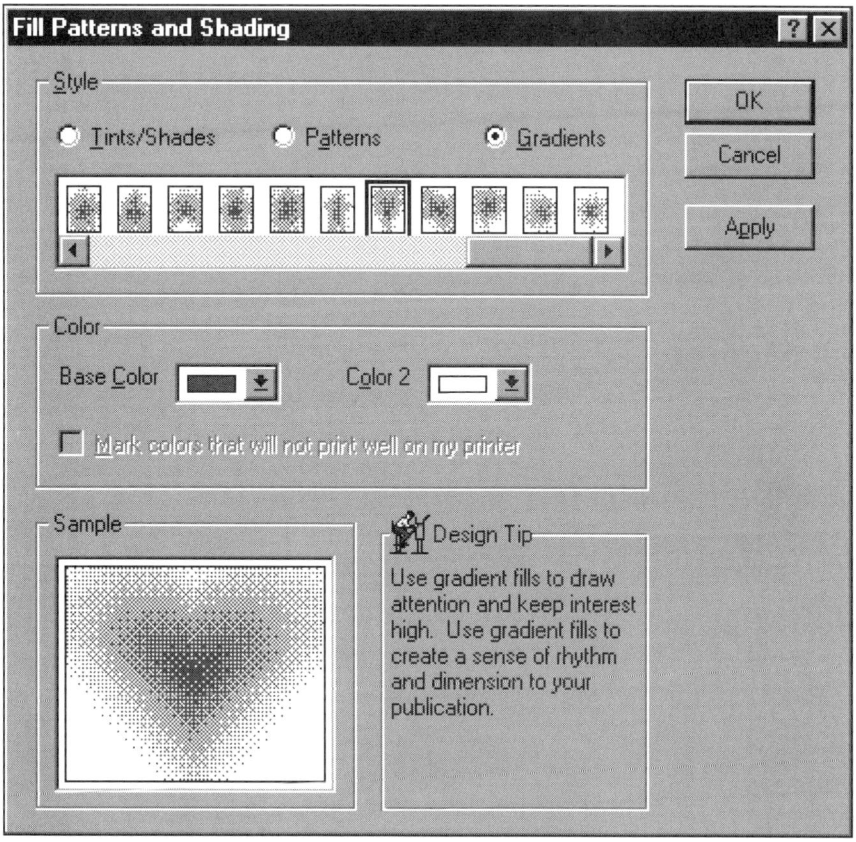

FIGURE 6.9 THE FILL PATTERNS AND SHADING DIALOG WINDOW.

Select the **Gradients** radio button, and select the gradient pattern you want. As you click on each choice, you can see how it looks in the Sample section. The pattern that is fifth from the right works best for this design, and Figure 6.10 shows the publication after adding the gradient heart.

FIGURE 6.10 IN THE PROCESS OF CREATING A VALENTINE USING THE CUSTOM-MADE HEART BORDER AND A LARGE HEART SHAPE WITH A GRADIENT FILL PATTERN.

To finish off this sample, you might want to add some text or WordArt. I chose to add some WordArt as shown in Figure 6.11. The only catch is that you have to remember to make the WordArt frame transparent, and it must be on top of the heart. If you move the heart on top of the WordArt, the words will be hidden.

FIGURE 6.11 A VALENTINE PUBLICATION.

In the context of the completed Valentine publication, the gradient heart fits the Microsoft Publisher definition of a *watermark*—a lightly shaded object appearing behind everything else on the page. Technically, to be behind everything else, an object has only to be on the bottom-most layer if multiple layers are in use. Most often, however, watermarks are placed in the *background*, and I'll explain that in just a moment.

Next I'll show you how I used a background watermark for one of my business letterhead designs. If you want to save this publication, do so now, and then create a new publication with a blank page. If you don't want to save this, you can simply insert a new page.

SAMPLE LETTERHEAD

The first page of my letterhead consists of three elements: a WordArt frame containing my name (I use this instead of a logo), a watermark, and a text frame containing my address, telephone, and fax numbers. The first thing to do is decide which elements go on the background and which belong in the foreground. The Publisher program includes a good demo explaining that the publication page or foreground is like a transparent sheet on top of the background page. Anything you put on the background will automatically appear on all subsequent pages.

I knew that I wanted the watermark on all pages, but I wasn't sure about the other two elements. I considered using the WordArt frame with my name on the first page only, and not on subsequent pages. That would mean placing the WordArt frame in the foreground of the first page only, while watermark and the address information would appear on the background. Ultimately, however, I decided to put all three elements in the background.

Working in the Background

Select **Go to Background** from the **View** menu or press **Ctrl+M**. When you start with a blank page, the background really doesn't look any different from the foreground. You can always tell where you are by looking at the status bar. Instead of showing a page number to the left of the zoom controls, it shows a little image depicting one page folded back from on top of another page.

Figure 6.12 shows my letterhead design. I began with the WordArt frame approximately 3.75" wide and 1.5" high. The font is Imprint MT Shadow and the size is Best Fit. Then I created a one line text frame along the bottom for my address and numbers. But what really makes this design is the third element, the watermark.

FIGURE 6.12 ONE OF DEVRA'S LETTERHEAD DESIGNS USING A WATERMARK.

Watermarks

A moment ago, I gave you the Microsoft definition of a watermark. Originally, before computers, a watermark was a design created in a piece of paper during the manufacturing process. Usually it was only visible when you held a page up to the light. Now, computers can imprint text as a watermark. For example, you may have seen pages with the word CONFIDENTIAL marked diagonally across the page from the lower left corner to the upper right.

You can also use images as watermarks. For this project I used a piece of clipart that comes with Microsoft Word. It's a Windows Metafile image called BOOKS.WMF. I used the **Picture File...** option on the Insert menu, and once inserted, rotated it slightly on an angle. Once placed, you need to select the color or tint. Because you don't want the watermark design to dominate, you need to select a light color. I felt that the original image would be too dark (it was black, white, and gray), so I used the **Recolor Picture...** option on the Format menu as discussed in Chapter 3 and selected Aqua from the basic colors.

Now move back to foreground (use the **View** menu or press **Ctrl+M** again), and try to click on your watermark. You can't, and you might even get a helpful message like the one shown in Figure 6.13. Watermarks are meant to be in the background, both literally and figuratively. Before you move on to the next section, add a new page to your current publication. If your watermark is properly placed on the background, your new page should have the watermark too.

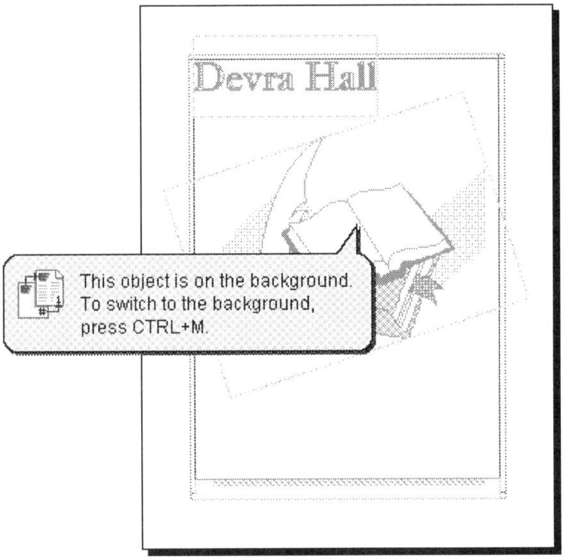

FIGURE 6.13 TRY TO SELECT A BACKGROUND WATERMARK FROM THE FOREGROUND. YOU CAN'T.

SAMPLE PHONE LOG

The next publication you'll create from scratch is a phone log. Again, start with a blank page, but this time use the Advanced Options to create a horizontal page by selecting **Landscape** format. The real purpose of this example is to show you how to create your own custom border art using Wingdings, but first let's put a simple table on the page. Use the **Table** object tool and drag out an area on your page. When the Create Table dialog window appears, enter **15** Rows, **5** Columns, and select the table format called **List 1.**

Select the table object and create grid lines using the Border option. You'll also need to resize the columns a bit to suit the application. I made the first two columns each about .75" inches wide, and the other three columns each about 2" wide. Then I formatted the first row so that the text would be centered, and I entered the following headings: Date, Time, For Whom, Caller's Name, and Message. Figure 6.14 shows the finished table. Now let's get to the custom borders made out of wingdings.

Date	Time	For Whom	Caller's Name	Message

FIGURE 6.14 THE TABLE FOR THE TELEPHONE LOG PUBLICATION.

Creating Custom Borders With Wingdings

You can create your own borders by placing wingding characters in a long narrow text frame across the top of a publication, then copying and rotating that frame for each of the other three sides of the page. Create the text frame, select one of the Wingdings fonts, and set the size to 24 pts. Then use the **Symbol...** option on the Insert menu and select a wingding character from the dialog window that appears. You can insert several different wingding characters, one at a time, or you can copy a single character repeatedly until the frame is full. Try to maintain even spacing between each character. I used the telephone Wingding and alternated with the **Tab** key as shown in Figure 6.15.

FIGURE 6.15 A TEXT FRAME FILLED WITH TELEPHONE WINGDING CHARACTERS ALTERNATING WITH TABS.

When your first text frame is completed, use the Edit menu options to **Copy** the frame and then **Paste** the copy on your page. (You can also use the right-click Text Frame Object menu.) When you Paste the object, it appears directly on top of the original. Click on it and move it down so you can see that there are two.

Now you need to rotate or flip this frame, but unlike some of the other objects you've worked with, there are no rotate speedbuttons for text frames. However, that doesn't mean you can't rotate the frame. You just have to use the **Rotate/Flip** option on the Arrange menu, and select your choice from the submenu that appears. The submenu choices are **Rotate Left, Rotate Right,** and **Custom Rotate....** The Flip Vertically and Flip Horizontally options are not available for text frames.

Click on the pasted copy, select the **Custom Rotate...** option, enter **180** in the Angle box of the Rotate Objects dialog window, and click on **Close**. Your pasted text frame should now be upside down, so drag it to the bottom edge of your page. Then Paste two more copies of the frame. Select one and use the **Rotate Right** option to stand the frame on end. Drag it over to the right edge of your page and resize it to fit. Click on the last copy and use **Rotate Left** option to stand the frame on the other end. Drag it over to the left edge of your page and resize it to fit.

To assist in creating a unified look, set three sided borders for each of the four text frames. Click on a frame, and access the Border dialog box. Select the top and two sides by holding down the shift key and clicking on each one in the Select A Side section, then choose **2 pt** thickness as shown in Figure 6.16. Do this for each of the four text frames.

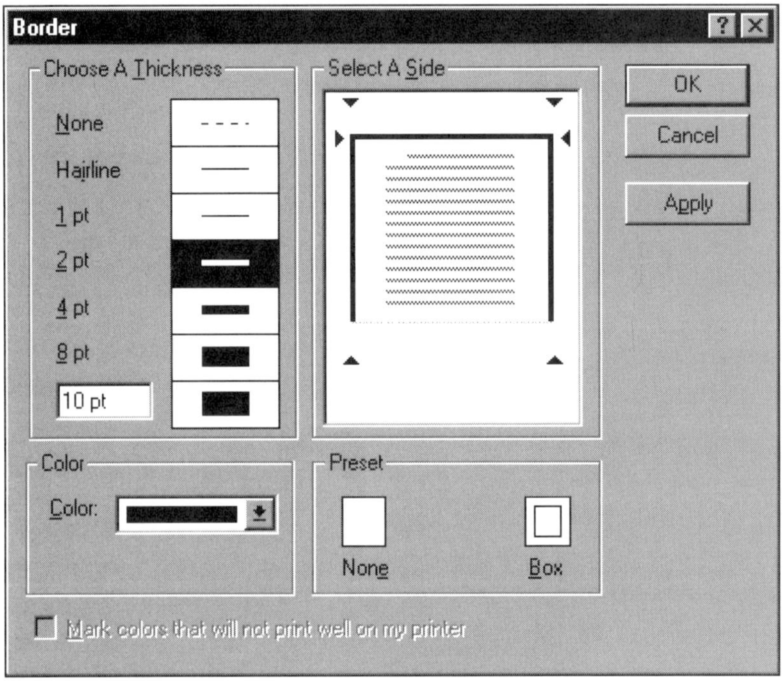

FIGURE 6.16 THE BORDER DIALOG WINDOW WITH THREE-SIDED BORDER SETTINGS FOR A TEXT FRAME.

When all four frames have three-sided border lines, you may find that you have adjust the frames slightly until they look just right. While my telephone wingding characters are not perfectly spaced, Figure 6.17 shows the Phone Log publication and gives you an idea of what your custom border might look like.

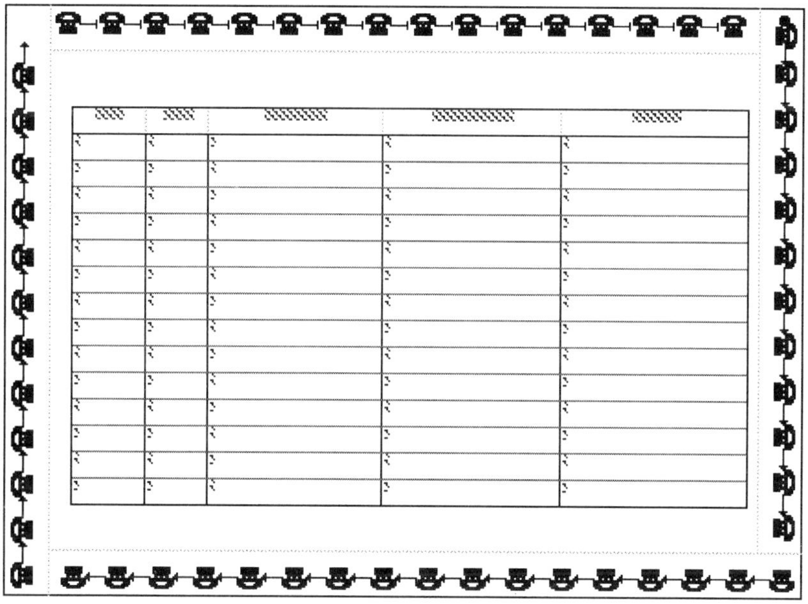

FIGURE 6.17 THE PHONE LOG PUBLICATION. THE CUSTOM BORDERS WERE CREATED WITH WINGDING CHARACTERS INSIDE TEXT FRAMES.

CREATING CUSTOM BULLETS

While we're on the subject of border art and wingdings, you can use wingding characters or a small part of border art to create your own custom bullets. These make great design effects.

Using Wingding and Symbol Characters as Bullets

To use a Wingding character (or any other symbol character) as a bullet, you need a text frame. Then use the Insert menu to place the character in the text frame. Choose the **Symbol...** option, and find the character you want. You can select a character from one of the three Wingding character sets, or use any other character or symbol that suits your fancy. Finally, select a size appropriate to your design.

Figure 6.18 shows a three-item bulleted list where the each bullet is a text frame containing an arrow character from the first set of Wingdings (it's the one on the second to last row, eighth from the right), formatted to 72 point size.

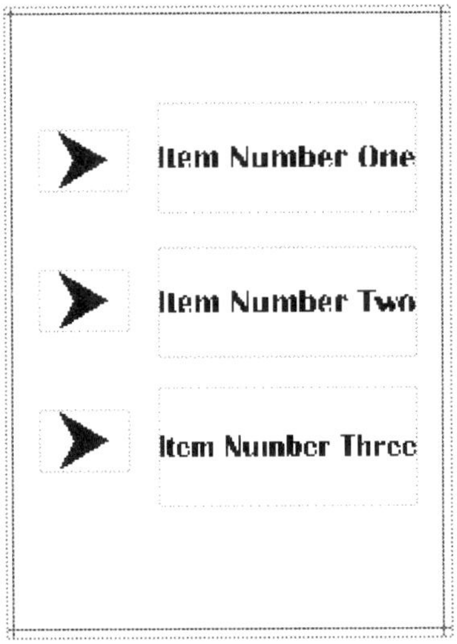

FIGURE 6.18 THREE-ITEM BULLETED LIST, WITH CUSTOM BULLETS MADE FROM A WINGDING CHARACTER.

Border Art Bullets

To create a bullet using a design from the BorderArt collection, you need to start with a box object. Once you create a box shape, select **BorderArt...** from the Format menu and choose your BorderArt style from the dialog window that appears. I used the Creatures... Butterfly design as shown in Figure 6.19.

FIGURE 6.19 A BOX OBJECT WITH BUTTERFLY BORDERART

Next you need to resize the box so that only one side is visible. Click on the box and drag the right side in until all you can see is one vertical line of butterflies as shown in Figure 6.20.

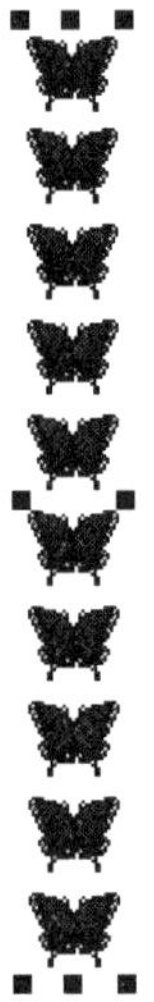

FIGURE 6.20 A BOX OBJECT WITH BUTTERFLY BORDERART, RESIZED SO THAT ONLY ONE VERTICAL EDGE OF BUTTERFLIES IS VISIBLE.

Finally, resize the box again, moving the bottom edge upward until all that is left is a single butterfly as shown in Figure 6.21. You can repeat this process to create as many bullets as needed, or you can copy the first one and paste as many as you need.

FIGURE 6.21 A BOX OBJECT WITH BUTTERFLY BORDERART, RESIZED BOTH HORIZONTALLY AND VERTICALLY, SO THAT ONLY A SINGLE BUTTERFLY REMAINS VISIBLE.

TIP

In addition to using enlarged wingdings and pieces or BorderArt as bullets, you can also use these objects as design ornaments in any publication.

SAMPLE FLYER FOR ANY OCCASION

You're going to use one of the PageWizard's flyer publications to experiment with Fancy First Letters. A Fancy First Letter, also known as a Drop Cap, is another design element used with text objects. It is not only decorative, but serves to draw the reader's attention. Too many on a page, however, will defeat the purpose. Like all good design features, use them sparingly.

Under the File menu, select **Create a New Publication...**, and then **Flyer**. When asked *What's the flyer for?* select **Other**. Then choose the **Basic** style and a **Landscape** format. When prompted to choose between Bulleted List and Paragraph, select **Paragraph**. And when asked whether you want ClipArt or space for a Photo, select **Neither**. Enter any headline you want, and choose **Neither** again when asked it you want to include an Entry Form or Phone Tear-offs. Finally say **No** to mailing. Figure 6.22 shows the flyer created by the PageWizard according to the choices just described.

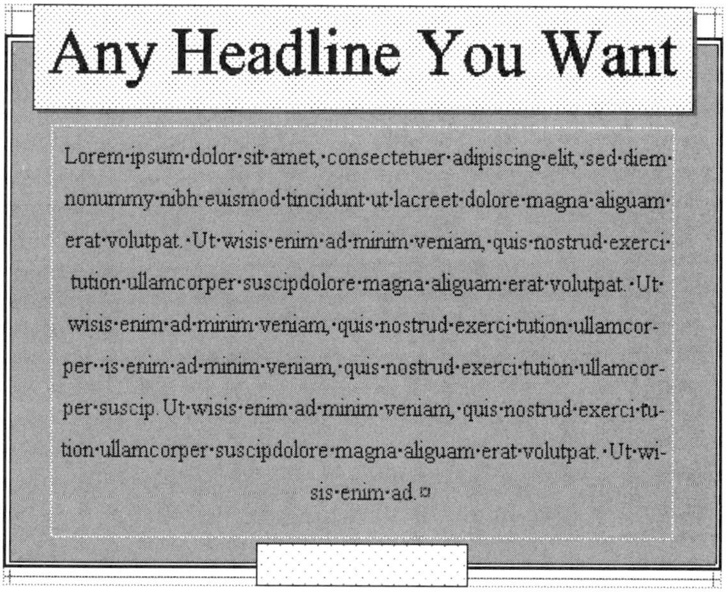

FIGURE 6.22 A FLYER FOR ANY OCCASION AS CREATED BY THE PAGEWIZARD.

Adding and Removing a Fancy First Letter

As usual, the PageWizard has set out to impress you with its Latin. But what we're really interested in here is the Fancy First Letter option on the Format menu. Click on the text frame containing the Latin paragraph, then select the **Fancy First Letter...** option to bring up the dialog window shown in Figure 6.23. When this dialog first appears on your screen, you will see that the settings indicate that your text does not have a Fancy First Letter. The dialog shown in Figure 6.23 reflects the selection I made to add a Fancy First Letter to the sample flyer.

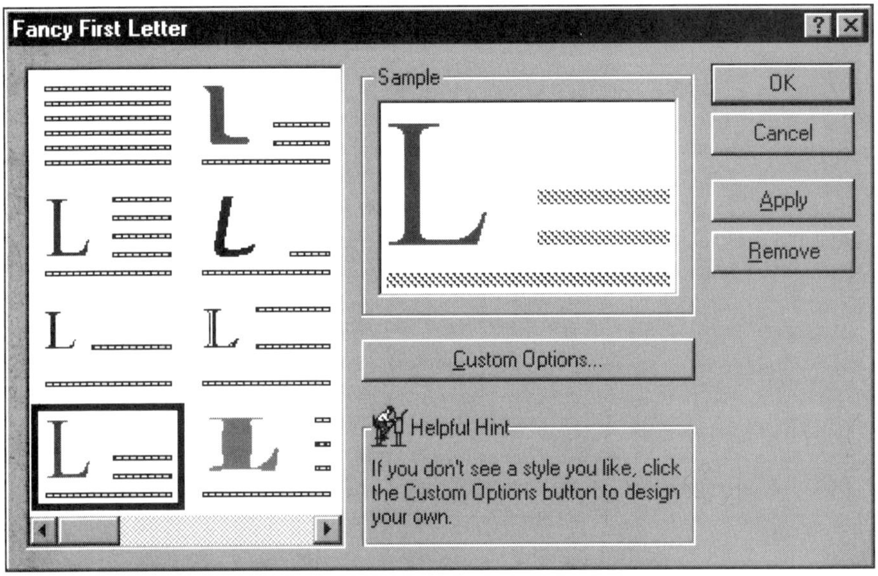

FIGURE 6.23 THE FANCY FIRST LETTER DIALOG WINDOW, REFLECTING MY SELECTION.

The left side of the dialog window contains a horizontally scrolling selection of 16 Fancy First Letter styles. Different styles not only use different fonts, but some take up more lines than others, and a couple of the styles use the first two letters. When you click on one of the styles, the Sample section in the middle of the dialog gives you a better indication of how your selection will look when applied. Pick one and click on **OK**. Figure 6.24 shows the result of my selection.

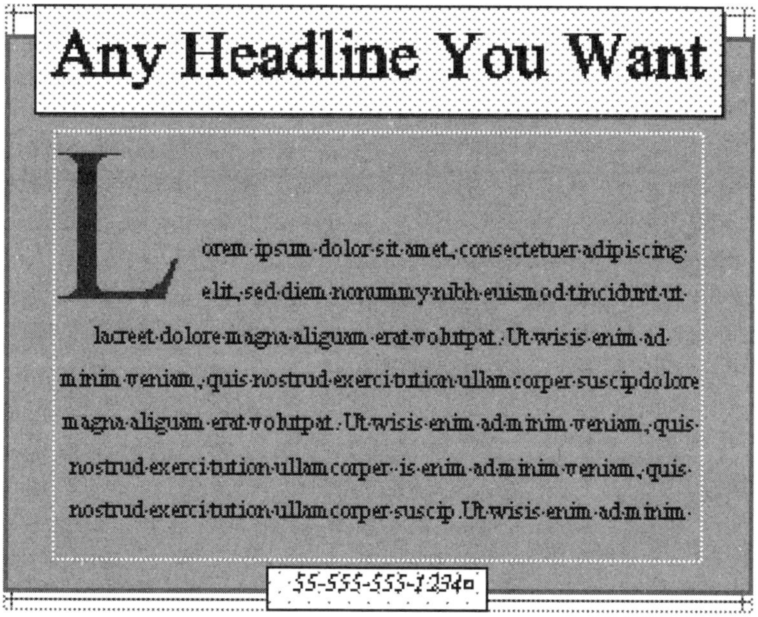

FIGURE 6.24 THE SAMPLE FLYER WITH A FANCY FIRST LETTER.

Changing the Look and Position of a Fancy First Letter

The dialog window also contained a Helpful Hint, suggesting that you might want to create your own Fancy First Letter style. Bring up the Fancy First Letter dialog window again, and click on the **Custom Options...** button to display the Create Custom First Letter dialog window shown in Figure 6.25.

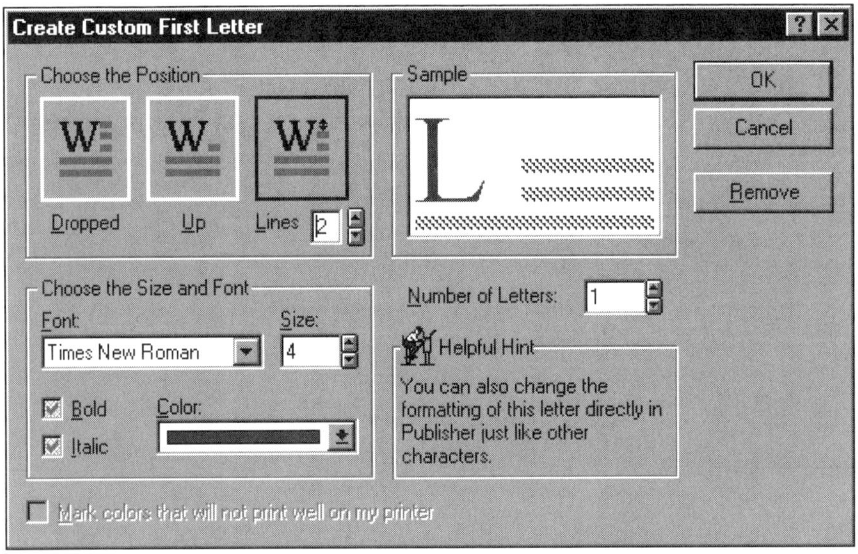

FIGURE 6.25 CREATE CUSTOM FIRST LETTER DIALOG WINDOW.

As the Helpful Hint in this dialog window points out, you can change the first letter formatting just like any other text formatting in a text frame. But this makes it so much easier! The settings shown in Figure 6.25 reflect the current settings, in other words the settings that match the First Letter style I selected a moment ago.

Position refers to whether the first letter extends below the first line of text (Dropped), above the first line of text (Up), or adjacent to a specified number of lines (Lines). The current position is set at 2 Lines. Click on the other position options and see how they alter the look of your current setting.

You can also change the Font, Size, Color, Bold, and Italic attributes from inside this dialog window. And lastly, you can apply your fancy style to any number of letters you specify. The first word is five characters, so I changed the Number of Letters to 5. Figure 6.26 shows the result.

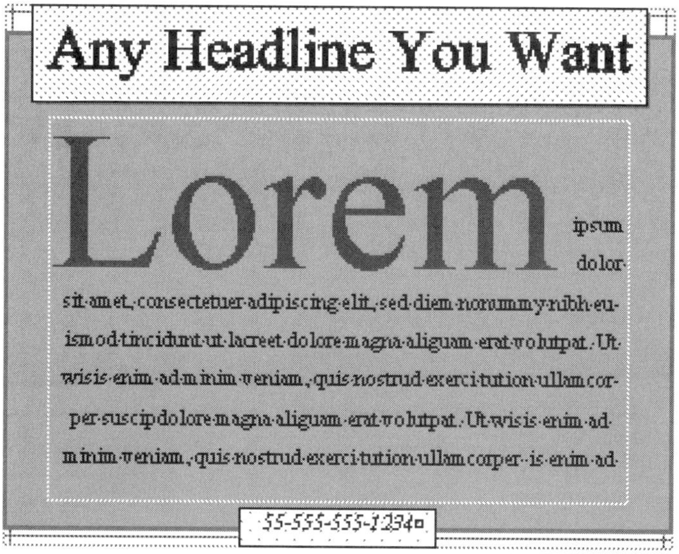

FIGURE 6.26 THE SAMPLE FLYER WITH A FANCY FIRST LETTER STYLE APPLIED TO THE FIRST WORD.

EXPLORING THE DESIGN GALLERY

In Chapters 2 through 5, I covered most of the object tools on the vertical toolbar. One of the remaining buttons, and the largest, is the Design Gallery button. It's the one that looks like a house. Similar to the ClipArt Gallery, the Design Gallery is a collection of design objects that you can add to your publications. Click on the button to bring up the Gallery dialog window.

NOTE

You can also access the Design Gallery by selecting that option from the Tools menu.

Categories and Styles of Gallery Objects

The Gallery objects are initially grouped into six categories. I say *initially*, because you can add, rename, and delete categories to suit your needs and working methods, and I'll show you how in a few minutes. First, let's browse around a bit. When the dialog appears, it opens to the category and style you used last. The first time you call up the Gallery dialog window it opens to the first category (Headlines), in the first style (Classic), as shown in Figure 6.27.

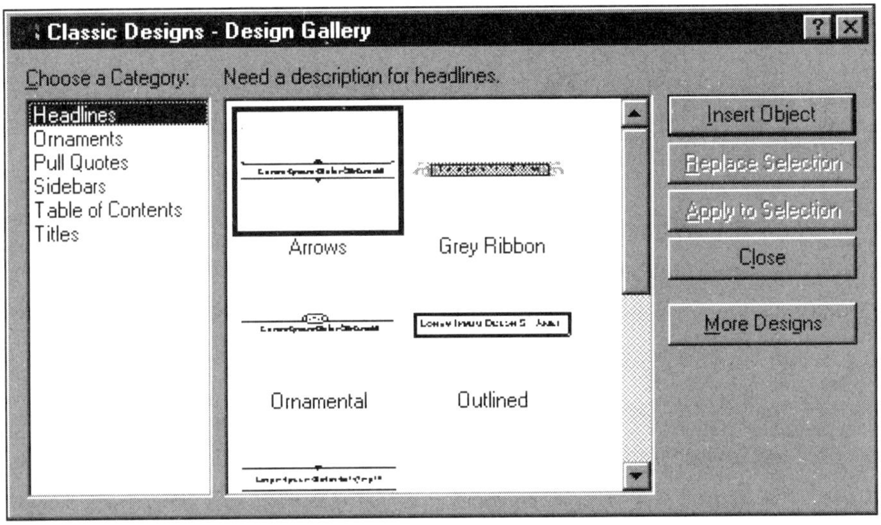

FIGURE 6.27 THE DESIGN GALLERY DIALOG WINDOW SHOWING HEADLINE OBJECTS IN THE CLASSIC STYLE.

Now select on the Ornaments category, and change the style by clicking on the **More Designs** button and choosing **Modern** from the pop-up menu. Your dialog should look like the one shown in Figure 6.28.

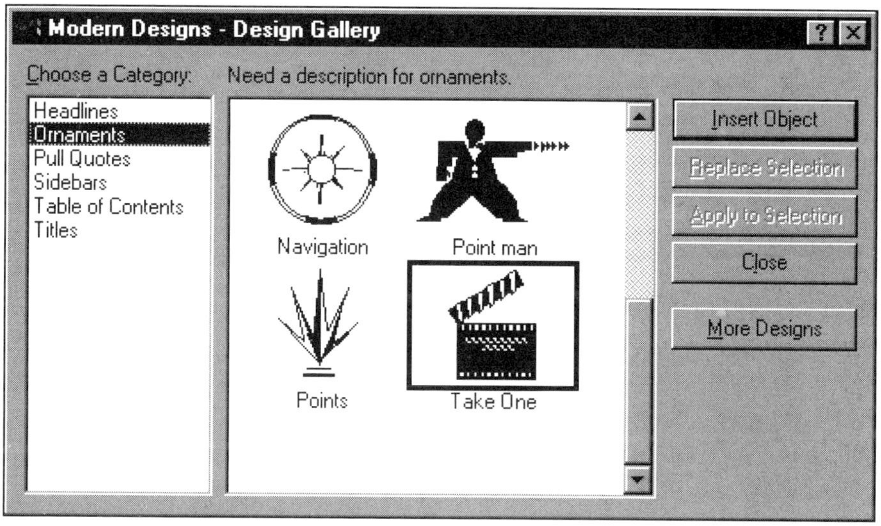

FIGURE 6.28 THE DESIGN GALLERY DIALOG WINDOW SHOWING ORNAMENT OBJECTS IN THE MODERN STYLE.

Next, check out the Pull Quote objects in the Jazzy style, and the Title objects in the Plain style, as shown in Figures 6.29 and 6.30 respectively. Pull Quotes are great for catching the reader's attention and getting them interested in reading the rest of the article. Keep browsing the categories and styles so that you get a feel for the objects that are available for your use. Also keep in mind that once you insert a Design Gallery object into your publication, you can alter the object as desired.

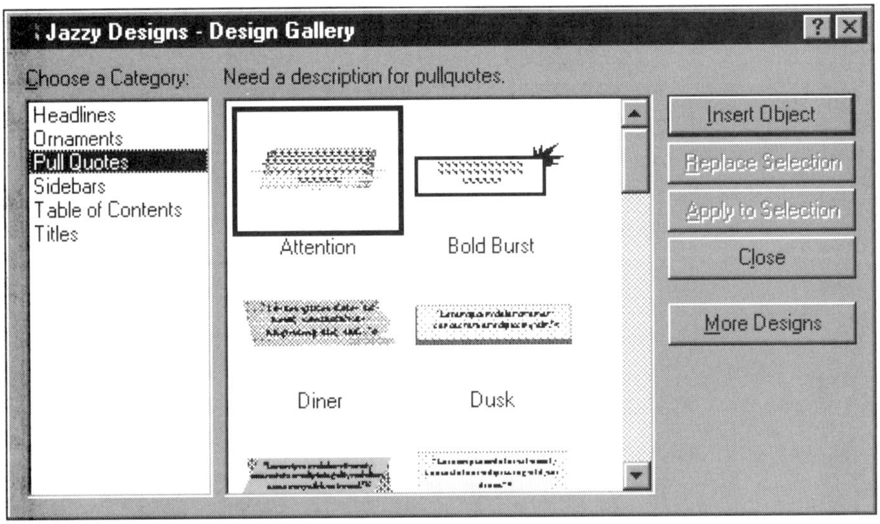

FIGURE 6.29 THE DESIGN GALLERY DIALOG WINDOW SHOWING PULL QUOTE OBJECTS IN THE JAZZY STYLE.

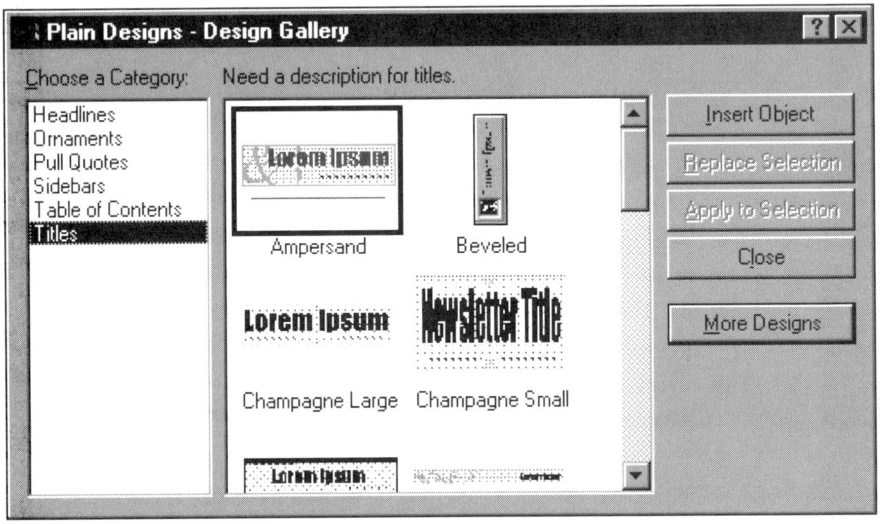

FIGURE 6.30 THE DESIGN GALLERY DIALOG WINDOW SHOWING TITLE OBJECTS IN THE PLAIN STYLE.

The four styles—Classic, Modern, Plain and Jazzy—should sound familiar to you, as many of the PageWizards asked you to select a style in which to create the various publications. Microsoft created the Design Gallery objects in these same styles so that when you use a PageWizard, you can add design objects that will match in style. Each style represents a design set.

While the styles match, the Gallery objects themselves are not the same as those used by the PageWizard. The Gallery objects are additional. Therefore, if there is an object that you really like in a publication created by a PageWizard, you might want to add that object to the Design Gallery yourself. How? It's pretty easy. First you have to decide whether you want to add it to the Design Gallery for a specific publication you are creating, or if you want to add it to the Classic, Modern, Jazzy, or Plain sections that are available to all publications. I'll show you how to do it both ways.

Organizing the Design Gallery

In addition to adding objects to the Design Gallery, both for a specific publication or for all publications, you can also add and modify the object categories, and you can also import design objects from other publications.

Adding an Object to the Design Set for the Current Publication

First you have to create and format the object. If you saved the Phone Log publication from earlier in this chapter, open it now so you can add the custom wingding border to the Design Gallery for that publication. Select the border (it should be a group object comprised of the four text frames), and select the **Add Selection to Design Gallery...** option from Publisher's Tools menu to bring up the Adding an Object dialog window as shown in Figure 6.31

NOTE

Alternatively, you can click on the Design Gallery button. Then when the dialog appears, click on the **More Designs** button and select **Designs for Publication Name**, where publication name is the name you assigned when you saved the publication. (So far, there are no objects in the design set for this publication.) Now click on the **More Designs** button again, and select the **Add Selection to Design Gallery...** option from the popup menu to bring up the Adding an Object dialog window as shown in Figure 6.31

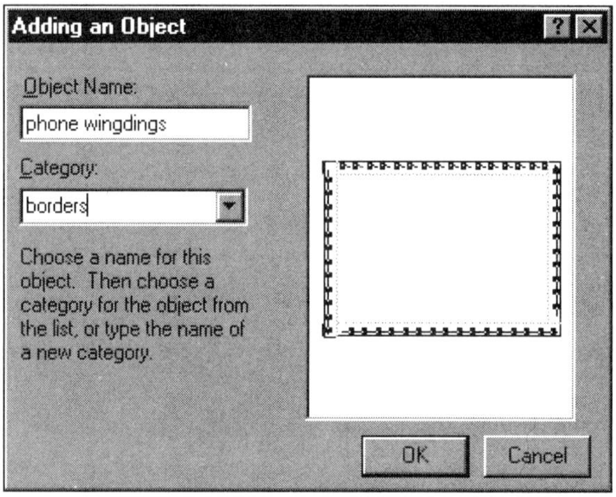

FIGURE 6.31 THE ADDING AN OBJECT DIALOG WINDOW USED WHEN ADDING OBJECTS TO THE DESIGN GALLERY.

Enter a name for the object in the Object Name box, and a category in the Category box. When you click on **OK**, a small dialog window appears with the new category name. Enter a description as shown in Figure 6.32.

NOTE

Once you have saved a design object for a specific publication, you have the option of selecting an existing category from the list box or entering a new category name.

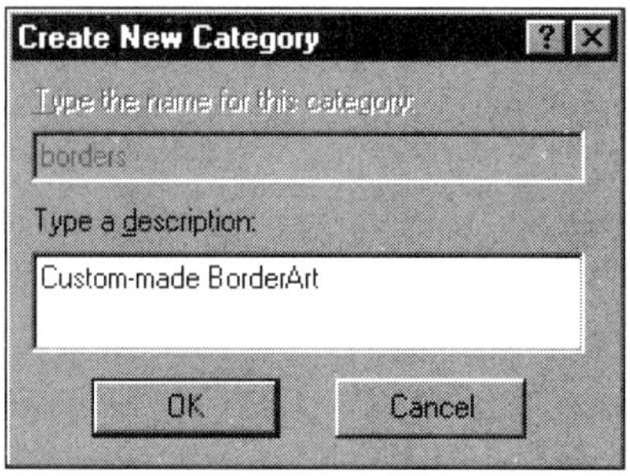

FIGURE 6.32 THE CREATE NEW CATEGORY DIALOG WINDOW USED WHEN ADDING CATEGORIES TO THE DESIGN GALLERY.

The next time you access the Design Gallery, the Gallery dialog window will look something like the one shown in Figure 6.33. Whenever you add a design object to the Design Gallery for your publication, it adds to the size of your publication file. If you add a lot of design objects, the file could get quite large. You might want to consider adding the design objects to one of Publisher's design sets as these are saved in their own separate publication files and will not impact your publication's file size.

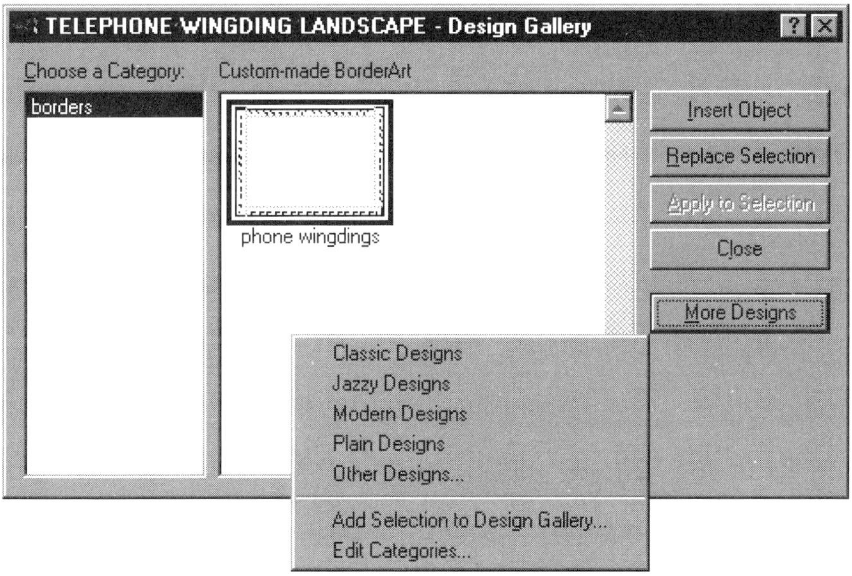

FIGURE 6.33 THE DESIGN GALLERY DIALOG WINDOW AFTER ADDING YOUR PHONE WINGDINGS OBJECT TO THE BORDERS CATEGORY.

Adding an Object to One of Publisher's Design Sets

Publisher Design sets are created and stored in their own publications. For example, the Classic Designs can be found in CLASSIC.PUB. Open that publication, create and format the object, select it, Click on the **Add Selection To Design Gallery...** option on the Tools menu, enter an Object Name and assign a category or create a new one. Click **Close**. Don't forget to save the publication. Next time you open the Design Gallery from any publication your new object(s) will be there.

Importing Designs From Other Publications

As you've now seen, the Design Gallery already accesses Classic, Jazzy, Modern, and Plain design sets no matter what publication you have open. If you want to use one or more design objects from some other publication, open the Design Gallery dialog window, click on **More Designs**, and select **Other Designs...** from the popup menu. Find the publication you want, select it, and click on **OK**.

For example, I already saved the corner hearts custom-made border in the Design Gallery of my Valentine publication. If I want to insert that border in the Phone Log publication, all I have to do is select **Design Gallery...** from the Tools menu, click on the **More Designs** button, and select **Other Designs...** from the popup menu. When the Other Designs dialog appears, I select the Valentine publication as shown in Figure 6.34 and click on **OK**.

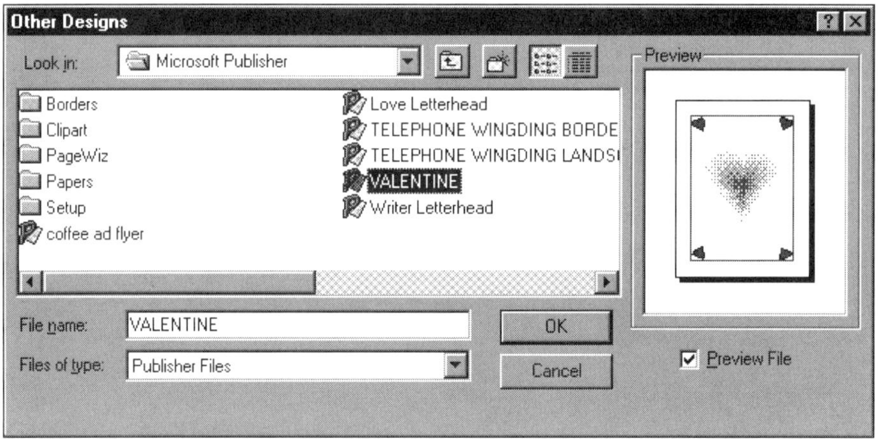

FIGURE 6.34 THE OTHER DESIGNS DIALOG WINDOW.

When the Design Gallery dialog window reappears, you'll see the Valentine Design Gallery displayed, and the Phone Log publications design set still available on the popup menu as shown in Figure 6.35.

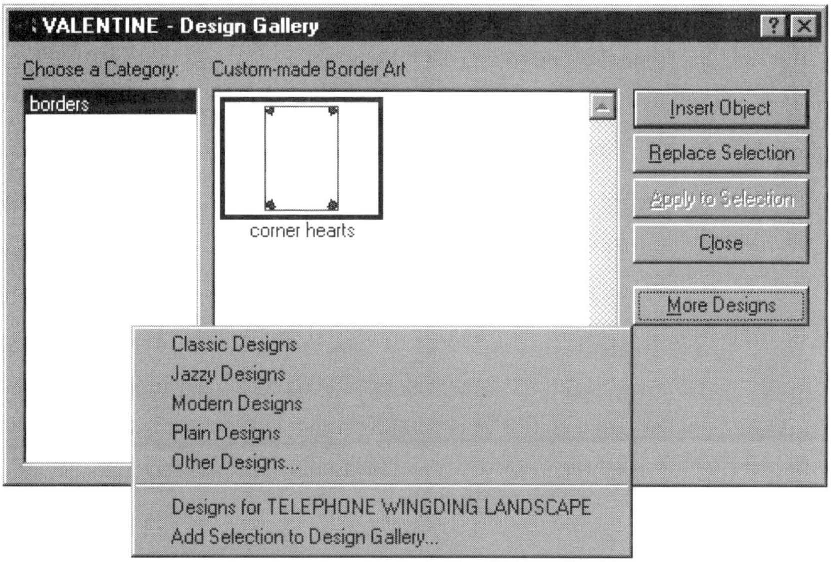

FIGURE 6.35 THE VALENTINE DESIGN GALLERY IS NOW OPEN, EVEN THOUGH YOU ARE STILL WORKING WITH THE PHONE LOG PUBLICATION.

Editing Categories

When you are working with the design set for your current publication, you can add new categories, as well as Edit, Rename, and Delete them. All you have to do is right-click anywhere in the Choose A Category section of the Design Gallery dialog window. When you select New Category from the popup menu, the same Create New Category dialog window you saw earlier appears. This time you have to enter both the category name and description.

If you select the **Rename This Category** option, the same dialog window appears only this time it's called Rename Category and the current name and description are displayed. The Edit Categories option brings up a different dialog that lists all of the existing categories, and contains four buttons: **Delete Category, Rename Category..., New Category...,** and **Close..**

You can also edit and add categories to the Publisher design sets, but just as with adding design objects to those sets, you have to open the Classic, Jazzy, Modern, or Plain publication first.

Don't forget to save the publication!

Adding Design Gallery Objects to Your Publication

By now you should be quite familiar with the workings of the Design Gallery. The only basic thing I haven't covered explicitly is how you actually place a Design Gallery object on your page. Once you find the object you want by browsing the categories and styles, you can either double-click on it, select it and use the **Insert Object** button, or right-click on it and select **Insert This Object** from the popup menu. Click on **Close** to make the dialog window disappear.

Replacing an Existing Object with a Design Gallery Object

If you select an object on your publication page, and then click on the **Design Gallery** object tool, the same Design Gallery dialog window appears. This time, however, the **Replace Selection** button is available. You can select a design object and use the **Replace Selection** button to replace the existing object on your page with the newly chosen object from the Design Gallery.

If you select an object on your publication page, and then by mistake you use **Insert Object** button in the Design Gallery, Publisher inserts your newly chosen object into the same frame as the existing object, resulting in two objects stuffed into a single frame. You can use the **Undo** option on the Edit menu to rectify such a mistake.

Changing Object Formatting using the Design Gallery

You can apply the formatting of Design Gallery objects to an object in your publication, provided that the design object is composed of a single object, such as a single text frame or shape. First select the object on your page to which you want to apply the formatting, then access Design

Gallery, find the element with the desired formatting, and click on **Apply To Selection**. If this button is not available, it is because you selected a complex object with formatting that cannot be copied.

SUMMARY

- BorderArt and Borders are two entirely different things.
- BorderArt can only be used with frames and boxes.
- A consistent look and feel is essential to good design. Design elements should be chosen carefully to blend into the feel of the publication you are creating. Contrasting elements should also be chosen carefully to create the appropriate visual impact for your audience.
- Watermarks can add a professional visual impact for your publication. Place the items for your watermark in the background of your publication. Switch to the foreground by pressing **Ctrl+M** and you'll be able to place anything you wish on top of the watermark.
- Wingdings make great custom borders. Create them by placing your wingding characters in long narrow text frames and then copy and rotate them for each of the other three sides of the page.
- Wingdings can also be used for your own custom bullets. Create a text frame and select **Symbol...** from the Insert menu. Then select a character from the Wingding character sets for your bullet.
- Drop Caps, or Fancy First Letters in Publisher's vernacular, create a professional look to your documents. Choose **Fancy First Letter** from the Format menu and select the settings that best fit your text.
- The Design Gallery is similar to the ClipArt Gallery and contains a number of colorful objects you can incorporate into your designs. You can also add designs of your own into the gallery.

CHAPTER 7

PUTTING IT ALL TOGETHER

- Creating multi-page documents
- Changing the style and feel of publications
- Using pull-quotes
- Tying together text on separate pages
- Editing text already in place

By now, you've seen lots of sample publications created by the Publisher PageWizard, and you've learned a lot about all the bits and pieces that make up a publication. In this chapter, you'll look at two more—a Business Hours sign and a sample Newsletter—and examine some of the design features used. Then I'll show you the last few tools and features that you can use to create one last publication—a semi-annual report—from scratch.

SAMPLE HOURS OF BUSINESS SIGN

Select **Create New Publication...** from your File menu and launch the Sign PageWizard. When asked *What type of sign would you like?,* select **Business**. Then, choose the Hours of Business sign and let the PageWizard **CreateIt!**

This publication (see Figure 7.1) consists of five objects. A WordArt frame, a custom shape, and a ClipArt clock, all layered one atop the other, plus two individual text frames. You experimented with layering in Chapter 6. Here you can see that the WordArt frame is on the topmost layer, and that it is transparent so that the yellow banner shape shows through. The shape is on the middle layer, and it obscures part of the clock, so it is not transparent. Finally, the clock ClipArt is on the bottom.

FIGURE 7.1 THE BUSINESS HOURS SIGN AS CREATED BY THE PAGEWIZARD.

Now take a look at this particular piece of ClipArt. It's all one object, but the design is of a round clock with a pale purple face and a greenish rim, on top of a dark purple square. The darker square adds dimension, gives the image greater impact, and creates a certain style for the sign. Check it out for yourself by substituting a different clock image and comparing the results.

Double-click on the frame to bring up the ClipArt Gallery, and select the **Business** category. You'll see that the ClipArt used by the PageWizard is called CLOCK3.CGM. Select the black and white clock (CLOCK1.CGM) and click on **Insert**. The result is shown in Figure 7.2. Now the sign is more conservative in feel. Some may prefer its simplicity, but it doesn't seem to have the same punch as the PageWizard's version.

FIGURE 7.2 THE BUSINESS HOURS SIGN, SUBSTITUTING THE CLOCK1.CGM CLIPART IMAGE.

Try one more substitution. This time select the FUNCLOCK.CGM image. The sign does seem to have a fun feeling now (see Figure 7.3). The yellow stars on the clipart even match well with the yellow banner shape giving it a unified look. Notice, however, that because the clock face is the same blue color as the square part of the design, it feels flatter than the PageWizard's choice.

FIGURE 7.3 THE BUSINESS HOURS SIGN, SUBSTITUTING THE FUNCLOCK.CGM CLIPART IMAGE.

Now let's move on the a more complex publication... a newsletter.

SAMPLE JAZZY NEWSLETTER

When asked *What style do you want?*, select **Jazzy**. Your newsletter should have three columns, and two stories on first page. The title of my personal newsletter that I send out once in a blue moon to friends is called Tempus Fugit, but you can enter any title you want. Include all three options offered: Table of Contents, Date, and Volume and Issue, entering whatever values you want. We're only going to look at the first page for now, so unless you're going to explore them on your own, there's no need for the PageWizard to create four pages. With only one page you will not need to print on both sides, so select **No** when prompted. Then let the PageWizard do its thing. Figure 7.4 shows a full-page view of the one-page newsletter.

FIGURE 7.4 FULL-PAGE VIEW OF A JAZZY STYLE NEWSLETTER CREATED BY THE PAGEWIZARD.

Overall balance is an important consideration. The reverse text frames (white on black) along the left side and top left corner could make the page side-heavy. However, the large title, placed at an angle, serves to draw the readers eye from the left toward the upper right. This, added to the Table of Contents heading in the lower right corner, plus the placement of the picture in the lower right quadrant, serve to balance the page. Also, the amount of white space around the headings and text of the articles helps counteract the dark elements.

The Table of Contents

The Table of Contents created by PageWizard is just a table object, with the first row only formatted for reverse text. If you want a different look, you can create your own or see if there's a table of contents object in the

Design Gallery that you like better. To replace the current object with one from the Gallery, click on it first to select it before opening the Design Gallery dialog window.

Remember consistency is an important consideration. You chose a jazzy style for the newsletter, so you should look at the table of contents objects in the Jazzy Designs set. Choose your category, then click on **More Designs** and select **Jazzy Designs**. With all of the reverse text in this publication, you'll need to find an object that will maintain the balance of the page. Bold Burst (see Figure 7.5) is probably your best bet, but you can experiment with others to see the effect. Select one and click on **Replace Selection**.

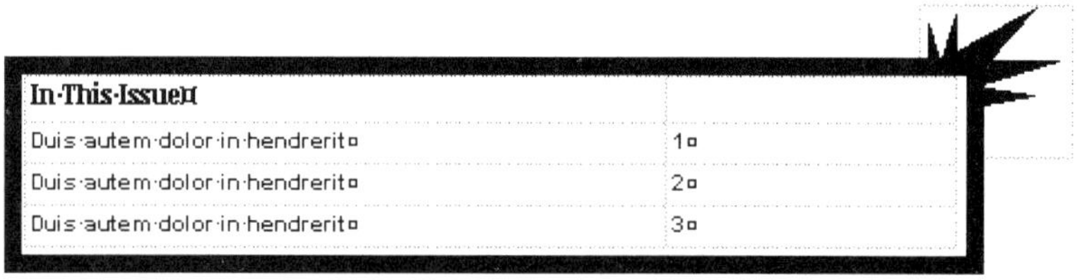

FIGURE 7.5 THE BOLD BURST TABLE OF CONTENTS OBJECT FROM THE DESIGN GALLERY'S SET OF JAZZY DESIGNS.

As you can see from Figure 7.6, this did not work out exactly right. The new object from the Design Gallery is a group object, and when Publisher replaced the original four-row table with this new element, the sizes were not a match. As a result, the table object within the group fell outside the boundaries of the box object. Furthermore, the group object as a whole collided with the page's background line object and page number.

FIGURE 7.6 THE BOTTOM PORTION OF THE NEWSLETTER AFTER REPLACING THE ORIGINAL TABLE OF CONTENTS WITH AN OBJECT FROM THE DESIGN GALLERY.

When something like this happens, you can choose the **Undo** option and go back to the original design. Or, if you like the style, you can resize the individual objects within the group so that they fit each other and the page. In this case, the fix is an easy one. First, ungroup the table of contents object. Then, select the box object and resize the bottom so that it encompasses the last row of the table object. Then regroup the box, table, and starburst objects, and move the group up just above the bottom line of the page. Figure 7.7 shows the new table of contents object on the newsletter page after the repair.

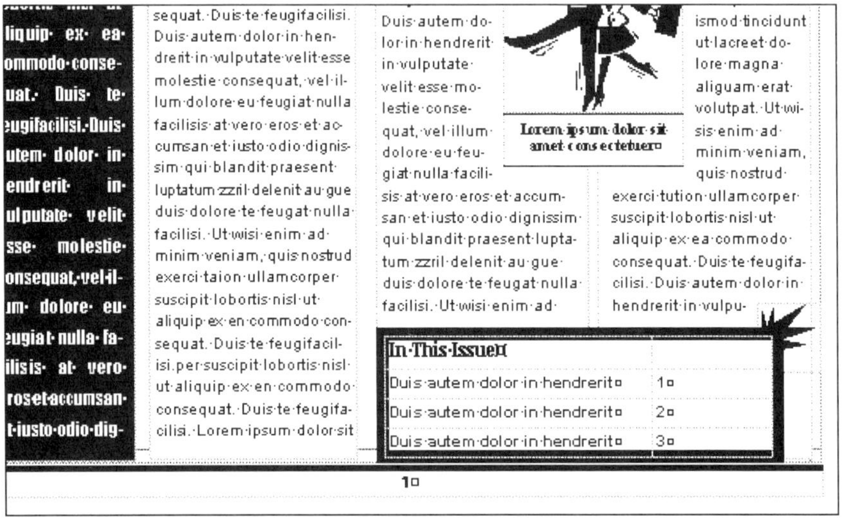

FIGURE 7.7 THE BOTTOM PORTION OF THE NEWSLETTER AFTER READJUSTING THE NEW TABLE OF CONTENTS OBJECT FROM THE DESIGN GALLERY.

The Picture and Caption

Unless a picture is completely self-explanatory, you should include a caption. When designing the layout and style of your captions, you want to be sure that your readers can clearly see which caption goes with which illustration. They should also be able to easily distinguish caption text from the text of an article. In the sample jazzy newsletter these goals are achieved by the use of white space.

Caption designs generally use formatting such as a smaller font, color, italic or bold print, or some combination of these formatting styles. Additionally, caption frames often have a line or border to separate them from the rest of the text. Here the font for the caption is Arial 9 point bold, in contrast to the article text which is plain Arial 10 point. Also, the caption frame has a thin top and bottom border line. The picture and caption frames join at the edge, and form a group object as shown in Figure 7.8.

TIP

The style applied to pictures and their captions should be consistent throughout the publication. It's also a good idea not to use too many different font types on a single page.

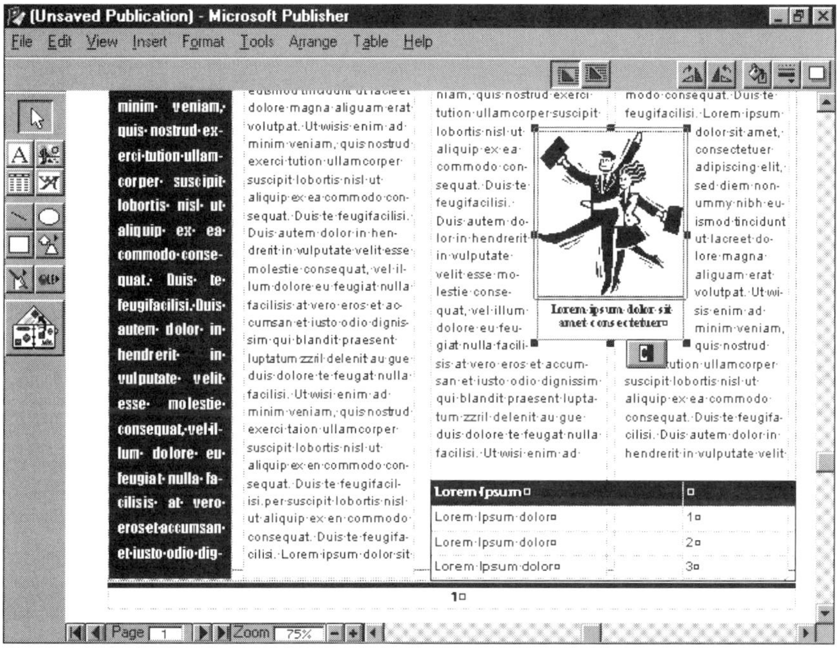

FIGURE 7.8 SECTION OF A JAZZY STYLE NEWSLETTER SHOWING THE PICTURE/CAPTION GROUP OBJECT.

Now let's take a look at another newsletter publication using a different design style.

SAMPLE TRADITIONAL NEWSLETTER

When asked *What style do you want?*, select **Traditional**. This newsletter should also have three columns, and two stories on first page. Again, you can enter any title you want. Include all three options offered: Table of

Contents, Date, and Volume and Issue, entering whatever values you want. Accept the default of four pages. Say **Yes** to room for a mailing label on the back, and **Yes** to printing on both sides of the paper. When the PageWizard is done, the first page of the newsletter should look like the one shown in Figure 7.9.

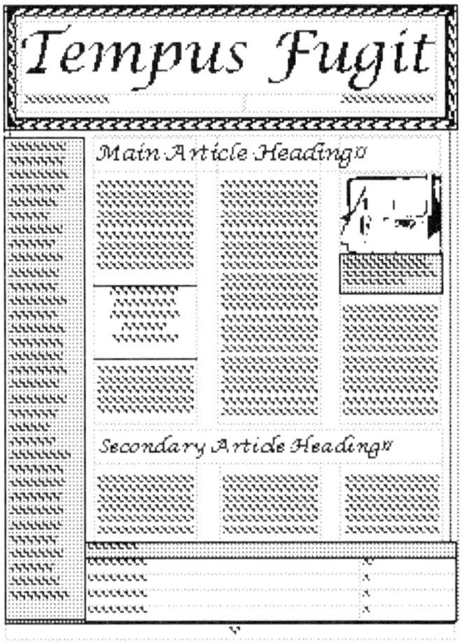

FIGURE 7.9 FULL-PAGE VIEW OF A TRADITIONAL STYLE NEWSLETTER CREATED BY THE PAGEWIZARD.

This traditional design has a boxier feel to it. Some might even describe it as neater. Compare the two. The jazzy design created the appearance of unusual shapes. For example, the two reverse-print frames (one in the top left corner, and one along the left side) created an L-shape. And the angle of the title frame was visually at odds with the rest of the page. The two articles were places unevenly on the page, one starting slightly higher than the other. And finally, the picture and caption were placed in the middle of two columns, not in one column or the other.

By comparison, everything on the traditional design page appears to be in its expected place. The title appears within a box with a BorderArt border, and sits neatly flush at the top of the page. The caption frame has a four-sided border forming a box, and both the pull-quote and the picture/caption elements are box-like in shape. Finally, all the columns are neatly aligned. The jazzy style maintained consistency in it's use of formatting, but it did not feel as stable, or perhaps I should say staid, as this design style. I guess that's while it's called traditional.

The Pull Quote

A pull-quote is a quote taken from the body of an article and set apart for the purpose of attracting the reader's attention to the article in question. You want to pick a quote that will, as the PageWizard suggests, *pique your reader's interest.* Pull-quotes should stand out. Just as with captions, your reader should have no trouble distinguishing a pull-quote from the body of the article. However, it should also be clear in which article the quote appears. The jazzy style newsletter had a pull-quote in the top-left corner of the first page, but it was not clear to me which article it was taken from. Personally, I prefer pull-quotes that appear somewhere within the body of the article.

The formatting for pull-quote style used in the traditional newsletter (see Figure 7.10), includes a top and bottom border line and ample white space to make it stand out from the article. Also, a different font style is used to provide greater contrast and visibility. The Font for the article text is Times New Roman, while the pull-quote font is Lucida Calligraphy. This is the same font style that is used for the title and article headings—all objects that you want the reader to notice at a glance.

TIP

It's never a good idea to use all capital letters in a heading because IT'S HARDER TO READ ALL CAPS. Research shows that people read by recognizing word shapes. Also, it makes some people feel as if you are yelling at them.

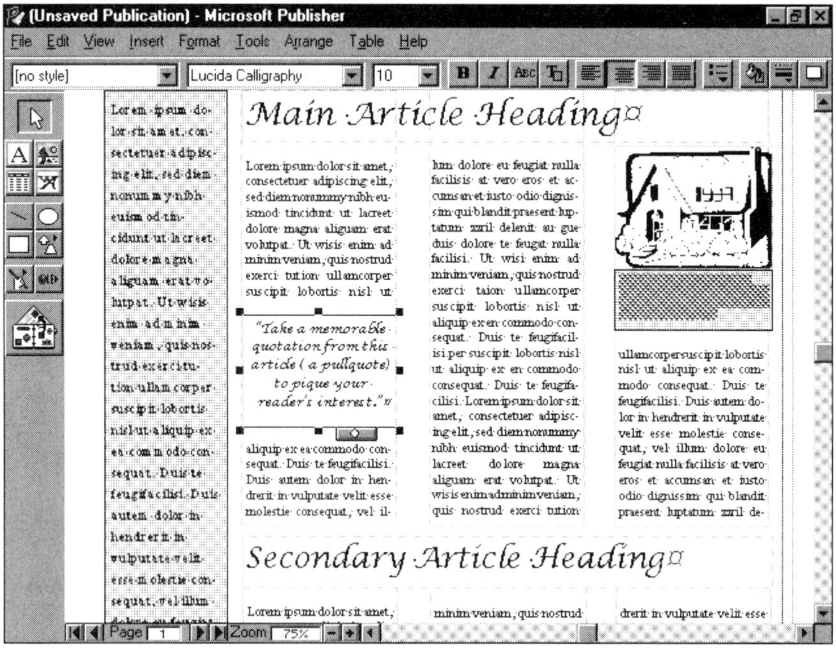

FIGURE 7.10 SECTION OF A TRADITIONAL STYLE NEWSLETTER SHOWING A PULL-QUOTE FRAME.

Facing Pages

Our instructions to the PageWizard specified printing on both sides of a page, so the newsletter layout is designed with facing pages. When you layout facing pages, you place certain elements on a right-page in opposite position to the same element on a left-page, producing a sort of mirror-like effect. This applies only to some, not all, of the objects. Use your statusbar buttons or the **Go to Page...** option on the View menu to move to page two. Then use the **Two-Page Spread** option (also on the View menu) to see pages two and three side-by-side on the screen as shown in Figure 7.11.

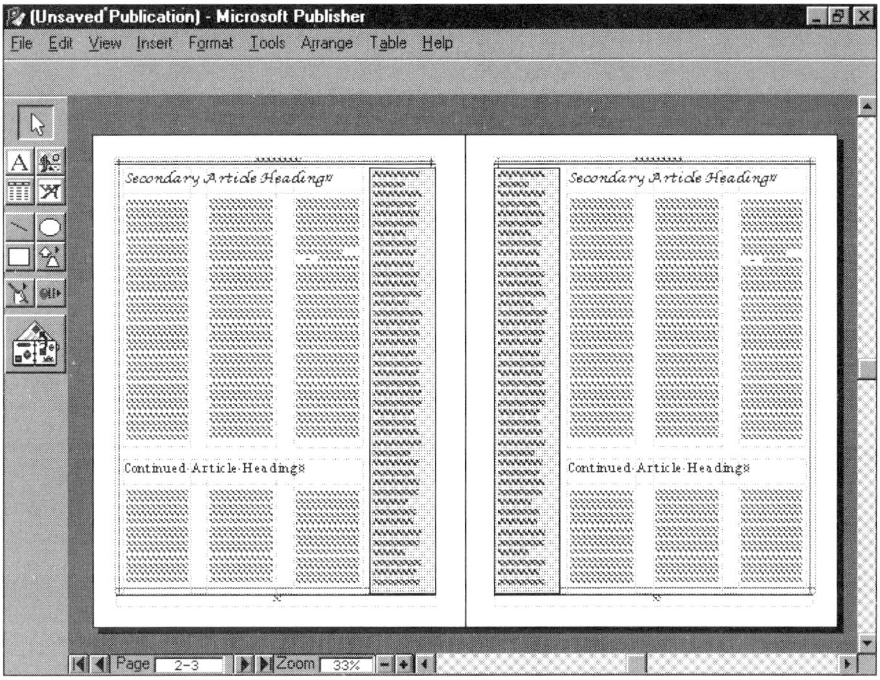

FIGURE 7.11 PAGES TWO AND THREE OF THE TRADITIONAL NEWSLETTER PUBLICATION.

It seems that the only mirrored objects in this publication are the shaded text frames. On the right-pages of the publication (pages 1 and 3) the shaded frame is on the left side, while it appears on the right side of the left-pages (2 and 4). Often, however, you will see publications where the page numbers appear on the top or bottom outside corner of a page. In these cases, the number would be in the left corner on a left page, and the right corner of a right page. If the placement was to be in the inside corner, then it would be on the right corner of a left-page, and the left corner of a right-page, just like the shaded text box you just saw.

The Background Page

In the traditional newsletter created by the PageWizard the page number is on the bottom center of every page. If you look closely, you can also see a black line at the bottom of every page. As you learned in Chapter 6, objects that appear in the background appear on *every* page. And that's where you'll find the page number and line object you see here. Press **Ctrl+M** to view the background and see for yourself.

My emphasis on the word *every* in the last paragraph could be a little bit misleading, because it implies that if you want to you mirror objects on right- and left-hand pages, you can't use the background. Not true! Publisher is smart enough to create right- and left-hand page backgrounds when a publication calls for facing pages.

Page Numbers

Publisher is also smart enough to number your pages for you. You could type in your own page numbers if you really wanted to, but then you couldn't put them on the background. (Remember, whatever is on the background appears on every page.) To create automatic page numbers on the background, create a text frame and use the **Page**... option on the Insert menu. What appears in the frame is the pound symbol (#). Take a look at it on your own screen. Then, when you move back to the foreground, you'll see it change from **#** to the actual page number.

The Last Page

Figure 7.12 shows the last page of the traditional newsletter publication created by the PageWizard. We told the PageWizard that the newsletter would be mailed out, and the layout for this page not only accommodates that request, but also manages to maintain design consistency on two levels.

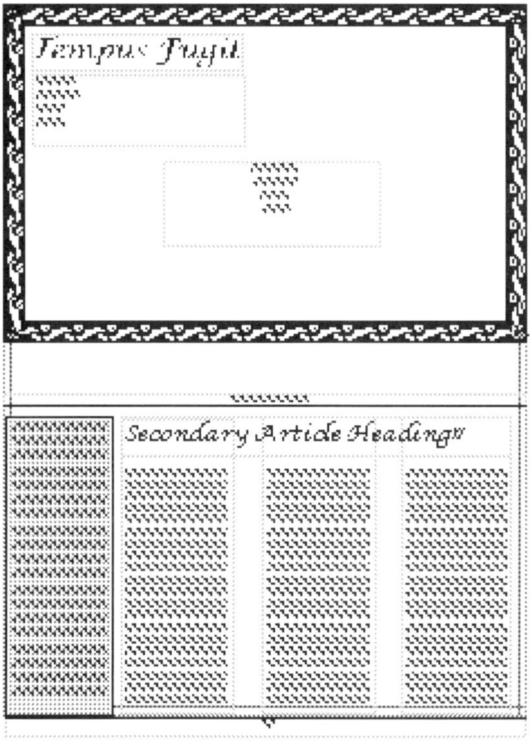

FIGURE 7.12 THE LAST PAGE OF THE TRADITIONAL NEWSLETTER PUBLICATION CREATED BY THE PAGEWIZARD.

As you can see, the page is split so that it can be folded in half and mailed. Also, for the purposes of mailing are two text frames for the addressee and the return address. These two text frames, along with a WordArt frame, are surrounded by the same BorderArt used to border the newsletter title on the first page. First impressions are said to be important. When someone receives this newsletter in the mail, the first thing they will see is the front of the mailing. Then when they open the newsletter, the same visual theme is maintained on the front page.

Page four is a left-page, so the bottom half of page four is treated the same as the other left page, with the shaded frame along the left side of the page. You will also find consistency in the use of the Lucida Calligraphy font for the title and the article heading. On this page in particular, it serves to tie together the top and bottom halves of the page.

Enough analysis and examination of PageWizard creations. It's time to create another publication from scratch.

SAMPLE ANNUAL REPORT

In this section you'll work on the layout of a four-page report. Like the traditional newsletter you examined in the last section, the report is also designed to be printed on both sides of the page. The first order of business is to create the background objects as shown in Figure 7.13. The design calls for page numbers in the lower outer corners. The page number itself should be red, and the text frame for the page number should be transparent and placed on top of a black diamond shape.

FIGURE 7.13 THE COMPLETED BACKGROUND (RIGHT-PAGE).

Once you create both the page number and the diamond shapes objects, you can hold down the **Shift** key and click on each one. Then, when they are both selected, bring up the **Line Up Objects...** dialog window by selecting that option on the Arrange menu. When the dialog window appears, specify Centers in both the Left to Right and the Top to Bottom sections and click on **OK**. This will place the page number frame directly in the center of the diamond. You may also choose to make these two objects into a group.

The background design also calls for two design lines, one along the bottom grid line, and the other along the outer grid line. The last object in the background is a WordArt watermark. The lettering, which reads 1995, is in the Slant Up (More) style, the font is Arial Rounded MT, and the font size is Best Fit. Because it is a watermark, the lettering is shaded instead of solid. Figure 7.14 shows the settings in the WordArt Shading dialog window. After you create the WordArt, select only that frame and use the **Line Up Objects** feature again. When you select **Center** this time, Publisher will center the WordArt frame on the page.

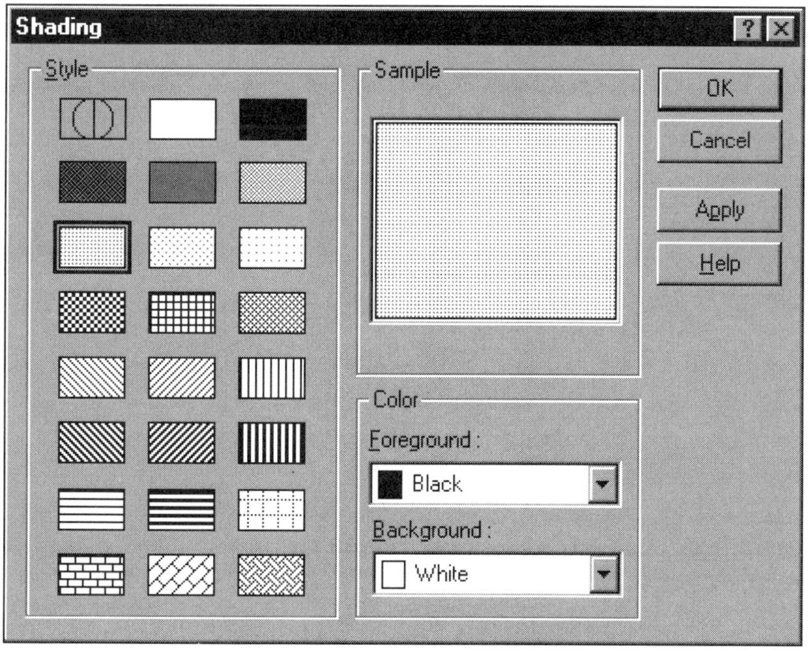

FIGURE 7.14 THE SHADING DIALOG WINDOW, WITH SETTINGS USED FOR THE WATERMARK.

Our next step is to set up some guide lines on the page that will make it easier to position the rest of the objects. Select **Layout Guides...** from the Arrange menu to bring up the Layout Guides dialog window. The settings for this report publication are shown in Figure 7.15. When the dialog first appears, the margins are set at a default of 1"—change this to .5". Then change the default for the Grid Guides from one column and one row, to three columns and five rows.

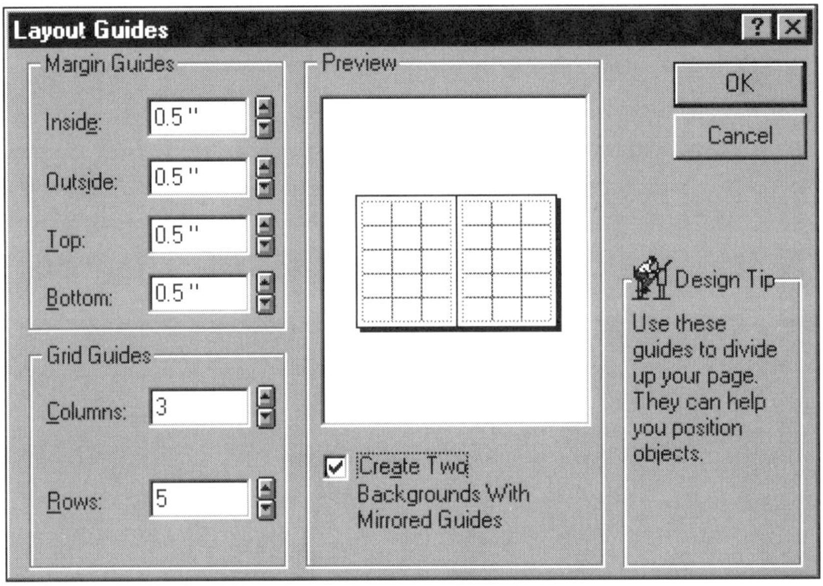

FIGURE 7.15 THE LAYOUT GUIDES DIALOG WINDOW.

Because the report is designed for printing on both sides, you can take advantage of the opportunity to use some mirror elements on facing pages. Place a checkmark in the box beneath the Preview section to create two backgrounds with mirrored guides, and watch the preview display change to show two pages. Click on **OK** to accept your new settings.

NOTE

Because you already placed objects in the background, Publisher will automatically create mirrored objects for facing pages. If you had not placed the objects already, you would have had to construct the left background and the right background separately.

Now would be a good time to add pages, so you can see the facing pages with your mirror backgrounds as shown in Figure 7.16. In previous chapters you have added an occasional page by click on the next page button on the status bar. When the next page did not exist, Publisher asked if you wanted to add a page. Using the **Page...** option on the Insert menu (**Ctrl+Shft+N**) gives you a great deal more control.

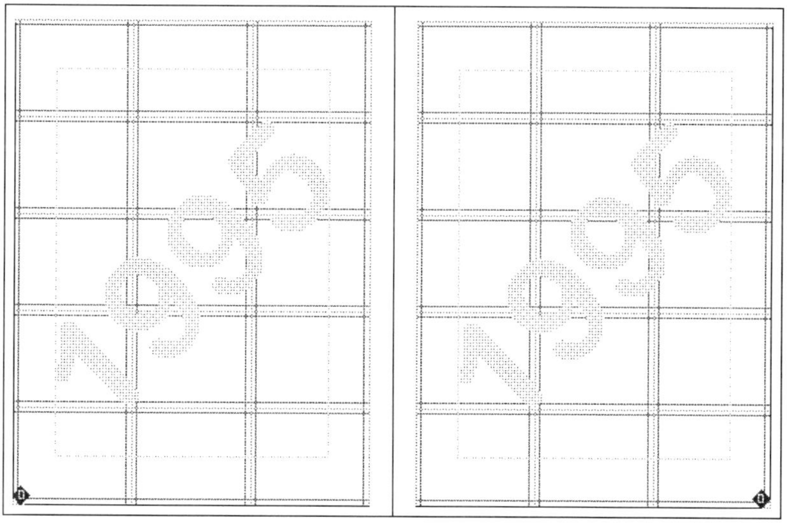

FIGURE 7.16 THE BACKGROUND OF FACING PAGES 2 AND 3, WITH GRID LINES SHOWING.

The Insert Page dialog window (see Figure 7.17) allows you to add several pages at a time, and specify whether you want the new pages to come before or after the current page. If you don't want blank pages, you can also instruct Publisher to create one text frame on each page, or duplicate all of the objects on a specific page.

NOTE

Blank page refers to an absence of objects in the foreground. Publisher automatically copies all objects on the Background.

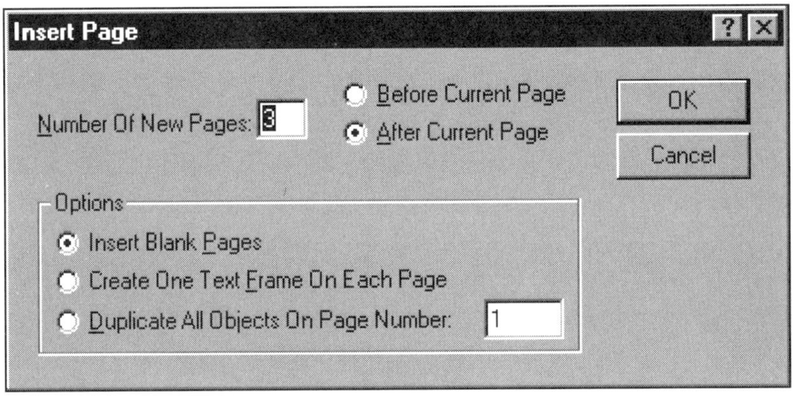

FIGURE 7.17 THE INSERT PAGE DIALOG WINDOW.

Now it's time to tackle the foreground, starting with page one. The first page of the report is a title page and contains only three objects: two WordArt frames and a picture frame for a company logo. The first WordArt frame, containing the Company Name, is 7 inches wide and 3 inches high. The lettering is of the Plain Text style, using the Bookman Old Style font with Best Fit and a shadow. The frame is positioned in the top left corner of the page.

The second WordArt frame is 4.5 inches wide and 1.5 inches high. The words Annual Report are also of the Plain Text style using the Bookman Old Style font with Best Fit, but no shadow. This frame is positioned so that it's bottom edge meets the second horizontal grid line. The picture frame, containing a clipart image, is placed just inside the lower-right corner lines. When you're done, your first page should look something like the one shown in Figure 7.18.

FIGURE 7.18 PAGE ONE OF THE SAMPLE REPORT PUBLICATION.

Now let's move on to the next page. Page two (see left side of Figure 7.19) is designed in a three-column layout, as are pages three and four. The first column of page two contains two sets of picture and caption frames in the same basic style as the ones you examined in the jazzy newsletter publication. The caption is 10 point italicized Times New Roman, and the frame, which has a top and bottom border line, appears immediately below the picture. It's a good idea to group the picture and its caption so that if you have to move them, they can move together. The first group is positioned in the top left corner of the page. The top edge of the second group should meet the second horizontal guide line.

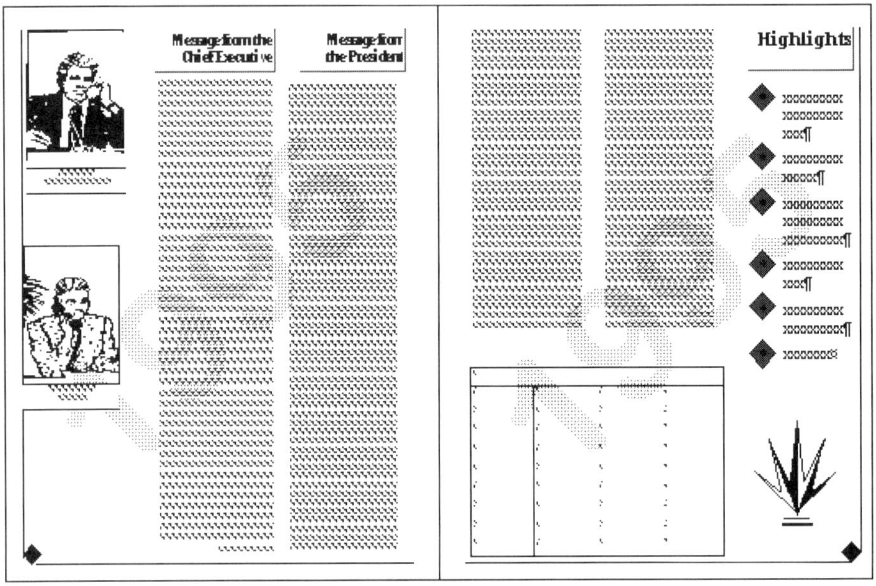

FIGURE 7.19 PAGES TWO AND THREE OF THE SAMPLE REPORT PUBLICATION.

Columns two and three each contain two text frames: a small frame at the top of the column for a heading, and a column-long frame for text. The heading frames have a 2 point red border on the right and bottom edges, and the heading itself is 20 point Rockwell Condensed Bold. You can type in the text, or insert an existing text file. The text format should be the same as the picture captions, Times New Roman, but one or two points larger size.

Page three begins with a continuation of the Message from the President. However, because it is a facing page, you can probably get away without another heading. The design calls for two text frames that take up the top three sections of the page. Most annual reports have some sort of table or chart. This report uses a table that takes up the remaining portion of columns one and two. Alternatively, if you had a chart created by some other program such as Excel, you might want to create an OLE object and link it to that chart.

The third column on page three contains a bulleted list, perhaps of company highlights and achievements. In addition to using a simple text frame and formatting the text as a bulleted list, this design also calls for red diamond shapes to be placed behind each bullet to add a little spot color and pizzazz. The Indents and Lists (Format menu) format settings specify 25 point round bullets, with text left-aligned and indented one-half inch. The text for each item is single spaced, with 12 points between items.

TIP

Bright reds, tan browns, and blues are generally good choices for spot color because they work well as a background to both black and white text, and can also be used for text.

To add the red diamond shapes, use the shapes tool to create a diamond, proportionally resize the shape to the appropriate small size, and fill it with red. Then, move it over one of the bullets and select **Send Farther** from the Arrange menu so that it appears behind the text frame. (Make sure the text frame is transparent.)

Because the round bullets are inside the text frame and not individual objects, you can't use the Line Up Objects to center the bullet inside the diamond this time. You can, however, take advantage of the Nudge feature. Select **Nudge Objects...** to bring up the dialog window shown in Figure 7.20. Here you can click on the appropriate arrow to nudge your object (in this case the diamond) by the specified distance.

Warning: As noted in the dialog window, you can use Alt+arrow keys to nudge objects directly. But be careful—if you add the Control key, you'll find that Ctrl+Alt+arrow key combination works to rotate objects (5 degrees at a time).

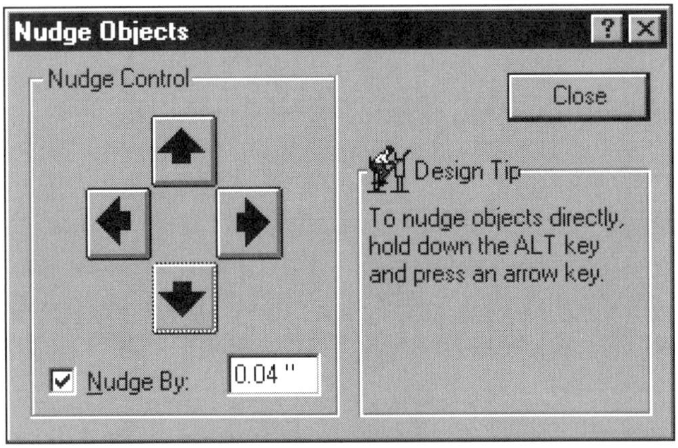

FIGURE 7.20 THE NUDGE OBJECTS DIALOG WINDOW.

The space remaining at the bottom of the third column is a good place for an ornament from the Design Gallery. It's always a judgment call as to whether or not you should fill up your space, or leave it blank. In this case, there was too much empty space, and I found an ornament in the Modern Designs set that was not only small, but full of space itself.

And now comes the fourth and final page (see Figure 7.21). The majority of this page is filled with a single article spread across three text frames, with an additional text frame at the top for the heading. The heading frame is of the same design style as all of the heading frames in this report: Rockwell Condensed Bold text in a frame with red border lines on the right and bottom edges. This time, because the article spans three columns without crossing over a page, the heading frame should also span three columns. This was the bottom border line provides the reader with a visual cue that the article continues in each column.

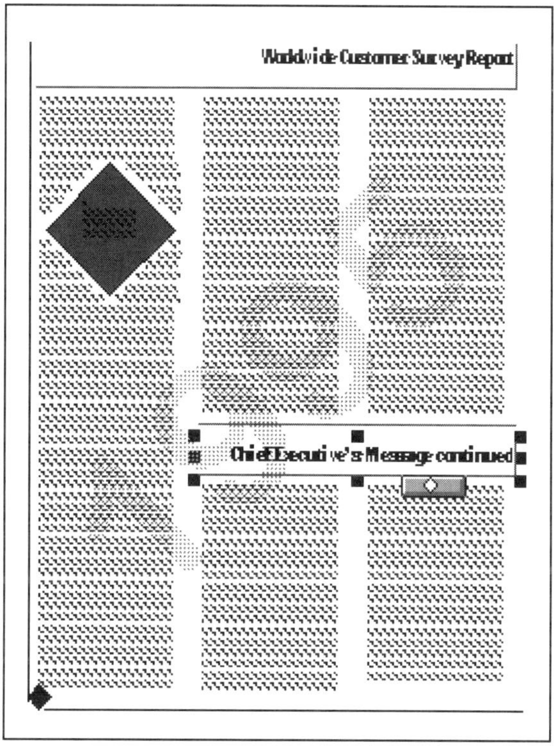

FIGURE 7.21 PAGE FOUR OF THE SAMPLE REPORT PUBLICATION.

There's a pull-quote in the second section of the left column, and again, the text of this quote is on top of a red diamond shape. What is important to note here is that the body text of the article wraps around the irregular shape of the diamond. To clearly mark the end of the article and separate it from the continuation of the Message from the Chief Executive directly below, add a red line.

There are two more text-related features that could be helpful to you at this moment. The first is the *Continued On Page #* and *Continued From Page #* automated option. Once you pour the overflow text from the page-two frame containing the Chief Executive's message into the frames at the bottom of page four, Publisher considers those frames to be linked. Once on page four, I don't think the reader needs to know on what page the piece began, but the Continued On information would be useful on page two.

Go back to page two and right-click on the frame containing the Chief Executive's message. Choose **Text Frame Properties...** from the popup menu, and place a checkmark next to the **Continued On Page...** option. Then click on **OK**. That's all there is to it. Because the frames are already linked, Publisher knows which page number to put in the reference. Figure 7.22 shows an enlarged excerpt of the bottom of the page, with the frame containing the continuation message. The frame object menu also appears in this figure.

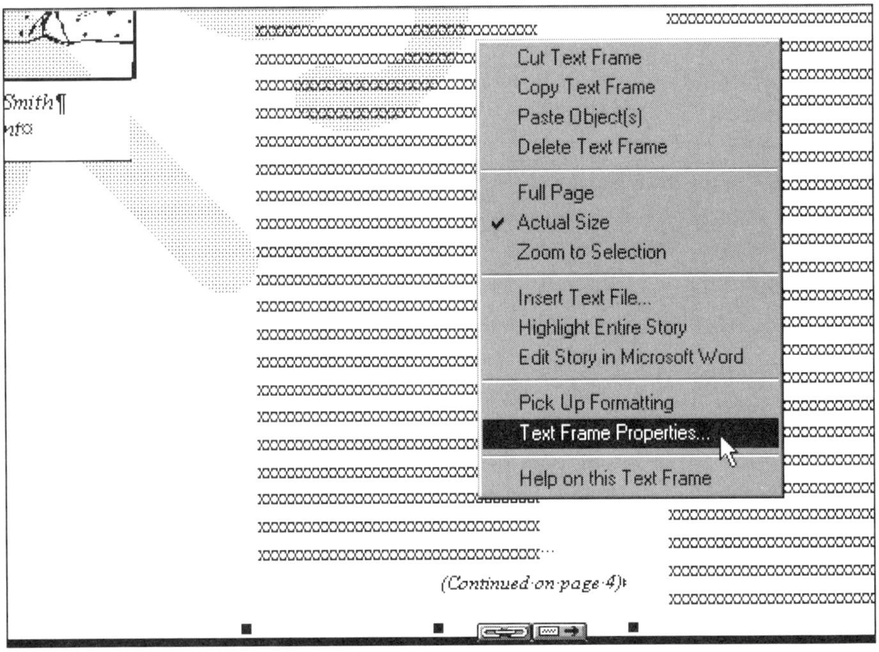

FIGURE 7.22 AN ENLARGED EXCERPT FROM THE BOTTOM OF PAGE TWO, WITH A FRAME CONTAINING A CONTINUATION REFERENCE. USE THE FRAME'S TEXT PROPERTIES TO SELECT THE CONTINUATION OPTION.

The second text-related feature that would be helpful now is the story editing feature. For small editing tasks, you can continue to edit text in your text frames. However, when editing long stories that span two or more pages, it is often desirable to be able to work with the text as a whole. If you look at the popup menu that is shown in Figure 7.22, you'll see the **Edit Story in Microsoft Word** option. Even if you did not create your text using Word, this option launches the Word program in its own window and opens your text. When you are finished editing, and exit from the Word window, your revised story appears in its text frames.

SUMMARY

- ✷ When you create a document using Publisher's Design Gallery, it's a good idea to only use elements from one section in any given publication. That will help you get a consistent feel to the entire document.
- ✷ Pictures in newsletters and similar publications typically have captions telling the reader what the picture is about. Captions usually have a different type weight, design, or even a different type face from the body text of the publication.
- ✷ You can easily number the pages of your document. Move to the background of your document by pressing **Ctrl+M**. Create a text box and select **Page...** from the Insert menu.
- ✷ Pull-quotes help draw attention to a specific article in a publication. You should select the quote carefully in order to draw your reader in. If the quote is unrelated to the text around it, your reader will feel frustrated.
- ✷ If you have Microsoft Word, you can edit a text file that you have already placed on your publication. Just right-click on the text area and select **Edit Story in Microsoft Word** from the popup menu.

CHAPTER 8

COMPATIBILITY AND SHARING

- Copying and pasting pieces of data created in other programs
- Importing existing data files created in other programs
- Linking and Embedding data created in other programs

In this chapter you'll find the basic information you need to incorporate data created by other programs into your publications. Methods vary depending on your needs. You can use the Copy and Paste functions available in all your Windows applications; you can import entire existing files created by other programs using the Insert options; or you can employ the power of OLE.

In addition, Microsoft has added a few convenient menu items that more easily integrate data from Microsoft programs such as Word and Mail. If you have Microsoft Mail installed on your system, you'll find that the **Send...** option on the Publisher File menu has ties to that program.

Most publications contain a lot of text, and Microsoft claims that most Publisher users create their text using Microsoft Word. So Publisher tries to integrate options by providing a menu connection to Word. This is not the only convenience however. As you'll see later in this chapter, if you choose to embed or link a text document, all you have to do to edit that document is double-click on the object to invoke the word processing program that created it.

INSERT ENTIRE FILES

You used the **Text File..., Picture File...,** and **ClipArt...** options from the Insert menu in Chapters 2 and 3. The **Text File...** and **Picture File...** options bring up dialog windows that allows you to select the file. The **ClipArt...** option launches the ClipArt Gallery dialog. In all three cases, whatever you select to insert is imported into your publication in its entirety. In other words, if you insert a text file, you get all of the text in that file. If you insert a picture or a clipart image, you get the whole image.

In order for the **Text File...** option to be available, you must first select a text frame. Then, when you select the file you want inserted, Publisher places a copy of the text from that file into the selected frame. Once inserted in the text frame, you can edit and format the text using any of the features in Publisher. When you insert a text file, Publisher can convert text from the following programs:

- Word 2.0, 6.0, and 7.0 for Windows
- Works 3.0 for Windows and Windows 95 word-processing files with the extension WPS
- Write 3.1 for Windows and Windows 95

- WordPerfect for MS-DOS or
- WordPerfect 5.0, 5.1, and 6.0 for Windows
- Plain Text
- Rich Text Format (files with the extension RTF)

Publisher can also handle many Macintosh word processing formats and a number of other formats. However, these will probably be the most common formats you encounter.

TIP

When you insert text or picture files, you have to know the name of the file you want. However, you do not need to know the name of the program that created the file.

When you insert a picture file, the Insert Picture File dialog window lists the following types of files from which you can choose:

- Windows Bitmaps
- Corel Draw Picture
- Computer Graphics Metafile
- Micrografx_Designer/Draw
- Encapsulated Postscript
- JPEG Filter
- Kodak Photo CD
- PC Paintbrush
- Tagged Image File Format
- Windows Metafiles
- WordPerfect Graphics

Once you insert a picture you cannot edit it. You can, however, resize it, recolor it, and use all of the other features covered in Chapter 3.

COPY AND PASTE

The copy and paste method is the easiest way to copy a piece of data from another program and place it in your publication. Copying and pasting text provides the simplest example. If you want to copy just a paragraph or two from a word-processing document, you would open your word processing program, copy the data, then switch back to the Publisher program and paste the data into the appropriate text frame.

The text you paste into the text frame is just a copy of text from your word processing file. Once inside your text frame, you can edit the text and formatting without having any effect whatsoever on the word processing file from which it came. This also means that once inside your text frame, you no longer have any indication of the source program that was originally used to create the text.

Copying and pasting data from other types of files is only slightly more complicated because you have choices to make about what type of object you want the pasted data to be. Here's an example. I decided that I wanted to place just a part of a graphic image in my publication. In the Chapter 6, Figure 6.2 showed the BorderArt dialog window with the People BorderArt displayed in the Preview section. For this example, I opened that image file (it's a TIF file) in the Microsoft Paint program as shown in Figure 8.1.

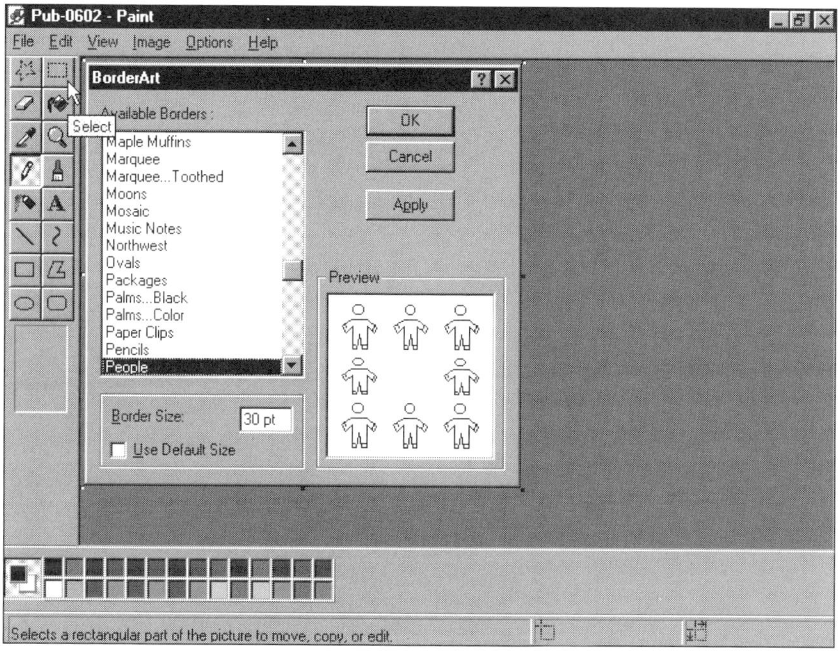

FIGURE 8.1 THE IMAGE FILE FOR FIGURE 6.2 OPENED IN THE PAINT PROGRAM.

Then I used the **Select** tool in the Paint program to drag out the area that I wanted to copy—in this case, the Preview window. Once the area was defined, I selected the **Copy** option from the Edit menu as shown in Figure 8.2.

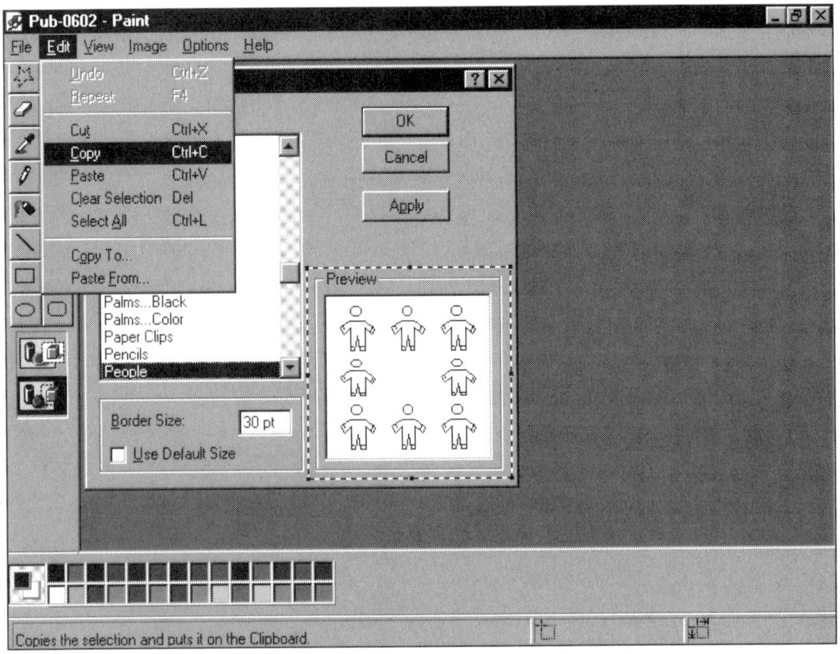

FIGURE 8.2 THE DOTTED LINE AROUND THE PREVIEW SECTION INDICATES THE AREA SELECTED TO COPY INTO THE WINDOWS CLIPBOARD.

Once the data was in my Windows clipboard, I switched back to the Publisher program. Now the decisions begin. There are two Paste options on the Edit menu: **Paste Object** and **Paste Special.** And this brings up a concept called OLE (Object Linking and Embedding). In this particular example, because we're working with a piece of data from a file and not the whole file, both options will create an embedded object.

If you select **Paste Object**, Publisher automatically creates the embedded object and it appears in a frame on your page. When you double-click on this object, you can edit it using the Paint tools that appear within the Publisher program.

But if you select **Paste Special...** the Paste Special dialog window appears as shown in Figure 8.3, and you get to make another decision. The Paste radio button is preselected, and the Paste Link radio button is not available (the option is grayed out), so that's one choice that's already made for you. (You can't create a link to data in the clipboard.) You do, however, have a choice of object types.

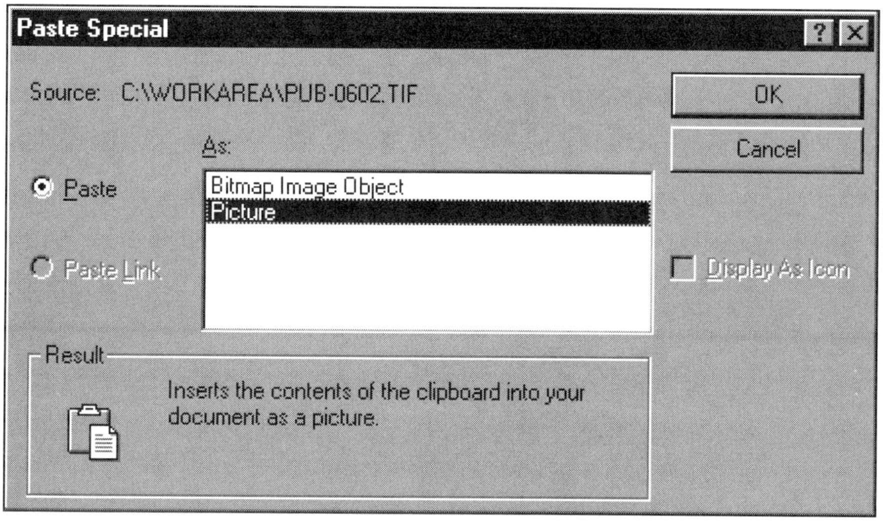

FIGURE 8.3 THE PASTE SPECIAL DIALOG WINDOW.

You can choose to embed the image as a Picture file, or as a Bitmap Image Object. If you choose **Picture**, your object will be device independent, meaning you will be unable to edit it. When you double-click on such an object, the Insert Picture File dialog appears. However, if you choose **Bitmap Image Object**, you can activate the Paint program tools from inside Publisher when you double click on the object.

OLE OBJECTS

OLE is one of those things that is more difficult to explain than it is to use. OLE stands for *Object Linking and Embedding*, and you don't need the skill—or nerve—of a matador to use it. In fact, WordArt is one type of OLE object, so you've already had some OLE experience.

For example, when you used the WordArt tool to create a WordArt object, or when you double-clicked on a WordArt frame from inside Publisher, you were working with an embedded object. As described in Chapter 5, the WordArt program tools appear within the Publisher window, and Publisher relinquishes control to the WordArt program while you work with the object. When you are done creating or editing the object, the WordArt program returns control to Publisher and the WordArt tools disappear.

An *embedded* object is one that is created by one program but resides inside a file created by another program. And because it resides in another program's file, it exists only within the document in which it is embedded. It has no existence outside of that document.

A *linked* object, on the other hand, has a life of its own, independent of the Publisher publication or other document type containing the link. For example, suppose someone in your office creates a spreadsheet and chart using Microsoft Excel, and you want to include that chart in your publication. Furthermore, let's assume that someone updates that spreadsheet weekly, still using Excel, which in turn modifies the chart.

The chart exists as an independent Excel file. As director of communications, you might be using Publisher to create an annual report for stockholders, and want to include the chart. All you have to do is create a linked object in your publication (I'll show you how in a moment.) Meanwhile, the marketing department is putting together a presentation using PowerPoint and they, too, want to include the chart, so they link it into their presentation file. The best part is, whenever you launch Publisher, or the Marketing team launches PowerPoint, OLE makes sure to update the link, using whatever data is in the source document (in this case, the Excel file).

Just as with embedded objects, when Publisher links this object to your publication, what appears is a copy. The difference is that the linked object is connected (linked) to the source. If you, or someone else, make changes to that object outside of Publisher (one of the benefits of using linked objects), those changes will be reflected in your publication when you open it again.

NOTE

The examples in this chapter use Microsoft products, but all programs that carry the Microsoft Windows 95 logo support OLE 2.0. Microsoft licenses the logo to any software publisher who meets certain compatibility standards. One of those standards is supporting OLE 2.0.

Inserting OLE Objects

When you click on the OLE button on the vertical toolbar, a pop-up menu appears listing various object types. You can select one of the types from the menu, or if the type you want is not shown, select **More....** to bring up the Insert Object dialog window. This is the same dialog window that appears when you click on the **Object...** option from the Insert menu.

The dialog contains two radio buttons: Create New and Create from File. When **Create New** is selected, an Object Type box shows all of the programs available on your system that support OLE as shown in Figure 8.4. If you select a type and click on **OK**, you will create an embedded object. Publisher creates the object frame and calls up whatever program you need to create that type. This is also what happens if you select an object type from the OLE button's pop-up menu.

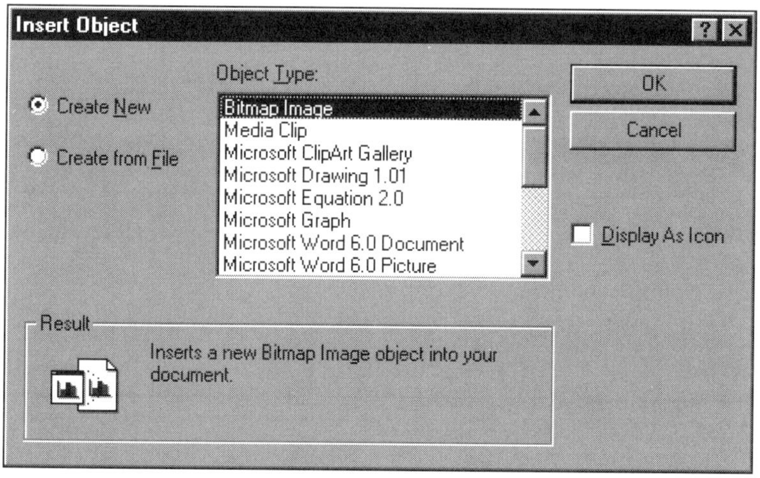

FIGURE 8.4 THE INSERT OBJECT DIALOG WINDOW WITH CREATE NEW SELECTED.

For example, if you selected **Microsoft Word 6.0 Document**, Publisher creates an object frame (not a text frame, because you will not be using Publishers text tools), and then calls the Word program. Just as with WordArt or Paint, the Word program's functions become available without actually launching the Word program itself.

When you select **Create from File**, the dialog window changes to look like the one shown in Figure 8.5. Instead of an Object Type section, you have a File box in which you must specify the name of the file you wish to insert. If you don't know the name of the file off hand, you can use the **Browse...** button to bring up the Browse dialog window and you can navigate through your system until you find the file you want.

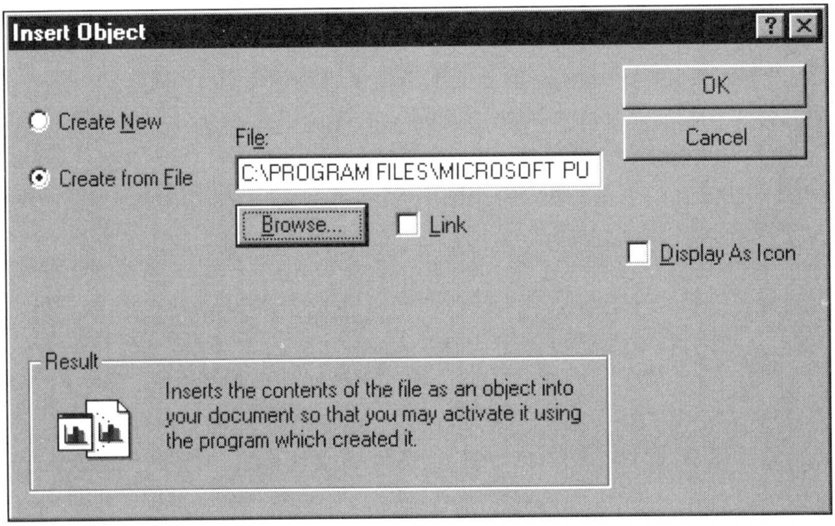

FIGURE 8.5 THE INSERT OBJECT DIALOG WINDOW WITH CREATE FROM FILE SELECTED.

Because you are working with a whole file, you now have the choice of embedding or linking. If you embed the file, it will reside inside your publication, and you will be able to edit it from within Publisher. If you put a checkmark in the Link box, Publisher will place a copy of the file in your publication and link that copy to the actual source file. If the source file is updated, those changes will be reflected in the copy inside your publication.

Displaying Inserted Objects As Icons

Both versions of the Insert Object dialog window also have a Display As Icon box. Figure 8.6 shows what the dialog window looks like with settings to create a new Microsoft Word object and display it as an icon. When you place a checkmark in the Display As Icon box, a picture of the icon appears, along with a Change Icon button that you can use to select a different icon if you don't like the one shown.

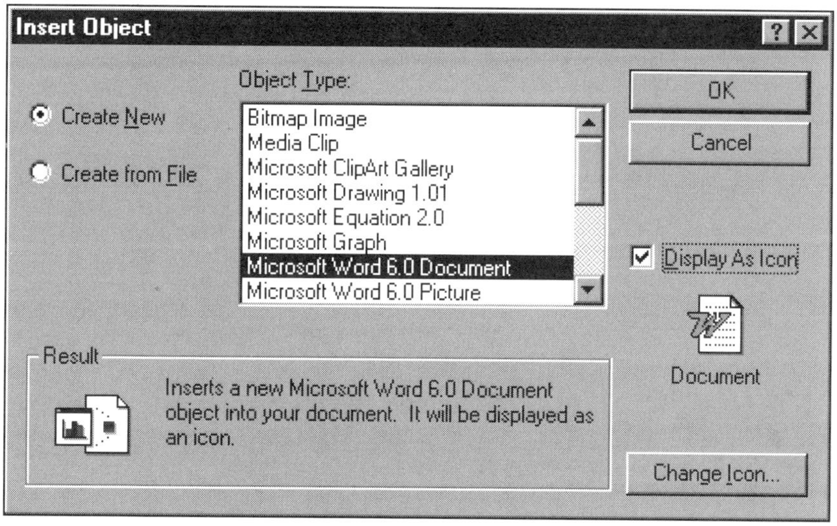

FIGURE 8.6 THE INSERT OBJECT DIALOG WINDOW WITH SETTINGS TO CREATE A NEW WORD OBJECT AND DISPLAY IT AS AN ICON IN THE PUBLICATION.

The Change Icon dialog window (see Figure 8.7) is easy to use. When you first insert an object and choose to display it as an icon, the Current and Default icons are the same, just as they are in Figure 8.7. (If you select a different icon, it will be reflected in the Current position.)

You can also select an icon that is associated with any file in your system. To do this, select the **From File** radio button and enter the name of the file. If you don't know the file name off hand, use the **Browse...** button to locate your file of choice. All of the icons associated with the named file appear in the scrolling window. Click on one to select it, then click on **OK**.

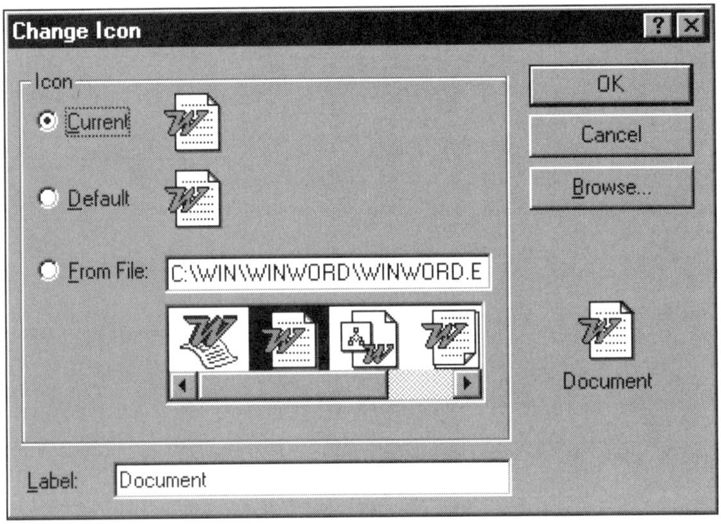

FIGURE 8.7 THE CHANGE ICON DIALOG WINDOW.

OLE 2.0 with drag-and-drop

OLE 2.0 has a drag and drop feature that provides you with yet another way to create an embedded object using a piece of data from a file opened in some other program. For example, all you have to do is highlight the text excerpt inside your Word program, or a table or chart in Excel, then hold down the **Control** key and drag the highlighted portion into your publication.

NOTE

You can also drag the highlighted data onto your Windows 95 desktop (Windows 95 refers to these files as scrap), and then drag it from there into your publication.

If you want an embedded object created using the drag-and-drop method displayed as an icon, you have to use the **Convert** option (see the section on Converting Object Types later in this chapter).

Updating Linked Objects

Earlier in this chapter I mentioned that Publisher automatically updates linked objects. That's true if you accept the default settings for a linked object. When the link is automatic, Publisher checks out the source document periodically so see if it has changed. You can, however, opt to update the link manually. Select **Links...** from the Edit menu to bring up the Links dialog window containing a list of all the links in your publication. Each listed link indicates the filename of the source file, the type of file, and whether the update is to be automatic or manual.

Figure 8.8 shows a Links dialog box with two links listed. The first link is to a bitmap image file with the file name CARS.BMP in my Windows directory, and it is set to update manually. The second link is to a text file (document) named TRAVEL.DOC, and the update method is automatic. If you select one of the listed links, you can click on the radio buttons at the bottom to change the update method. To update manually, select the appropriate link from the list and click on the **Update Now** button. If Publisher knows for a fact that the object is already up-to-date, the Update Now option will not be available.

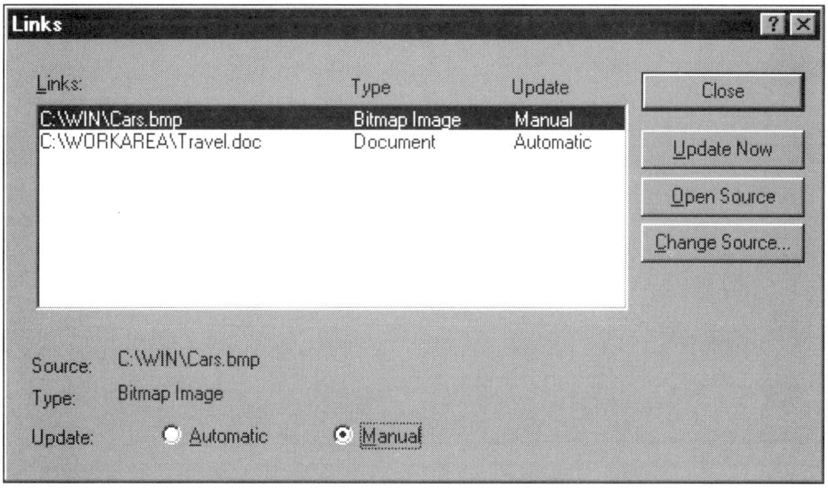

FIGURE 8.8 THE LINKS DIALOG WINDOW.

NOTE

Publisher also automatically updates a link object whenever you activate the object by opening it up in the source program, and whenever you print your publication.

Editing OLE Objects

All OLE objects have Edit, Open, and Convert menu options, but how those options take effect depends on the specific object. For example, while embedded objects are easily edited from within Publisher, you also have the choice of opening the original source program in a separate window and editing the object from there. The Edit option brings the source program tools into the Publisher environment. The Open option launches the source program in its own window. All editing of linked objects, on the other hand, must be done from inside the source program, so the Edit and Open options both do the same thing—launch the source program in a separate window

WARNING

Remember that if you decide to edit a linked object, your changes will alter the source document and therefore effect everyone else's use.

You can find the Edit and Open options by selecting the last item on the Edit menu (the one after the Links option). This item changes depending on what type of object you have selected. For example, it might say Bitmap Image Object, Bitmap Image Link, Microsoft WordArt 2.0 Object, Microsoft Word 6.0 Document Link, and so on. But whatever the option says, when you select it, a submenu appears with three options: Edit, Open, and Convert. (I'll cover the Convert option in a moment.) You can also find these options on the pop-up menu when you right click on the object.

You can also edit a linked object by using the **Open Source** button on the Links dialog window (see Figure 8.8). This button launches the program that created the linked object. Unlike embedded objects whose editing tools appear within the Publisher environment, linked objects must be edited from within the program that created the file, so Publisher calls the source program but it opens inside it's own window. You can get the same results by double-clicking on a linked object frame.

Converting Object Types

Some objects can be converted into different types. When I talked about copying and pasting earlier in this chapter, I described an example where you had to choose the object type, and you had two choices: Picture or Bitmap Image Object. Whatever choice you make is not irreversible because you can Convert the type.

When you select the **Convert...** option from the Edit submenu, or use the object's popup menu, as described in the previous section, the Convert dialog window appears as shown in Figure 8.9. This dialog window shows that the object in question (Current Type) is a Bitmap Image that is about to be converted into a Picture or Device Independent Bitmap. Note the message in the Result section! This change will be permanent. Once you convert it into a Picture, Publisher will no longer consider this a Bitmap Image.

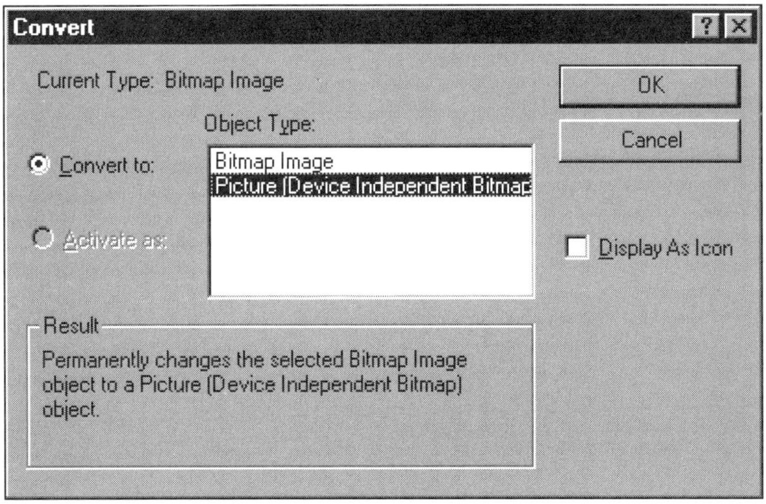

FIGURE 8.9 THE CONVERT DIALOG WINDOW.

Also notice that you can use this dialog window if you want to display the object as an icon. Once you use this dialog window to convert an object showing visible data, into and icon, you will have to double-click on the icon to open the source program in a separate window and view the contents there.

Deleting and Replacing Links

If you no longer wish to maintain a link to a particular file, you can delete the link or you might choose to maintain the link but with a different source file. To delete a linked object, you can select the object and use the **Delete Object** option on the Edit menu, or simply right-click on the object and select the option from the popup menu. To replace the linked file with a different source, choose **Links...** from Edit menu to bring up the Links dialog window shown above in Figure 8.8, and click on the **Change Source** button.

Changing the Source of a Linked Object

The Change Source button brings up the Change Source dialog window shown in Figure 8.10. From here you can select a different file to replace the one that is currently linked. You could delete the linked object and simply create a new one, but using Change Source allows you to preserve the object frame and formatting.

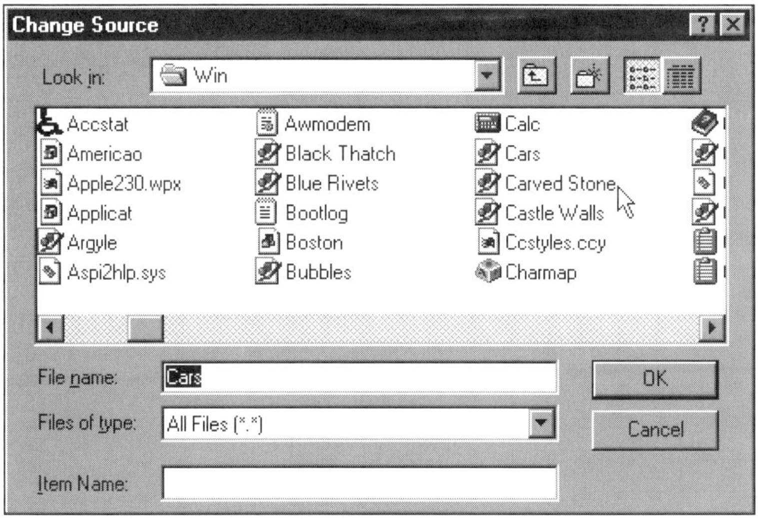

FIGURE 8.10 THE CHANGE SOURCE DIALOG WINDOW.

For example, I formatted my Cars image frame with a thick border and a shadow as shown in Figure 8.11. Then I used the **Change Source** feature to replace the Cars image with an more abstract bitmap image called Carved Stone. (Both of these files are in your Windows directory if you'd like to experiment yourself.) The result is a new image inside the same object frame with the same border and shadow as shown in Figure 8.12.

FIGURE 8.11 A BITMAP OBJECT LINKED THE CARS IMAGE. THE OBJECT FRAME HAS A WIDE BORDER AND A SHADOW.

FIGURE 8.12 THE SAME BITMAP OBJECT, NOW LINKED THE CARVED STONE IMAGE. THE OBJECT FRAME REMAINS UNCHANGED.

SUMMARY

✷ Inserting a simple piece of text is easily accomplished using standard Windows cut and paste (or copy and paste) functions.

✷ If you want to embed an object, you can include a link to the original file using Publisher's Paste Object function. Then, when you double-click on the object, you can edit it using the tools of the program that created it (if that program supports OLE).

✷ Linked objects can either be automatically updated (which they are by default) or they can be updated manually. If you the object is automatically updated and someone changes the original document, the next time you open the Publisher document the changes will show in your work.

✷ Objects can be converted from their original type to native Publisher formats. Select the **Convert...** option from the Edit menu or use the popup menu from the object itself. These conversions are permanent. After you convert the object, the link will be lost.

CHAPTER 9

OUTPUT

- Using the Layout Checker
- Getting Help from the Print Troubleshooter
- Printing publications on your own Laser or Inkjet Printer
- Using an outside print service

Most often, your method of output is likely to be printing on your own laser or inkjet printer. With the enhancements that were made to the Windows 95 version of Publisher (especially those relating to the ability to create color separations), more and more users are beginning to use the program to create publications and output them to a file that they give to a professional print shop for production.

In this chapter I'll talk about all three types of output, as well as the Layout Checker and Printer TroubleShooter features that help make these tasks easier. I'll also talk about the use of color, printing booklets, and printing envelopes. Let's start with the Layout Checker feature because that's the first thing you will want to do before actually sharing a publication with others, no matter what your method of output.

LAYOUT CHECKER

Before you use the Check Layout feature, you really should give your publication the visual once-over. Be sure to **Hide Special Characters** (**Ctrl+Shft+Y**), **Hide Boundaries and Guides** (**Ctrl+Shft+O**), and use the **Full Page** option (**F9** toggles between actual and full page view). Once you're satisfied with how it looks, use the Layout Checker to look for specific layout problems you may have missed.

The Layout Checker works a little like the spelling checker in your word processing program. You start it by selecting the **Check Layout...** option on the Tools menu to bring up the dialog window shown in Figure 9.1. Here you specify the areas that the checker should look at. You can choose **All** to examine all the pages in your publication, or you can select a specific range of pages. By placing or removing a checkmark at the bottom of the dialog window, you can specify whether you want the Background checked as well.

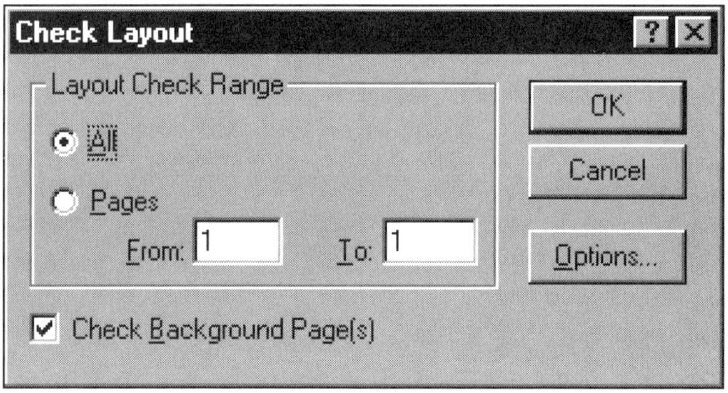

FIGURE 9.1 THE CHECK LAYOUT DIALOG WINDOW.

The Check Layout dialog window also has an **Options...** button that brings up a second dialog window shown in Figure 9.2. Using this dialog you can decide what types of problems you want the Layout Checker to look for. You can select **Check For All Problems**, as shown, or you can choose one or more of the four specific problems.

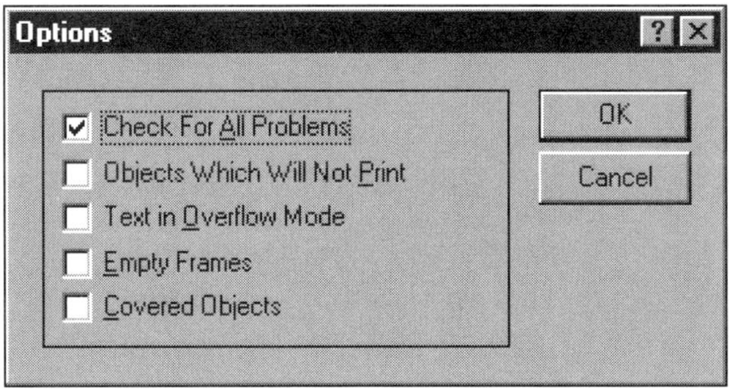

FIGURE 9.2 THE OPTIONS DIALOG WINDOW FOR THE LAYOUT CHECKER.

The four specific layout problems are:

- Objects Which Will Not Print: Use this option to have the Layout Checker identify any objects in your publication that will not print. One reason Publisher may not be able to print an object is if it falls outside the printable area of your page.
- Text in Overflow Mode: This option tells Publisher to let you know if any of your text frames contain text that does not fit inside the frame. Such text is stored in an overflow area and does not print.
- Empty Frames: Frequently, people create publications by placing all the frames first, and then adding the content to each frame. Using this option is a good way to make sure that you remembered to insert all your text and images in their frames. However, if you deliberately created empty frames, perhaps to indicate where the outside print shop should place photos, then you might not want to use this option.
- Covered Objects: This option looks for objects that are covered by other objects. At times when you intentionally cover one object with another, you may want to skip this option.

While checking, a Layout Checker dialog window appears on your screen. If a problem is detected, Publisher displays the problem and suggested solutions in the dialog window as shown in Figure 9.3, and selects the offending object(s). If desired, you can correct the problem then and there, without ever closing the Layout Checker dialog. When you're done making the correction, click on the **Continue** button in the dialog window. If the suggestions in the dialog window don't give you enough information, you can click on the **Explain...** button and the appropriate Help topic appears.

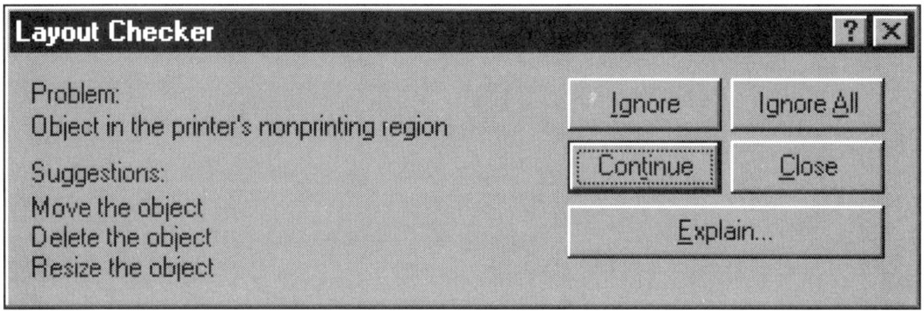

FIGURE 9.3 THE LAYOUT CHECKER DIALOG WINDOW REPORTING A PROBLEM AND SUGGESTING SOLUTIONS.

As mentioned above, there are times when Publisher perceives a problem that is not a problem to you. You don't have to fix a problem identified by the Checker if you don't want to. You can choose to **Ignore** that instance of the problem, or **Ignore All** instances of that problem. When the Layout Checker has completed its task, a Publisher message appears. If the Layout Checker did not detect any problems, the Publisher message reads *The layout check is complete. The Layout Checker did not detect any layout problems.*

If one or more problems were found, the Checker gives you the opportunity to check the publication again. If you corrected the problems as they arose, this is a useful feature that allows you to make sure your corrections worked. If you chose not to make corrections, you would click **No** to bypass this opportunity.

NOTE

Depending on the size and complexity of your publication, or the area you selected too check, the Layout Checker may work very fast. If the check goes quickly, and if the Checker did not find any problems, the Layout Checker dialog window may appear and disappear so fast that you barely notice it.

USING YOUR OWN LASER OR INKJET PRINTER

If you have a black and white printer, you are limited to printing black & white publications that include shades of gray as well. Depending on your printers resolution capabilities, you can print black and white publications from 300 dpi (or dots per inch) to 2400 dpi. The higher the dpi, the finer the picture quality and the more shades of gray. If you have a color printer, that supports resolutions up to 600 dpi, you can print your own color publications as well.

TIP

Here are two ways you can introduce color into your black and white publications: print on color or patterned paper, and use color foils (only works with laser printers).

NOTE

Those of you without color printers will have to use an outside service to handle spot color and full color publications (see

Print Setup

When you select the **Print Setup...** option on the File menu, the Print Setup dialog window appears as shown in Figure 9.4. You can use this dialog window to select page orientation, specify paper size and paper source, access the printer's Properties window, and even change your printer selection. Before I talk about some of the printer properties, let me digress for a moment to warn you about the perils of changing printers and the use of the manual paper source.

Beware! Changing printers can be dangerous to the health of your publications. If you change your printer after creating a publication, Publisher recomposes your publication. Why? Because font support, print regions, and other features can differ from printer to printer. If you use fonts in your publication that are not supported by the new printer, Publisher automatically substitutes fonts that are supported. While Publisher strives to use similar-looking fonts, the substitution could change the look of your publication, and the way the text lines break or fit in the frame. You might even end up with some overflow text. Also, if the print region on the new printer is smaller than the printable area supported by the previous printer, you could also end up with objects that cannot be printed. Therefore, it is always a good idea to re-check your publication whenever you change printers.

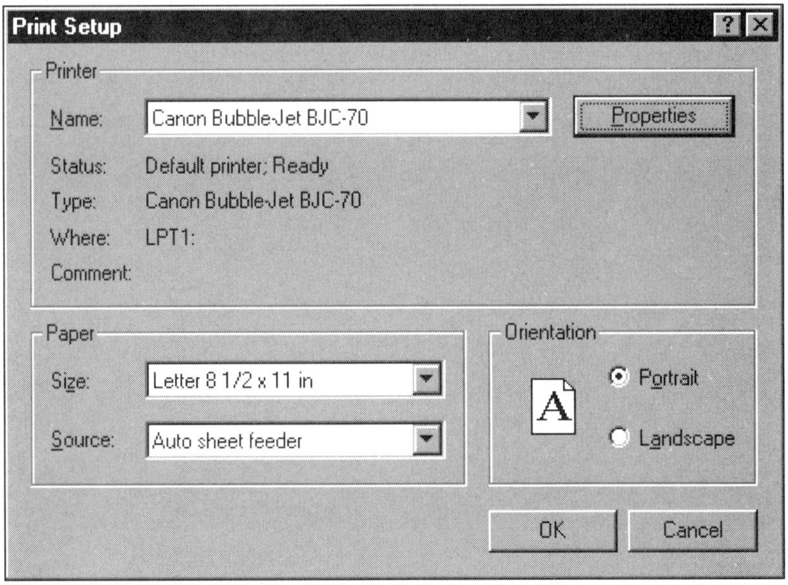

FIGURE 9.4 THIS PRINT SETUP DIALOG WINDOW APPEARS WHEN YOU SELECT THE **PRINT SETUP** OPTION FROM THE FILE MENU.

A moment ago I mentioned the Paper Source setting. Usually this option is set to Auto Sheet Feeder. However, if you want to print on envelopes or odd-sized paper, you will need to set this option to Manual Feed. Unfortunately, not all printer support this option.

Now, back to Properties. When you click on the **Properties** button in the Print Setup dialog window, the Properties window appears containing the tab pages and options that your selected printer supports. Figure 9.5 shows the Graphics tab page on the Properties window for my Cannon Bubble-Jet color printer, while Figure 9.6 shows the same tab page for a black and white Apple LaserWriter printer.

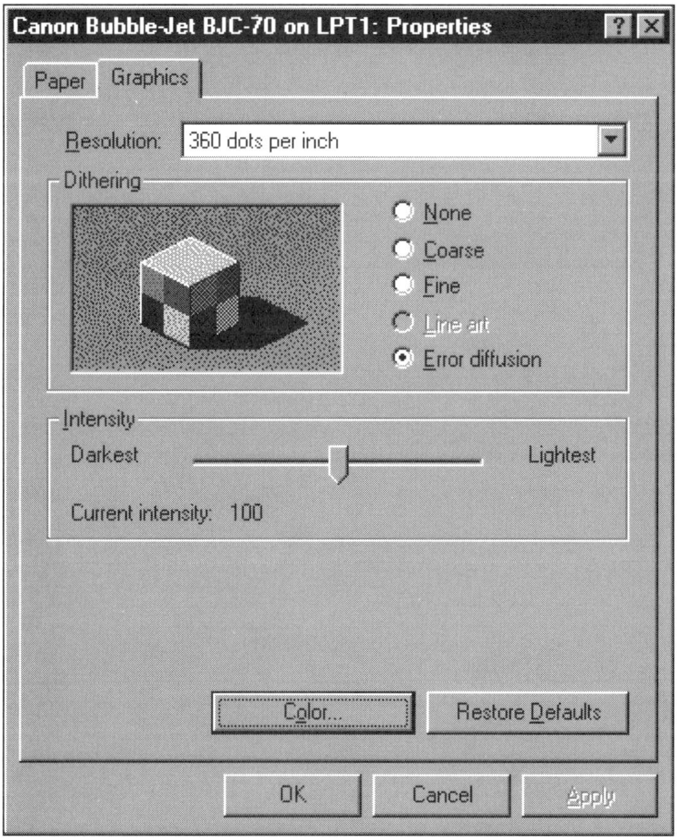

FIGURE 9.5 THE GRAPHICS TAB PAGE ON THE PROPERTIES WINDOW FOR A CANNON BUBBLE-JET COLOR PRINTER.

You can see that while both dialogs contain settings for Resolution, the black and white printer's graphic options include settings for halftones while the color printer's graphic options include settings for Dithering and Intensity. The properties tab pages vary from printer to printer.

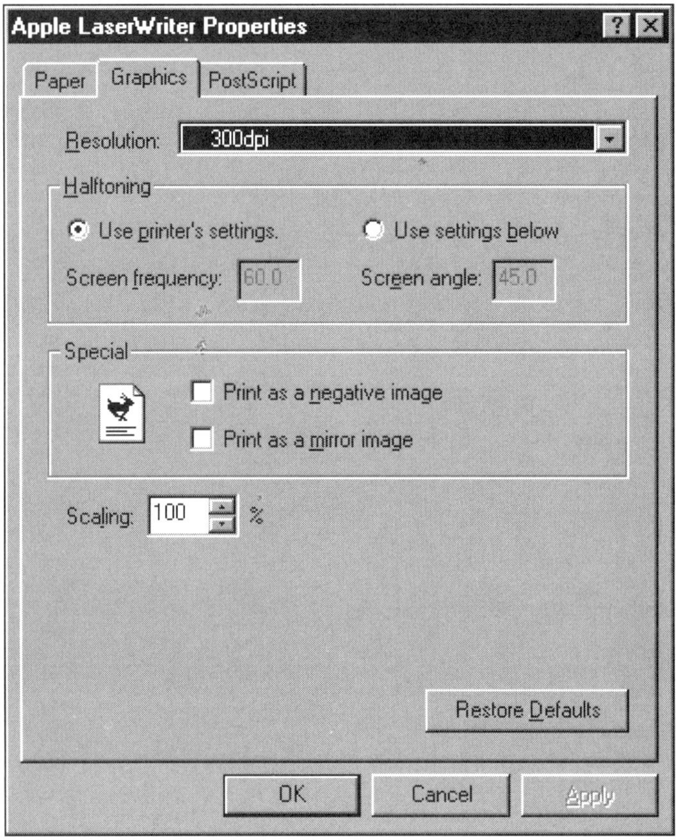

FIGURE 9.6 THE GRAPHICS TAB PAGE ON THE PROPERTIES WINDOW FOR A BLACK AND WHITE APPLE LASERWRITER PRINTER.

Dithering is what produces gray scale tones and blended colors. You don't have to use dithering, but if you are working with photographs or images (gradients) that do not have well-defined edges, you should use

Error Diffusion. The Line Art option is ideal for graphics with sharp definition between white, black and gray shadings.

Intensity actually means the amount of energy in the color. In practical terms, this actually means the amount of color the printer will attempt to saturate the region with. Try not to change this setting too often, particularly if you are sending materials out to a service bureau. You could just end up with a messy glob of toner or whatever material your printer uses. Or you could end up with areas that don't print on your paper that you intended to have ink on them.

The **Color...** button brings up the Graphics - Color dialog window shown in Figure 9.7. Here you have six options, three relating to color control, and three relating to color rendering intent. Color control let's you indicate whether you want to print in black and white only, color without image color matching, or color with image color matching.

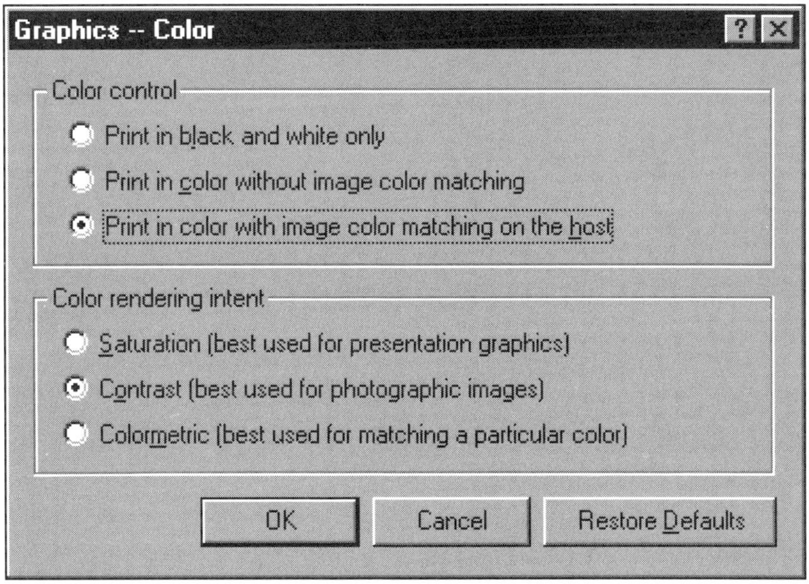

FIGURE 9.7 THE GRAPHICS - COLOR DIALOG WINDOW ACCESSED FROM THE GRAPHICS TAB PAGE OF THE PROPERTIES WINDOW FOR A COLOR PRINTER.

Image Color Matching (ICM) is a method Windows uses to match printer colors with your screen colors. Not all color printers are capable of ICM and you should check with your printer manufacturer to see if they support it.

TIP

Access the **Options** dialog window from the Tools menu and make sure that the Improve Screen and Printer Color Matching option is selected. Also, whenever you use the color dialog windows to select colors for objects in your publication, be sure to use **the Mark Colors That Will Not Print Well On My Printer** option.

Some printers support duplex printing (printing on both sides of the paper). If your printer supports this option, you'll find it on a Properties tab page called **More Options**. If you don't have a Properties tab page by that name, then your printer can't print on both sides. If you really need double-sided printing, you might want to consider printing a master—each page separately—then using the services of a copy shop that has photocopiers that support duplex copying.

WARNING

Some people manually feed a page into their printer a second time, but this is not recommended! You run a very good chance of getting ink or toner transferred to the printing mechanism of your printer.

The Print Setup option is not the only way to access these settings. Most of these same options can be accessed from the Print dialog window as well.

Print

The **Print...** option on the **File** menu brings up the Print dialog window as shown in Figure 9.8. The top section of this window provides you with the same basic information and choices as are available to you when you click on the **Printer Setup** option on the File menu. Here you can use the drop-down window to change the printer type, and click on the

Properties button to access the dialogs for setting the Paper and Graphics options. Also in the top section is the Print to File checkbox. If you select this option, Publisher will prompt you for a filename and location once you click on **OK** to being printing.

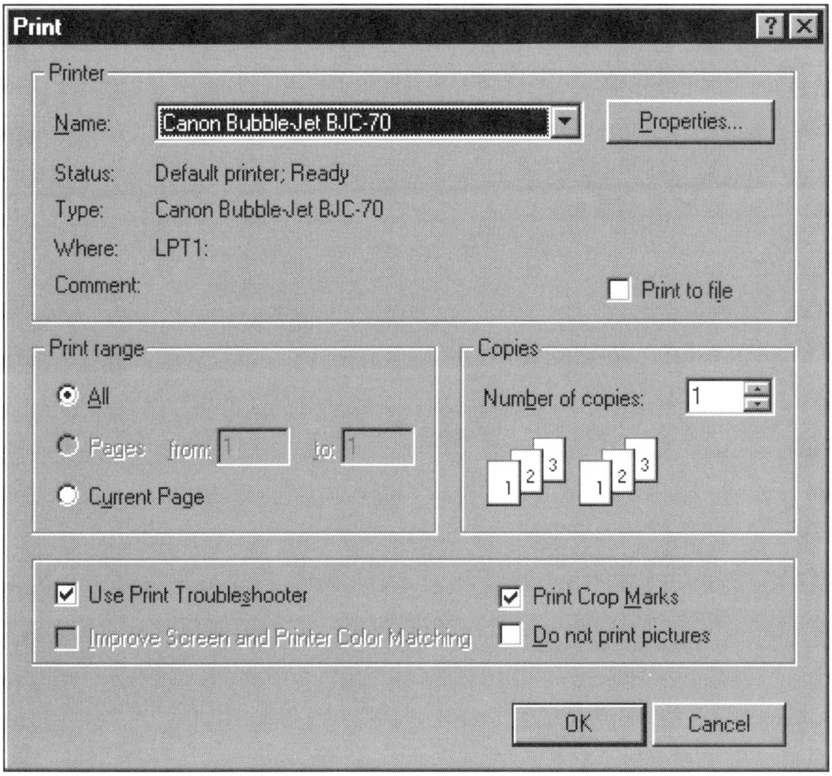

FIGURE 9.8 THE PRINT DIALOG WINDOW.

The center section of the Print dialog window contains two areas. On the left are the settings for Print Range, used to indicate which page or pages you want to print. You can print **All** pages, the **Current** Page, or a specific range of Pages. On the right you indicate the Number of Copies desired.

The bottom section contains four checkbox options, as follows:

✱ Print Crop Marks: Crop marks show you where to trim pages when the publication size is smaller than the paper on which it is printed. For publications that require assembly of multiple pages, crop marks show you where to match up the pages.

TIP

If you are going to print out camera-ready pages on your own printer, and take them to an outside printer, be sure to include crop marks.

✱ Use Print TroubleShooter: The Print TroubleShooter is a Help feature. When you place a checkmark in this box, Publisher waits until your job has finished printing and then prompts you to indicate whether the publication printed successfully. If you indicate No, the Help window appears displaying the TroubleShooter topics to help you find solutions to whatever problems may have occurred.

NOTE

The topics offer step-by-step instructions and occasionally suggest consulting the Windows 95 Print TroubleShooter if Publisher's TroubleShooter doesn't do the trick.

✱ Do Not Print Pictures: Printing pictures takes a lot of time and toner (or ink). If you want to print drafts of your publication, you might want to use this option to print everything but the pictures.

TIP

You might also want to lower your printer's resolution when printing drafts. (Use the Properties button and then select the Graphics tab page as described earlier.)

✱ Improve Screen and Printer Color Matching: This option helps to make your color output match as closely as possible the appearance of the colors as seen on your monitor. If your printer and monitor do not both support ICM profiles (ICM stand for Image Color Matching), this option will not be available.

At the very bottom of the Print dialog window are two or three buttons, depending. The OK and Cancel buttons are always there, on the far right. If a page of your publication takes up half a page of space, or less, an additional button—Page Options...—appears in the lower left corner of the dialog window. Click on it to bring up the Page Options dialog window shown in Figure 9.9

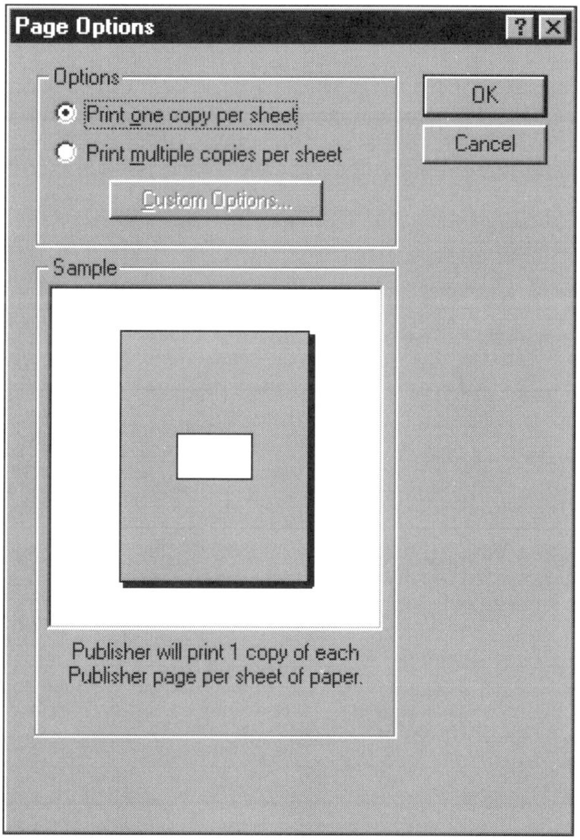

FIGURE 9.9 THE PAGE OPTIONS DIALOG WINDOW FOR A BUSINESS CARD PUBLICATION, SET TO PRINT ONLY ONE CARD PER SHEET.

When your publication takes up half a page of space, or less, you have the choice of printing multiple pages (as many as will fit) on a single sheet of paper, or specifying only one page per sheet. If your publication consists of only one page, then Publisher can print multiple copies on a single sheet of paper.

You made this selection one before, in Chapter 2, when the Business Card PageWizard asked you for your preference. In that case, the PageWizard took care of the settings. When you are creating your own publications, you make your preferences known using this dialog window. And unless you specify otherwise, Publisher's default setting prints multiples per page.

When the **Print multiple copies per sheet** option is selected, the **Custom Options...** button becomes available. Click on it to bring up the Custom Options - Small Publications dialog window shown in Figure 9.10. This is where you get to set the margins and spacing between copies. You can enter the settings yourself, or place a checkmark in the Automatically calculate spacing box to let Publisher do it for you.

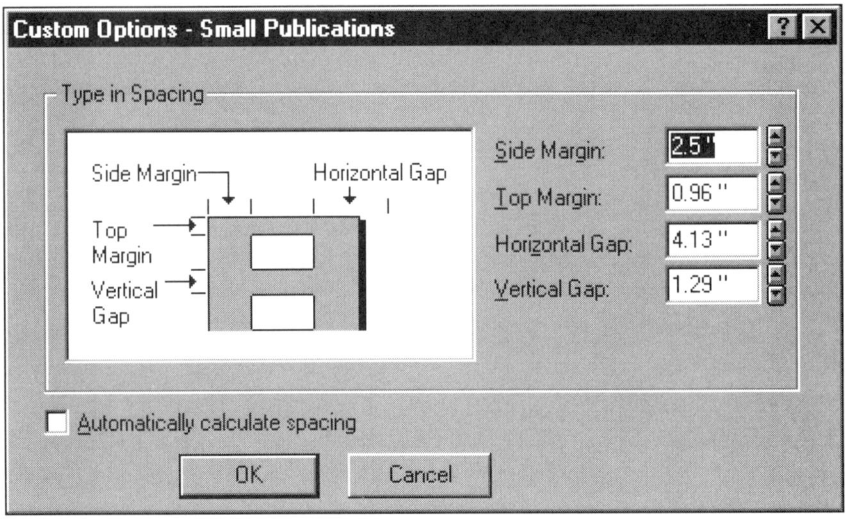

FIGURE 9.10 THE CUSTOM OPTIONS - SMALL PUBLICATIONS DIALOG WINDOW.

USING AN OUTSIDE PRINT SHOP

When you decide to use an outside printing service, Publisher prints your publication to a file that you can take on a disk or send via modem. When you select **Outside Print Setup...** from the File menu, a series of Wizard dialog windows appear, prompting you for the information needed to prepare the output files. You have to complete the Outside Print Setup before you can use the Print to Outside Printer and Print Info Sheet options.

Outside Print Setup

The first step is to specify the type of print job. Select one of the options from the first Outside Print Setup dialog window shown in Figure 9.11. The dialog windows vary slightly depending on whether you choose black and white, full color, or spot color output.

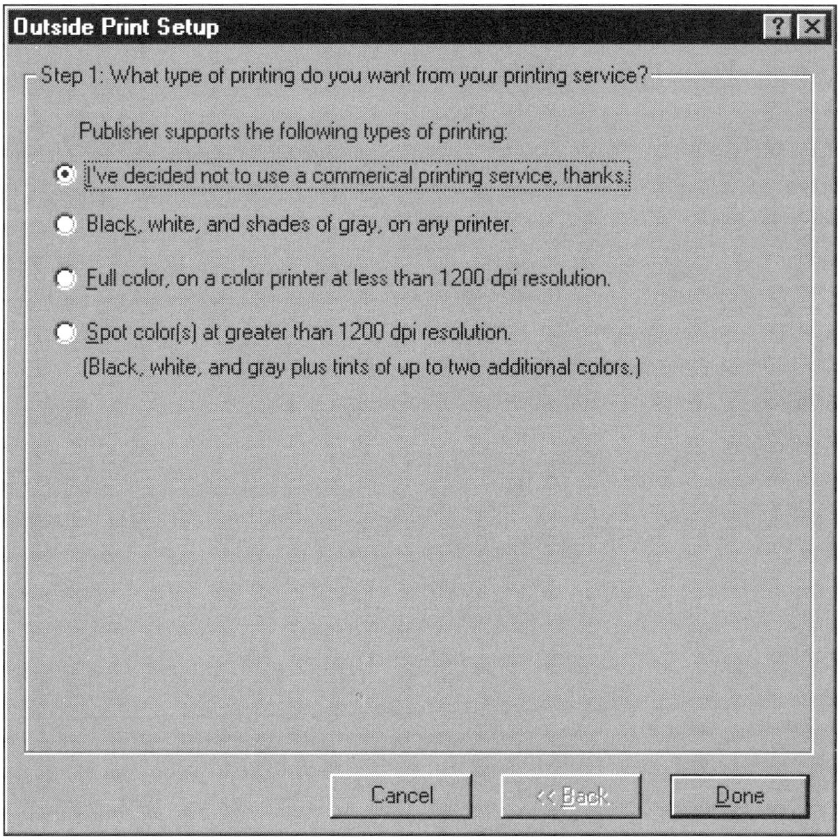

FIGURE 9.11 THE FIRST OUTSIDE PRINT SETUP DIALOG WINDOW.

Black, White, and Shades of Gray

Once you define your publication as black, white, and shades of gray, the second step is to specify which type of printer will be used to print your publication. As you can see in Figure 9.12, you can choose Publisher's outside printer driver, or select a specific printer. The Publisher printer driver is a generic postscript driver compatible with the majority of printers used by outside print services, and supports the advanced printing features. However, selecting a specific printer might be more desirable if you know for sure the exact printer used by your outside service. To do this, click on the double-arrow button to bring up a Print Setup dialog window. Select your printer and click on **OK**.

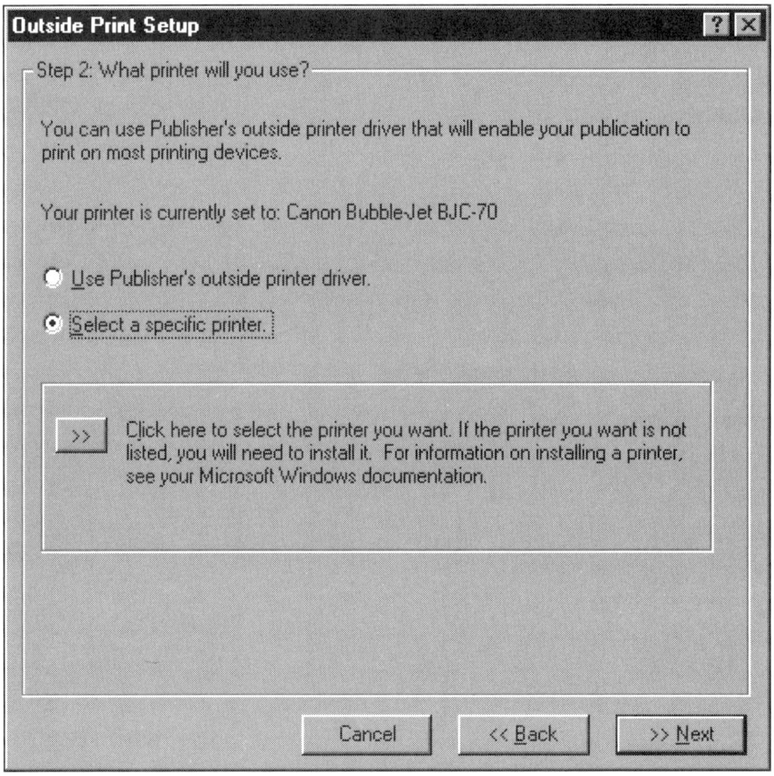

FIGURE 9.12: THE SECOND OUTSIDE PRINT SETUP DIALOG WINDOW WHEN PRINTING BLACK AND WHITE OR SPOT COLOR PUBLICATIONS.

You get to select options for your black and white publication using the third and final Outside Print Setup dialog window shown in Figure 9.13. If your outside printing service tells you they want to print your publication on oversized paper, be sure to select the option that allows Publisher to automatically select an Extra paper size. Most print services also want to see print markings on the output. These marks, which include crop marks, registration marks to assist in the alignment, and spot color names, print outside the boundaries of your publication's page.

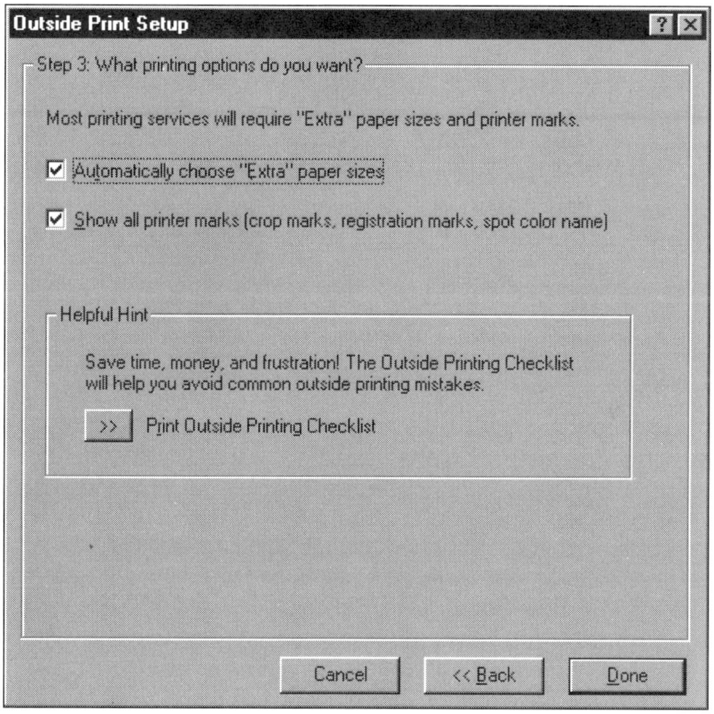

FIGURE 9.13 THE THIRD AND FINAL OUTSIDE PRINT SETUP DIALOG WINDOW WHEN PRINTING BLACK AND WHITE PUBLICATIONS.

You also have the option of printing the Outside Printing Checklist. This five-page document presents you with a series of questions and issues that you should discuss with your outside printing service...preferably before you create the final version of your publication.

Spot Color

When you select Spot Color, the first dialog window changes to include the Select Spot Color(s) section as shown in Figure 9.14. Spot color refers to the use of two base colors in addition to black and white, and includes the use of grays and any shades of the two base colors. Publisher supports the use of two spot colors, automatically creating color separations for the outside print service. Use the drop-down selection boxes to pick the color(s) you want. If you are using a second spot color, be sure to place a checkmark in the box as well.

TIP

You can end up with more colors by overlapping the use of the two base colors. For example, if a yellow object overlaps a blue object, the overlapping area will appear green.

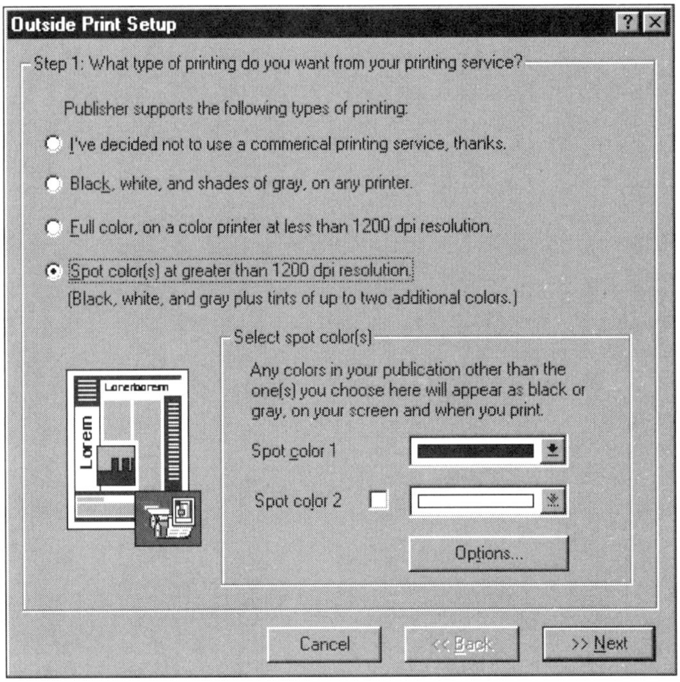

FIGURE 9.14 THE FIRST OUTSIDE PRINT SETUP DIALOG WINDOW WHEN YOU SPECIFY SPOT COLOR.

You also have some options when using spot color. Click on the **Options...** button to bring up the Spot Color Options dialog window shown in Figure 9.15. Overprinting allows black text or objects to print over areas in your publication that have color. You must select this option if you want black text or object to print on top of color objects. If this option is not selected, Publisher will not print the color or colors of the object that is behind the black text or object. This is only relevant when producing color separations. When you print a publication on your own color printer, everything prints.

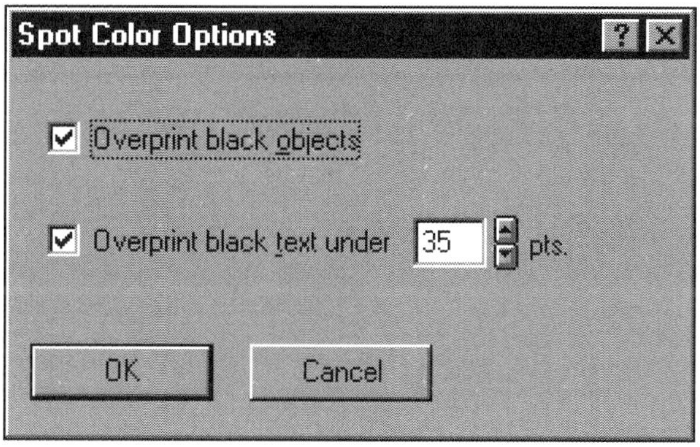

FIGURE 9.15 THE SPOT COLOR OPTIONS DIALOG WINDOW.

The second and third Outside Print Setup dialog windows for spot color publications are identical to the ones used for black and white publications (see previous section).

Printing Color Separation Proofs

Once you are set up for spot color printing, a Print Proof option becomes available on your File menu. The Print Proof dialog window is shown in Figure 9.16. Make sure there is a checkmark in the Print Color Separations box and click on **OK**. Publisher will print a maximum of three pages for each publication page. One for black, one for spot color #1, and a third separation if you are using a second spot color. It's a good idea to print proof pages and examine them before taking your job to the outside service bureau.

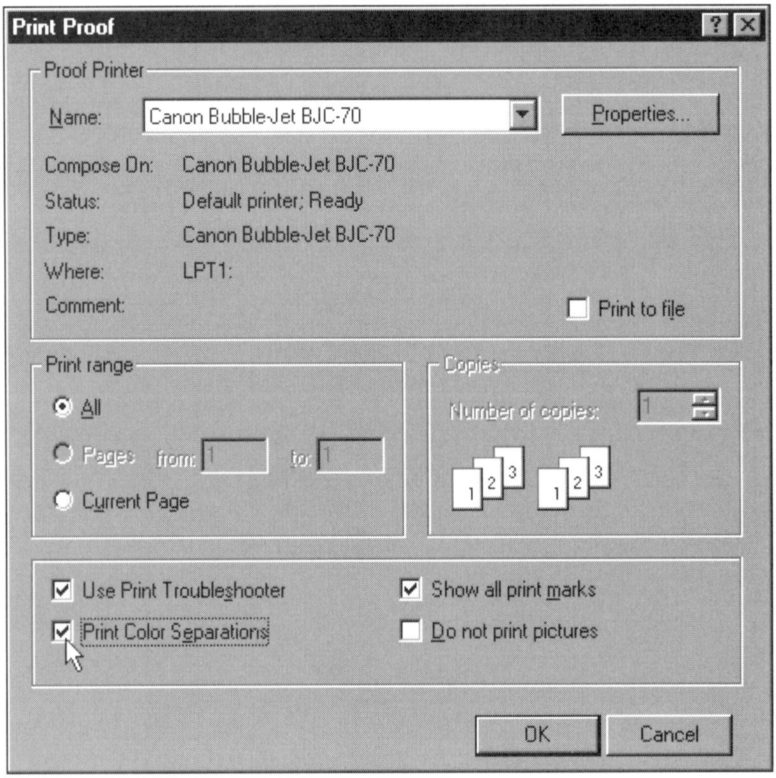

FIGURE 9.16 THE PRINT PROOF DIALOG WINDOW.

Full Color

When printing full color, there are only two Outside Print Setup dialog windows, both of which you've seen already. In the first dialog window you specify the type of print job, in this case full color. And in the second dialog window you choose between the Publisher printer driver and a specific printer of your choosing. That's all there is to it.

Print to Outside Printer

Once you have completed the steps to setup your publication for an outside print service, you can use the **Print to Outside Printer...** option on the File menu. The Print to Outside Printer dialog window is shown in Figure 9.17.

Most of these options should be familiar to you, as they are the same as the options on the Print dialog window used when printing on your own laser or inkjet printer. (See the Print section earlier in the chapter).

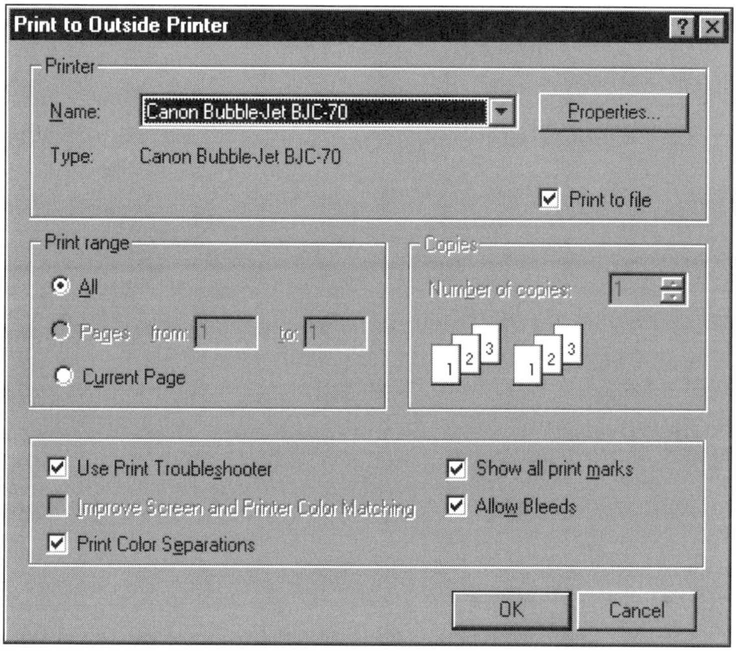

FIGURE 9.17 THE PRINT TO OUTSIDE PRINTER DIALOG WINDOW.

Depending on which type of output you selected during setup, some options may not be available. For example, if you setup for full color printing, the Print Color Separations option will be grayed out. There are a few other small differences between this dialog window and the other Print dialog window. When using an outside service, you have the option to show all print marks, whereas when you use your own desktop printer, the option is to show crop marks only. That is because registration marks and color separation names are not applicable to desktop printing.

Another difference is that if you select the Print to file option when using Print to Outside Printer, that file will be a Postscript file so ask your service bureau what sort of files they prefer.

Print Info Sheet

Unless you're an old pro or have created other publications with the same basic characteristics for the same outside print service before, it's a good idea to use the **Print InfoSheet** option on the File menu. As it will say at the top of your InfoSheet, *check to see if this information will work with your printing service.* A quick check could save you from wasting a considerable amount of time and money. Figure 9.18 shows the information provided on the InfoSheet after I prepared my Writer Letterhead publication (the one with the watermark I showed you in Chapter 6):

Check to see if this information will work with your printing service

- **Filename:** WRITER LETTERHEAD
- **Created using:** Microsoft Publisher 3.0 for Windows
- **Page size:** 8.5 x 11 "
- **Sheet size:** 9.5 x 12 " (Letter Extra)
- **Number of sheets to print:** 1
- **Total pages printed:** 1
- **Colors:** Spot color job with one spot color in addition to black.
- **Onscreen colors used:** Spot Color 1 - 0R, 0G, 255B
- **Printer marks:** Crop Marks, Registration Marks
- **Formatted for printer:** MS Publisher Imagesetter
- **Horizontal/vertical resolution:** Device Default Resolution
- **Attached Proof was printed on:** Canon Bubble-Jet BJC-70

List of fonts used:

Times New Roman

List of special effects used:

Rotated Pictures

Recolored Pictures

WordArt Frames

FIGURE 9.18 SAMPLE INFOSHEET DATA.

SUMMARY

✷ Give your document a once-over before you print. Be sure to **Hide Special Characters** (**Ctrl+Shft+Y**), **Hide Boundaries and Guides** (**Ctrl+Shft+O**), and use the **Full Page** option (**F9** toggles between actual and full page view).

✷ The Layout Checker is a valuable tool that can help you find areas in your document that may not print correctly

✷ Always check with your service bureau *before* you send materials to them. You will save yourself time, money, and endless aggravation.

Microsoft Publisher 95

Index

A

B

C

D

G

H

I

N

O

P

Q

R

S

U

V

W

Z